HARDSCRABBLE

———○⟨⟩◆⟨⟩○———

A NARRATIVE OF THE
CALIFORNIA HILL COUNTRY

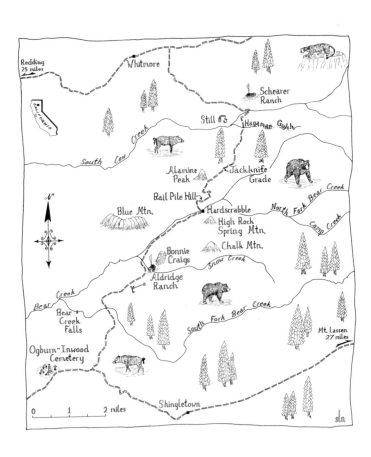

Redding
25 miles

Whitmore

California

South Cow Creek

Still 6̄

Schearer
Ranch

Hagaman Gulch

Alamine
Peak

Jackknife
Grade

North Fork Bear Creek

Rail Pile Hill

Blue Mtn.

Hardscrabble

High Rock
Spring Mtn.

Chalk Mtn.

Camp Creek

Bonnie
Craigs

Snow Creek

Aldridge
Ranch

Bear Creek

South Fork Bear Creek

Mt. Lassen
27 miles

Bear
Creek
Falls

Ogburn-Inwood
Cemetery

Shingletown

0   1   2 miles

stn

HARDSCRABBLE

A NARRATIVE OF THE
CALIFORNIA HILL COUNTRY

ANITA KUNKLER

Edited, with commentaries and notes, by
WILBUR S. SHEPPERSON

A BRISTLECONE PAPERBACK
UNIVERSITY OF NEVADA PRESS
RENO, NEVADA 1975

Library of Congress Cataloging in Publication Data

Kunkler, Anita, 1907-1967.
    Hardscrabble: a narrative of the California hill
country.

    (A Bristlecone paperback)
    Autobiography.
    1. Shasta Co., Calif. — Description and travel.
2. Ranch life — Shasta Co., Calif.   3. Kunkler, Anita,
1907-1967.   I. Title.
F868.S49K86   1975   979.4'24'050924   75-29216
ISBN 0-87417-044-3

CONTENTS

EDITOR'S COMMENTS AND
ACKNOWLEDGMENTS

HARDSCRABBLE is the autobiographical account of the first eighteen years (1907-1925) in the life of Anita Vivian Aldridge Kunkler. Most of the work was written during the forties and fifties as short stories and single episodes, and then reorganized into a more thematic and chronological form in the sixties. A friend of the author typed the manuscript without changes or corrections in punctuation, spelling, or style, and the work was completed only a few months before Anita's death in December 1967. The memoir is set in the mountains of Shasta County, California, but the traditions and background of the Aldridge family lead back across the United States to the hills of eighteenth-century North Carolina. Anita's adventures are basic, unadorned, and no doubt common to thousands of isolated country folk tucked away and out of sight in a state otherwise famous for its glamour and prosperity.

The editor has retained the basic arrangement, general sequence, and development found in the original manuscript. A few episodes have been deleted, either because they did not relate to the author's life, or because they were peripheral to the overall theme. Some slight reordering of topics, paragraphs, and chapters was necessary in order to be consistent and to maintain a logical, chronological flow of events. Most chapters stand as they were written — independent and generally complete entities. The author's spelling, capitalization and punctuation have been standardized only minimally. Dates, locations, and explanatory footnotes have been provided for comprehension's sake, and some redundant or gramatically awkward words and phrases have been deleted or corrected. Much attention has been given to preserving the author's spirit, intent, and literary flavor, and no censorship has been imposed.

Many individuals, as well as research organizations, record offices, and libraries, have contributed to the editing and foreword of HARDSCRABBLE. Grateful acknowledgment is given to the Research Advisory Board of the University of Nevada for their financial assistance, and to Professors Jerome Edwards, William Rowley, and Michael Brodhead for advice given during the editing. Particular thanks is extended to Walter and Martha Aldridge of Shingletown, California. They presently own and operate Bonnie Craigs Ranch, which includes the land obtained by William Aldridge when he first settled in California in 1862. Mrs. C. B. Aldridge Quint of Redding was especially helpful in providing records and documents relating to the history of the Aldridge family. Finally, the writer is deeply appreciative of the cooperation and aid given by Lloyd ''Poke'' Kunkler* of Paynes Creek, California, and by Earl and Beverly Kunkler of Incline Village, Nevada. Earl and Beverly, the son and daughter-in-law of Anita, have provided valuable advice and assistance; and Anita's husband, Lloyd, not only made the publication possible but is himself a key character in the last chapters of the memoir.

Reno, June 1974   W.S.S.

---

*Lloyd Kunkler died at Paynes Creek in August 1974.

FOREWORD

SOME FAMILIES and groups crossed the American continent because they were obeying a religious belief. Others sought political opportunity, social change, or escape from the law, and many planned to farm, trade, dig gold, or in some way become prosperous and perhaps wealthy. But thousands of individuals drifted across the country without any clear or fixed purpose. They trekked west because movement was in the air — they became caught up in the great drama of migration. They had absorbed the strange American dream: a faith in themselves, in action, and in the future. Such people were rarely deterred by hardships or dangers — neither unfriendly natives, nor the perils of travel, nor sickness, nor weather, nor distance intimidated or dismayed them. And they fared surprisingly well; watchful providence or native resourcefulness allowed them to prevail.

The Aldridges were such a frontier people. Family lore suggests that they came from Wales and settled in Maryland sometime in the late sixteen hundreds. Nicholas Aldridge apparently participated in the extensive migration of yeoman farmers who moved south from Virginia, Maryland, and Pennsylvania into the North Carolina piedmont in the years following 1745. Contemporary observers have left pointed descriptions of the ignorance and squalor of some of these Scottish, Scotch-Irish, and Welsh migrants; but at the same time, they have testified to their rugged individuality and their total disdain for aristocracy and all forms of social superiority.

Nicholas Aldridge settled in Orange County, North Carolina, and during the 1760s became engaged in the Regulator agitation which swept through that section of the piedmont. The movement was an intense reaction against the arrogance, wealth, and power of the tidewater plantation owners who ran the colony and systematically exploited the upland frontiersmen. Colonial records indicate that Nicholas participated in the violence which broke out in 1768, and further suggest that when the militia marched in to quell the rebellion, his land was confiscated. Scores of the local farmers fled west into and over the mountains, and thus the Aldridges next appear some seventy-five miles to the southwest in Rowan County. During the American Revolution, the family again had trouble with the authorities. In 1781 they petitioned the Commissioner of Confiscated Property, in an effort to retain their Rowan County land. This time the government had seized their property on suspicion that Aldridge had bound his son William "in Arms against the State." Apparently the Aldridges, like many of the piedmont families, had supported the British during the revolutionary conflict. It was their way of striking back against the hated tidewater dominance. In this instance, however, their protestations of unlawful seizure were successful, and after the treaty of peace with Great Britain, local legislation, and lengthy litigation, Aldridge was legally awarded clear title to his land in 1786.

William had been born in the 1750s and, after moving to Rowan County, had married Hannah Bell in December 1772. Among their several children was William Jr., who in turn was married in the early 1790s. His first son, John, was born in Rowan County in 1792. Between 1801 and 1803, both William Sr. and William Jr., as well as other relatives, sold their property. Sometime after October 1803, the family, led by William Aldridge, Sr., took the route that North Carolinians had followed since Daniel Boone cleared the Wilderness Road in 1775 — over the mountains through the Cumberland Gap and into east-central Kentucky. Although the Aldridges of North Carolina had bought and sold several small pieces of land and had petitioned the government for the return of their property, none of the four generations, from Nicholas through John, had been able to read or write, and all had signed legal documents with their mark.

The Aldridge lifestyle seems to have changed little in Clark County, Kentucky. They were small farmers who devoted much time to hunting, fishing, and handling livestock. William Sr. died in 1807, and William Jr. in 1832; both were buried near Winchester. In the meantime, John married Mary Jane Greening in November 1814, and when their second son was born in 1819 they named him William, in honor of his grandfather and great-grandfather. During the late 1830s, depressed farm prices and a prolonged period of economic struggle stimulated migration and drove marginal farmers from the Ohio Valley. John decided to move west to Missouri. Although most of the family elected to remain in Kentucky, John and Mary were accompanied by their son, William, and a daughter, Martha.

The Missouri period in the Aldridge odyssey is historically uncertain and confused — facts mingle with myth and legend; stories conflict, and the reminiscences are blurred. Thousands of people were moving into, through, and out of the state during the period. Renegades sometimes terrorized the countryside, and disagreements often resulted in violence. The family lived in the western part of the state and engaged in farming and the transportation of grain and other supplies to the staging center at Independence. Young William became a teamster, and hauled produce for a friend and neighbor by the name of Aaron Barrows. Once, when he and Barrows returned from the thirty-five-mile journey to Independence, they found Barrows's house burned and his family missing. One account suggests that the family had been murdered. Soon thereafter, in 1846, William married Mary "Polly" Allen, who had recently arrived with her parents from Tennessee, and the next spring they all started for Oregon.

Beginning in 1843, a sizeable flow of people left Western Missouri for the overland trek to the Pacific Northwest. Polly Allen's uncle had joined one of the earlier parties and pushed on west. In 1840, John Aldridge's daughter Martha married Andrew Welch, and they too were attracted by the stories they heard about Oregon. Peter H. Burnette's lecture tours throughout Western Missouri prompted hundreds of families to leave for the Willamette Valley during the mid-forties. Thus in the spring of 1847, John and Mary Aldridge, Martha and Andrew Welch, William and Polly Aldridge, and Polly's parents, the Allens, along with several unmarried children, joined others at Independence for the move west.

At fifty-five years of age John Aldridge was not a young man, but the desire to open up another country, to blaze a new trail, to pioneer in one more wilderness, and to see Oregon as his forefathers had seen North Carolina and Kentucky, had become irresistible. The propaganda about the West and the growing "Oregon fever" kindled the imagination of an already restless spirit. Only challenge and difficulty could satisfy such an instinct.

After surviving a variety of conflicts and hardships, the Aldridge party arrived in Oregon City, Oregon, in October 1847. In November, Lucinda was born, the first of William Aldridge's fourteen children. In August 1848, the bill creating Oregon Territory was passed by Congress, and in October of that year William and Polly filed their land claim in Polk County. The following year, William's parents, John and Mary, filed a similar claim by placing an ''X'' on the official document. John's North Carolina heritage revealed itself when he named a small stream and a nearby settlement ''Pedee,'' after a Carolina river. Although most of the family remained permanently in Polk County, William and Polly were soon attracted to an area some fifty miles south, in Lane County. In 1856 they moved with their five children to land now occupied in part by the Eugene airport. A few weeks after their arrival in Lane County, their sixth child, David Ritten Atheson (''Att'') Aldridge, father of Anita Kunkler, was born.

By 1861, William and Polly were again on the move, and, with their rapidly growing family of ten children, they decided to settle in the hill country of Northern California. Clearly, the Aldridges did not think of themselves as among the vanguard of a historic movement. They did not wish to carve out a domain from which their children could dominate a valley. Even the liberal inducement of 640 acres of free land offered by the Oregon Donation Act of 1850 was insufficient to hold them. They were not concerned with becoming the ''salt of the earth'' or the ''backbone of America'' but almost automatically tested themselves against hardships and dangers. No reward was expected except the personal satisfaction of having ''measured up'' against the harsh forces of nature. Years later, when asked why he had left the extensive land grants which he and his parents had claimed in Oregon, William suggested that he had probably moved to California in search of his Missouri friend and benefactor, Aaron Barrows. Barrows had left Independence on a wagon train bound for California at about the same time that William had left for Oregon. They had agreed to seek out each other in the West, but the friend was never found.

A substantial number of Oregonians were moving into Northern California in the fifties and sixties, and Shasta County, on the upper reaches of the Sacramento River, provided a natural gateway for travel both north and south. The first settlement of the region had been made in the mid-forties, when Pierson B. Reading and Samuel J. Hensley contracted with John A. Sutter to trap and raft logs down the river. In 1850, Shasta became one of California's original twenty-seven counties; and later the same year, the trading post of Shingletown was established about halfway between the Sacramento River and Mount Lassen. The next year, the settlement became a station on the Nobel Pass trail, which ran west from the Humboldt River in Nevada, along Honey Lake, past Mount Lassen, to Shingletown, and then on into the Sacramento Valley. But while migrants passed through the eastern part of the county, most of the population growth in the fifties and sixties was in the mining areas of Whiskeytown and French Gulch, and around the county seat of Shasta City.

Millville, six miles east of the Sacramento River, and Shingletown, twenty-five miles up in the mountains, came to represent more remote and often rebellious centers of activity. In 1861, Millville petitioned to become the seat of a new county to be carved from the southeastern corner of Shasta County; and at about the same time, the entire area developed considerable pro-Confederate sympathies. A sawmill had been started at

Shingletown in 1852, and the migrants on the Nobel Trail had steadily increased during the fifties; but it was not until about 1860 that farmers of the Aldridge type began to stake out homesteads in the narrow creek valleys, and officially register their timber claims.

William Aldridge drifted for a few months in the mountains to the east of the river. Several times he walked the more than three hundred miles to his home in Oregon and then back to California. At one point, he was on Antelope Creek in eastern Tehama County, and later he lived in the forest along South Cow Creek in Shasta County. But in early 1862 he moved five miles south, over the Blue Mountains, and, along with the family, built a house near the confluence of Snow Creek and the North Fork of Bear Creek, some six miles north of Shingletown. The deed of May 3, 1862, indicates that the Aldridges took over the homestead of James and Elizabeth McCoy and paid $1,400 for the claim of 160 acres and McCoy's personal property. The 1862 tax rolls show William Aldridge owning one cow, one wagon, four horses, and twenty hogs. When William had left Lane County, Oregon, he had purchased a wagon and horses from a rancher who gave him a branding iron. The $\mathcal{Y}$ became the brand for the Aldridge ranch (Bonnie Craigs), and the iron was still in use as of 1973.

The Aldridges of California lived in a society so new that its members were bound to each other by few and slight ties. They had a pattern, a foundation, and a past — but, like most hill country settlers, they gave little thought to the Victorian claims of inner virtue, religious vision, or indomitable faith. Hardships and exertion had long been their constant companions, and the nature of frontier life had long since rendered them pragmatic. Nor did California agriculture prove a utopian find: there were mean log huts, a crude diet of wild meat and fruits, and a physically crushing life for women and children. They accepted California with its rowdiness and its vice, and they were only vaguely aware of the state's new myths and values.

But despite their many migrations, the Aldridges of California were still the Aldridges of the Appalachians and the Ozarks. Their colonial heritage, along with their hill-country habits, their traditional culture, and their new environment, blended and helped shape the family's destiny. These frontier folk had no formal education, but they were canny and resourceful; they were unsophisticated, but sturdy and self-reliant; they were friendly and hospitable, but violently independent. And whether because of heredity or American geography or economic necessity, they were rebels — they opposed tidewater aristocrats, colonial governors, Revolutionary War leaders, and Unionist advocates. William's sympathies lay with the active Confederate movement of southeastern Shasta County and, along with many of his neighbors, he questioned the boisterous patriotism of the merchants, newspapermen and ranchers west of the Sacramento. There was a bull and bear fight at Millville in which the bull, named Jeff Davis, supposedly killed the bear, Abe Lincoln. The Shasta *Courier* repeatedly denounced the ''traitorous'' actions of some of the people of the Millville and Shingletown area. On May 30, 1863, it declared, ''The time has come when these worshippers of Davis will not be allowed to insult the ears of Union men with impunity.'' The next year, William and Polly named their eleventh child Jefferson Davis Aldridge; and until his death in 1891, William continued to avow the rebel cause.

But, as during the previous centuries, the family had little time for the luxury of either national or local politics. Instead they were engaged in a struggle for simple survival. Anita has graphically detailed the frontier conditions faced by her grandparents on North Bear Creek.

Here, they began their battle to eke a living from the poor sandy soil, which was filled with rocks, some of which were of boulder size. In spots, the sandstone lay but a few inches beneath the soil. Water from a spring, which arose at the base of a high, gray cliff, found its way down the mountain and was used for irrigation. The cliff, which towered behind the house, was the only spectacular thing about the place.

Some nights, they saw campfires of wild Indians on top of the cliff. These Indians raided the garden from time to time, and one time, when the entire family had gone for the day, the red devils destroyed and carried away all their household things. The only thing overlooked was the big iron pots Grandmaw Mary [Polly] cooked in over the fireplace and her spinning wheel.

Grandad was a giant of a man, over six feet tall and weighing better than two hundred pounds. Despite his size, strength, and determination, the task of wrestling a living from this untamed place taxed him to the utmost. With the help of the entire family, he felled trees, grubbed brush and cleared away rocks. Almost every year there was a new baby until the final number stood at fourteen.

With the family's needs becoming so very pressing, David Atheson, or "Att," as he was known, went to work early in life.[1] He later declared that despite the family's extensive spinning and weaving of clothes, he was twelve years old before he received his first pair of pants and was at last able to discard his

1. The hill people of Northern California followed President Andrew Jackson's dictum that it was a damn poor man who could spell a

xvii

long-tailed, smock-like shirt. He was in his teens before he earned his first pair of shoes by hiring out as a teamster. While young, he hunted rabbits and squirrels, and protected the crops from marauding animals; but as he grew older, he quickly excelled at hunting deer, bear, wild hogs, and bobcats. At nineteen, Att was employed as a buckaroo, driving cattle between Northern California and Eastern Oregon; and in early 1875, he secured a job as a type of pony express rider, carrying mail out of Lake View, Oregon. He soon fell in love with a girl by the name of Anita and was planning to propose marriage when the girl eloped with a fellow mail courier. In deep depression, he quit his job and returned to Shasta County. Thirty-two years later he insisted upon naming his last child Anita.

Once Att had returned home, most of his older brothers left for more profitable employment. William Aldridge was then in his late fifties and had failing eyesight; therefore, Att slowly assumed many of the family responsibilities and the managerial duties connected with the ranch. A much younger and slightly retarded brother, William Lee, became his constant companion and admiring follower; the two remained close friends throughout life. Young Bill was an unusually mild-mannered and imitative youth who sometimes needed help in defending himself in a big and boisterous family and in competing in a rowdy community. Although Att was high-spirited, he was always conscious of his brother's needs, and saw himself as Bill's protector.

It had become a common practice for the Aldridges to round up fifteen to twenty wild hogs each autumn and fatten then for the winter meat supply. In 1875, Att and Bill decided to turn

---

word only one way. Some five different spellings of Att's name have been found: Atterchen, Atterson, Atchison, Atheson, and Atcherson. The name was probably selected in honor of the prosouthern senator from Missouri, David Rice Atchison.

hog-catching into a lucrative business. Att's excitement in relating the story to Anita years later revealed much about his rural interests and the community's rustic lifestyle.

That summer [1875], I began wonderin how I could make some money. The oaks was bendin and bustin with acorns that year. That put an idea in my head. If our corn turned out big, and we could get ten, twelve ton of these acorns picked up, we might make a heap of money catchin wild hogs and sellin them, if we was men enough to drive them to the railroad. I'd noticed there was more slick ears in the woods than I ever seen before. Early that fall, me and Bill lit out and brought in a couple of dozen wild hogs fer our winter meat.

We fixed up the big corral so it was bull-tight fer a place to hold a big bunch. I figured we had enough corn with the acorns to get a bunch gentle enough so as we could drive them to market. Wild hogs in those day weren't like the few that range down in the thicket now [about 1915]. There was old boars, ten, twelve years old, that had tusks as long as a billy goat's horn. To catch and fetch in one of those old boys, you had to step damn lively, and have some darn good dogs. I fired the younger kids into pickin up acorns, and they had a pile of them ten feet tall in no time. Early one mornin, me and Bill took our three dogs and lit out lookin fer hogs. We struck hog signs right away. From their tracks, I knew it was a sow and eight or ten half-grown shoats. Down the ridge a ways, we jumped them, and the dogs went lookin fer the shoats. One by one, they tracked them down and caught em, and we tied them tight with piggin strings we'd fetched along fer that purpose. We felt pretty good about our catch. Nine shoats and the old sow. In no time, we'd have the corral full; and if we could get anywhere near the price bein paid fer tame hogs, we'd be makin a hell of a lot of money. I couldn't think fer the life of me why I hadn't thought of this before. We dragged the shoats up where the sow was and then the job of sewin their eyes shut with needle and a stout thread began.

You gotta use a lot of gumption drivin wild hogs, even with their eyes sewed shut. But once they find out they can't see to run, they settle down and go along with their noses on the ground, feelin their way, and stay bunched together. They keep listenin fer a feller and keep goin in the opposite direction from where they hear you. The secret is to always keep yourself in the opposite direction from the way you're wantin them to go.

We kept on catchin hogs every day until we had a whole corral full of them. Among the bunch, we had twelve to fifteen of those big wicked boars, like I was tellin you about, real old tuskers. I had no idea that we'd get more than four bits a head fer the likes of them, but they put up such a dang-busted fight, we'd brung them in to prove to them and to ourselves that we could do it.

We had five hundred and forty-two when we counted the lot. As you know, most everyone calls me Att. It was about this time the fellers around the country began calling me "Wild Hog Att."

Although the hogs escaped from the corral, inflicted injuries on their captors, and consumed more acorns than was planned, in late autumn they were fattened sufficiently to be sold at the stockyards at Anderson, thirty miles away. Among the many hazards of the drive were the numerous cliffs and ravines of the mountains, and the necessity of fording several streams, including the Sacramento River, in the lowlands. A few hogs were lost along the way; but the Aldridge children stayed close and even swam the rivers with the livestock. In 1875, Att received $1,350 for 540 hogs delivered to the railroad siding at Anderson. For Att and his family, the experiment had proven a phenomenal financial success — and one that was to be repeated over the following years.

During Att's youth, Shasta County was still sparsely settled and primitive, and it abounded with fish, game, and wild animals.[2] In 1870, the county contained only four thousand persons, mostly in the communities of Shasta and Millville, or in the mining districts. The wild hogs and native Indians did not disappear until the forests were systematically cut, toward the end of the century. Indians poached from the Aldridge garden until the 1890s, and the last grizzly bear to be killed in California was shot in 1895 at Inwood, some four miles from the Aldridge ranch. Although Shingletown was founded as a trading post, it quickly became a lumber center. At an elevation of 3,488 feet, it was situated just above the steep fall line and at the lower or western edge of a forested plateau. The heavy forest extended some fifteen miles to the east before it was broken by the volcanic rock and the rugged terrain of the Lassen Peak

---

2. Shasta County, like other frontier communities, became famous for its uncouth tastes in naming its towns. One local historian has suggested that Horsetown, Churntown, Muletown, Middletown, Spring Creek, Dog Creek, Whiskey Creek, and Eagle Creek are almost classical when compared to names of other Shasta County towns.

district. The Shingletown post office was established in June 1874, and about 1880 the mass export of lumber products began. By the 1890s, Shingletown teamsters were hauling about four million board-feet of lumber, a million shakes, and ten thousand posts a year down the steep slopes to the Sacramento River or the adjacent railroad.

During the last two decades of the century, the communities of Shingletown, Inwood, and Whitmore became famous for their dances, all-night parties, and masquerade balls. Thanksgiving, New Year's, Saint Patrick's Day, the Fourth of July, and other holidays brought boisterous frontier-type celebrations to the lumbering towns. Att was the caller for many of the square dances. He was handsome, congenial, and had a good sense of humor; he enjoyed dancing, drinking hard liquor, and fiddle-playing. But he was neither a lumberjack nor a reckless spendthrift, and his greatest pleasure was a ten-day hunting trip in the high country with his horse, dogs, and gun. He was by instinct a frontiersman — an excellent shot with a rifle, an experienced tracker of wild animals, and an able horseman. Although he was a storyteller and, when drinking, a noisy exhibitionist, most of all he enjoyed being alone in the mountains. He seized upon every opportunity to hunt and trail game, and he knew every precipice, canyon, cave, and thicket in the region.

Att also understood human nature; he quickly learned the value and uses of money; and he became an authority on livestock. He developed a fine style as a bargainer and trader. He once informed a stocks-and-bonds salesman that the only stock he would buy had to have four legs and no paper certificate under it. The mundane activities of planting, harvesting, mending fence, milking cows, and other farming chores bored him. Whenever possible, he shifted these duties on to other people.

He quickly sensed the need for extensive irrigation works, and he engineered the construction of several ditches and the watering of all available land in the immediate valley. As he grew older, the excitement of hunting and the more prosaic pleasure of irrigating the clover and planting fruit trees became his chief avocations.

Att was some thirty years of age when he became acquainted with an attractive thirteen-year-old girl, Sarah Elizabeth Parker, who lived about eight miles up the valley on the headwaters of North Bear Creek. Her father Steven Parker had migrated to California from Illinois, and in the mid-seventies he met and married Maria McElroy of the Stockton area. One of Maria's grandparents was Cherokee; another was descended from a coastal tribe living north of San Francisco. Maria was a colorful, pipe-smoking, venturesome woman. The Parkers were drifters who often moved two or three times in a year, and possessed only meager items of personal property — a wagon, a team of horses, some chickens, and a very few household utensils. Steven was one of the many poachers in the Shingletown area who cut trees and split them into posts, pickets, and shakes, which he sold to buyers from the central valley. Since he did not own the timber, he had to work on public land; and if he happened to be on private property, it became expedient to move on before the owner learned of his activity.

In the mid-eighties, the Parkers settled in the forest on a tributary of North Bear Creek known as Camp Creek. Sarah had been born near Stockton on September 22, 1873, and, although quite young when the family moved to Camp Creek, she was the oldest of the family's three daughters and had to assist her father in the forest. Indeed, she became an expert in the art of falling trees, sawing cuts from the logs, splitting out the bolts, and checking and riving. After two or three years, the Parkers decided that their daughters should be educated. Since there was no school in the vicinity, they moved some nine miles down North Bear Creek, and built another shake cabin near one of the oldest and best-known schools in Shasta County.[3] The daughters attended Bear Creek School for two years until, in the winter of 1888-1889, the family dedicded to relocate in Yolo County.

Before the Parkers moved south, Att and Sarah, or "Sadie," as she was known, had become engaged, and Att had filed a claim for government land three miles up North Bear Creek from his parents' ranch. It was an untamed piece of mountainous property which had less than twenty acres of creek bottom suitable for farming; the remaining acreage was quite hilly and rocky. During 1889, Att built a house, a barn, some sheds, and a corral near the creek; but it was extremely difficult to clear the boulders, brush, and trees from some additional eight acres. However, by late autumn he had moved in with his wagon, three horses, two cows, four hogs, and six dozen chickens. The feature which most pleased Att, after his year of hard work, was the emotional satisfaction of decorating the front gate and selecting a name for the ranch. As Anita later explained: "The thing he liked best of his handiwork was an arch he constructed atop the frontyard gate. On this arch he had fashioned from manzanita limbs, cut and bent to form each letter, a motto: WELCOME TO HARDSCRABBLE — the name he had given his homestead. Some might say it was a crude thing, but it had grace

---

3. The Bear Creek School, first opened in 1862, was financed by local subscription. The building was moved several times, but by the 1880s it was permanently located at the falls on South Fork Bear Creek. Several of the teachers during the late nineteenth century were German men from the Whitmore area.

and dignity as it sat perched on a thick, hand-hued cedar board, cut to the shape of a rainbow.''

By Christmastime 1889, the Parkers were on the move again. They drifted back north and temporarily settled near Red Bluff. Att immediately went to see Sadie. They were married, and three days later they arrived back at Hardscrabble. As they drove up to the arch, Att, who was almost thirty-five, romantically assured his new, seventeen-year-old bride who had never known a permanent home, ''You will never have to move around again. This is home for always.'' Years later, their daughter sensed that, despite consuming problems, Att and Sadie had succeeded at Hardscrabble.

> My Mother was happy, and left no stone unturned to make the place shine from physical effort and the special touch that every good wife puts into making a home. They worked side by side, clearing land and digging a ditch for irrigation water. It was rough digging. Part of it wound around a steep hill which was solid rock. This had to be drilled and dynamited. Mom turned the drill and Dad did the striking with a double jack-hammer to get holes down, to dynamite the rock. This done, more land clear, they planted it to garden and redclover.

Sadie was soon pregnant. A midwife from over the Blue Mountains was alerted, and on March 30, 1891, Estella May was born. Two years later Agnes joined the family; and in August 1895 the midwife again crossed the mountains to deliver a son, Albert Carl. Less than a month before Albert's birth, Estella had become ill from eating too many almonds. Att had raced over twenty miles to Millville to seek a doctor and then galloped back up the hot, narrow valley. The doctor arrived later in the evening, but Estella had died. Att's young saddle horse also died later in the night.

For over a decade, Att and Sadie and the two children lived quietly in the little clapboard dwelling sandwiched between the road and North Bear Creek. South of the road was the steep and boulder-strewn Chalk Mountain (Att called its northern spur "High Rock Spring Mountain"), and north of the creek was Rail Pile Hill and Alamine Peak. Several springs flowed from the north side of High Rock Spring Mountain. The little streams found their way across the road or through culverts, and provided water for Att's expanding orchard and the springhouse where the family kept their milk, cream, and butter. Sadie churned the rich cream into many pounds of butter and Att delivered it to the store at Shingletown, where it was eagerly purchased by the cooks from logging camps and lumber companies. Att slowly enlarged the homestead until he owned some five hundred acres; but he did not expand his farming operations. Sadie worked with him in the fields. They used a scythe and hand cradle to cut the small patches of hay and clover, and then employed an "Injun sulky" to gather it up. The sulky was pulled by two people, each with a strap over one shoulder and under the opposite arm. The tongue of the sulky was balanced between the two workers and provided a steering mechanism. Sadie not only helped pull the rake, she also assisted in mending the fence, often looked after the livestock, did much of the milking, and performed many of the barnyard chores.

In early 1907, twelve years after the birth of Albert, Sadie learned that she was pregnant again. The thought disturbed her deeply, and throughout Anita's childhood and early youth Sadie often informed the household that having a child late in life was a serious mistake. Att, on the other hand, was delighted with the prospect of fathering another son. He decided that the family had enough money for Sadie to go to her mother's home in Anderson for the birth, and to secure the services of a doctor. On October 23, 1907, Sadie gave birth to a healthy daughter. The child was named Maude Irene by grandmother Parker; but five days later when Att arrived in town, he not only expressed disappointment that the baby was a girl, but angrily vetoed Maude Irene as a name. He chose Anita Vivian instead. Over the following months, the fifty-one-year-old Att seemed to forget that the child was a girl. He called her ''Scrub,'' and a communion of spirit and an understanding which was not shared by other members of the family developed between the two. Even as a small child, Anita absorbed Att's interest in animals, his love of the wilderness, and his inherent loneliness. She has drawn a poignant sketch of herself and of the family lifestyle at Hardscrabble.

> I was a funny-looking little kid. As thin as a scarecrow, with big hands and feet. Hair a yellow straw color, very long and straight. Mom braided it in pigtails. She parted it in the center and pulled it up and back so tight it gave me an owlish look in my rather too large, green eyes.
>
> When a child is brought up in a backwoods country and without the companionship of other children their age, which was my fate, it is difficult for anyone who has not experienced it to understand the different complexes as to likes, dislikes, viewpoint, and behavior in general that one has.
>
> I had a favorite spot to play across the road in front of the house. It was under some large oak trees. There, I played in the sand for hours, talking to myself a lot of the time, in make-believe of some-

thing I was playing. If I grew tired of this, there was always the calves, and sometimes I had a pet fawn or the little pigs. I would climb into the pigpen, go into the little ones' bed, and play with them, pretending I was one of their kind. They seemed to welcome me, and we were all friends.

The road ran in front of our house. There was occasional travelers that came that way. I kept my ears peeled for the sound of their approach. When I'd see or hear a stranger coming, I'd scurry for the wagon shed to hide in the shake pile. The shake pile was bundled shakes piled in such a fashion that there was small hallways inside the pile.

Some travelers stayed all night. When this happened, the only way Mom could get me out of the pile was let me starve or freeze out. If that didn't work, she would coax until she lost patience, then get me and drag me into the house by force. I'd set my feet and bawl loud, hoping Dad would hear me and make her let me go. In madness, she would say, ''Shut up, or I'm gonna knock the puddin out of you.'' Inside, I'd shut up because I did not want to draw the attention of the strangers. At the table, I was so bashful I could only pick at my food; but after Dad and the strangers had retired to the living room, I'd wolf down enough food to fill three kids my size. I was always hungry.

My family usually had what they called a ''sing'' after the work was done for the day. Agnes at the organ playing chords, we'd sing for an hour or more. Mom was a good soprano, Agnes alto, Al sang tenor, and Dad a deep bass. I added my squeaky voice, which was always off-key, but they said I sang good, that I did "Jim Dandy." They just put up with me.

As a child, Anita indulged in mischievous and sometimes dangerous games. She had encounters with rattlesnakes, played with a pet dog which had rabies, secretly kept coyote pups as pets, made dog harnesses out of valuable leather straps, constantly got bruised and injured, and went hunting with her father almost as soon as she could walk. The rural drifters and local figures of rumor and mystery particularly intrigued her. Tom Moore "was evil-looking, one eye gone, an ear which looked to have been torn off or chewed off, and he had a scar which ran from his temple to one corner of his mouth. He was tall and bony, and spoke as if he was from the deep South." He lived in a small shack on the ridge near Jump-up Springs high up on Chalk Mountain. He had no employment and seemed to enjoy Att's conversation and the food given him by Sadie. One day, Tom surprised Anita while she was playing in the blackberry patch. Much against her will, he lifted her off the ground — only to be attacked by Att's dogs. In desperation, he found refuge on the roof of the smokehouse. When Sadie found out that he had tried to hug Anita, her voice trembled with excitement and fury, and, with a shotgun pointed at the intruder, she ordered him from the farm. Tom was not seen by the Aldridges again.

In a remote and outwardly placid community, such encounters created a state of emotional anxiety for months: although few of the lonely and solitary individuals who eked out an existence on society's fringes were either mysterious or criminally inclined, they fired the imagination of isolated families and struck concern into the hearts of rural women and children.

Anita's childhood seclusion and rural isolation allowed her to highlight unusual encounters and experiences, and gave her time to fashion them into a high folk memoir. With fine sensitivity, she catches the seasons changing, the sunlight through the trees, birds in flight, and the wonders of animals and nature. In thought and expression, she relies upon the most direct and eloquent forms. She is her story's protagonist, unveiling her inner thoughts and personal life. She sees the conflicts, aggressions, absurdities, and weaknesses in others. She sees the members of her immediate family, and a few outsiders, playing their many roles. She sees natural obstacles such as mountains, floods, and bobcats, but to her they are only circumstantial. Her delightfulness and drama come from within — from her zest, her *joie de vivre*. Anita becomes a fully rounded character, who — although quite young — thinks rationally, feels deeply, and remembers well.

The headlong push over the Appalachian Mountains, across the Mississippi River, and finally to the Pacific Coast reoriented the American outlook and helped to mold a western character. The story has been told many times, but it is forever popular. The drama of the western trek and especially the rush of the forty-niners produced a particularly large body of exciting and imaginative literature. Scores of participants in the migration provided rich and colorful accounts of every phase of the movement, and a generation later the aging pioneers built on that heritage by authoring a new set of recollections and reminiscences. Far less thought and concern has been shown for the second and third generation of hill country Californians: the gold was gone; the dramatic discoveries and intensity of feeling that had attracted both participants and observers had died away. The cities of the central valley and the coastal areas had drawn the commerce and the industry of a growing state away deliver babies; moonshine flows freely; and national, state, and even local regulations are viewed as foreign infringements. Never again will meat for the table be regularly supplied by the rifle, fruit grow wild for the picker, timber be cut by drifting squatters, or men work, fish, or drink at their own discretion. It is the end of an era. HARDSCRABBLE'S inhabitants are among the last of what was once the great American majority.

The author of HARDSCRABBLE was neither trained nor experienced at writing, but she expresses her feelings with directness and clarity, and can savor and relive whatever happened to her. Many diaries and memoirs are lugubrious, monotonous and evasive fragments of a life; but Anita does not tantalize us with the memory of an era that is gone and from which we hear only echoes. She allows us to listen in on a real past; she provides us with a delightful continuity; and she restores our sense of intimacy in history. As the chief character, she emerges strong and aggressive, but unfailingly sensitive and feminine. She does not allow time to make her memory rigid or nostalgia to deface her perspective. She is always able to see through the deposit of years and reexperience her girlish enthusiasm without becoming bewildered or sentimental. Of course, life in the hill country of Shasta County was often routine and unspectacular; but through her power to recall, select, and place in perspective, she has translated her experiences into both a valuable historical document and a vital human reminiscence.

The tales of Anita's youth are always vivid in her memory. As stories of childish daring, haphazard growth, personal involvement, and real adventure, they are told easily and straightforwardly — the reader is reminded of *Huckleberry Finn* or *True Grit*. And yet individual incidents, like the one in which her father pursued a wildcat with mystical determination, suggest *Moby Dick* or *Track of the Cat*. The stories never tease the reader with momentous questions that subsequently are dismissed as unanswerable. The author shows little interest in progress, public morality, social injustice, or enlightened society. As a child, she is seldom cautious or formal; rather, she is blessed with determination, an earthy kind of wit, and a deep love of nature and the outdoor life. Her uneducated intelligence, humble understanding, fidelity, and consistent good humor attract and convince the reader. Her involvement is beyond ego: she uses the memories of childhood to come to terms with her existence. She sees as a poet, and she views the past with love. She is by instinct a storyteller, and her style is strong and poignant. HARDSCRABBLE is as much a novel as a memoir.

Since Anita grew up in the back country, she readily understood her elders' audacious hyperbole. HARDSCRABBLE is a written outgrowth of that oral tradition, reflecting the peculiar sense of place and continuity of experience which was so necessary for human sustenance. The author portrays people but does not evaluate them; she reveals a mood but does not pass judgment. She writes for her own satisfaction and for the pride and pleasure of her family. Yet her story is selective, interpretive, and full of imagery, and it should help give her kind of people a place in the Western sun.

Contemporaries of Anita wrote of the picturesque glory of the California hills, and of the churches, schools, libraries, and other marks of civilization supposedly sought by the early settlers. Anita is much too close to her roots to speak of "picturesque glory" or "marks of civilization." She tells of a people who filled no particular niche in society. They were not part of the corporate settlement. They were neither above nor below anyone; neither leaders nor followers; neither employees nor employers. They were not persecuted, nor did they persecute. Rather, they were independent, with little anxiety for social station, and generally content with free, uninvolved survival. Her family neither belonged to nor attended church. They embraced no religious faith. Her father argued that ''talkin to your grub'' and ''beggin to some . . . Supreme Bein'' was ''hog wash.'' They did not support the Masons, the Oddfellows, the Rotary, the Chamber of Commerce, or the Ku Klux Klan. Anita would not have enjoyed the Girl Scouts; she attended the young ladies' sewing circle only once.

Anita was not a prophet of progress, a chronicler of growth, a dreamer, or a mystic. Instead, she reflects a sense of the heroic, of the pastoral, of the vanishing frontier. She offers us the atmosphere of lingering promise — a bit of the fable that was frontier America, that was golden California.

W.S.S.

1

BULLFIGHT AT HARDSCRABBLE

A S I LOOK back through the years to my first memories of Hardscrabble, I see it, a rather beautiful mountain ranch, set in a little valley with high hills on its
north and south boundaries.

High Rock Spring Mountain was to the south, and Rail Pile
Hill and the Lick Springs and Alamine Peak to the north. You
could see Blue Mountain in a westerly direction, and eastward
you could see but to the farthest end of the meadow; the view of
the hills, which lay beyond, was screened by the tall pine trees
which grew there at the meadow's edge. Bear Creek skirted the
meadow on its northern edge. Moss-covered, sandstone cliffs
covered the hill directly south and in front of the house.

The house was unpainted, its roof of shakes. It might have
been termed a mountain shack by a passerby who had not seen
and felt the warmth and well-being that glowed within its walls.
In spring and summer, flowers bloomed everywhere near the
house. Violets, pansies, roses, sweet williams and many others
made the yard a place of beauty, and the sweet smell of the
honeysuckle, which covered the front porch, scented the entire

place. That, and the smell of new-mown hay, ripe cherries, and June apples, is the thing I remember most vividly.

Row upon row of hog sheds nestled over near the gully. The barn and corrals were below, on a little rocky flat. The wagon and woodsheds were near the north side of the house. South sat the smoke house where the hams, bacon, and sausage were smoked. This is also a place I shall always remember for its delicious smells and the sight it presented with the smoked meat hanging from its rafters.

The strawberry and currant patch grew between it and the irrigation ditch. The ditch-water went babbling along through the yard, crossing a high, leaky flume across Rock Spring Branch; and then it hurried on down the ditch, which ended at the Clover Patch on down the canyon.

Chicken hens, forever busy at their egg-laying job, hurried around and cackled and chicked, while the rooster flirted among them, keeping the barnyard gay with his crowing. You could hear a cowbell tinkle over on the hillside, while near the barn lot you could hear the contented grunts of the sows as they nursed their pigs while laying in the shade of the big oaks which grew there.

The spring where we got our cold drinking water was another pleasant place. The moss was ankle-deep around it. This was the home of one of my friends, a little bright-green frog which I called, "Hoppy." He could jump six feet, and when he croaked you would have guessed he was as big as a bullfrog, if you hadn't seen him. Mom kept big crocks of butter and gallons of cream there in the cool. The spring, and a burlap cooler she had made, was our refrigeration.

Inside the house, there was no elaborate fixings or furniture. The kitchen was a place of many delicious smells: preserves simmering on the back of the Home Comfort wood range; the tantalizing aroma of homemade bread, fresh from the oven; and usually a ham or roast in the oven. This kept my appetite whetted to a peak all the time.

The living room I can remember mostly for its warmth in the cold winter evenings. When memory takes me back through the haze of years past to one of these evenings, I see us all setting around the old heater, eating popcorn and apples. Mom, at peace with the world, painstakingly darning socks, flashing smiles at us when she looked up fron her work. Her face was almost beautiful, despite the evidence of hard work she had done. Her hands were toilworn and red. She was pleasingly plump and a little over five feet tall. Her dark hair was always coiled on top of her head, with ornamental combs holding stray locks in place in the back. Her eyes were black. And I can see Dad, with hair almost entirely gray, setting in his rocking chair, stroking his mustache, spinning yarns, and spitting tobacco juice in his spittoon. His face was long and narrow, with deep dimples in each cheek, which came and went as he talked and smiled. Thickset, bristly eyebrows set above his gray eyes gave him a touch of harshness in appearance.

It was a red-letter day for me when we went hunting, when someone came to visit, or even when a stray animal wandered down the road. One of my first recollections is of a long-horned Spanish bull which drifted to Hardscrabble. We first seen him on the flat across the creek from the corral. He was courting one of our cows. Our bull, ''Pitt,'' scented the rascal and came trotting down the ridge, bellowing and bawling to beat the band. He came on down the road in front of the house. He was mad and getting madder every step he took. His ''boo-boos'' and brassy-sounding bawls shook the air as he passed by, telling the stranger, ''You get the hell away from Roxie, she's mine. I'm gonna whip the socks off of you.''

The black one heard his threats and answered right back — with his ''boo-boos'' and brassy bawl as loud as Pitt's — and seemed to say, ''Hooey. Come on, you big bully, try and run me off! If you think you're gonna whip me, you had better think twice, cause I'm meaner than the devil himself.''

We could see him at the far edge of the flat. He was pawing the ground with one foot and then the other, sending great plumes of dirt in the air, it coming down on his back in a cloud of dust. Pitt was not stopping to listen. He went on, wringing his tail, bawling and boo-booing louder than ever. He swiftly crossed the creek and he, too, stopped to paw the earth. Then he flew in a chaparral and ripped it to pieces. His dark red body glistened in the sun. The black one came towards him, his head high, displaying his long, murderous horns to the best advantage. He was sounding off in a series of screaming bawls, the sound of which set my skin crawling.

The canyon was aroar with the echoes of this fight talk from the bulls. Dust was raising from the pawing of both the bulls as they grew near each other. They sparred with one another by bowing up and eyeing each other. After all this fight talk, they finally clashed.

The combustion of their mighty strength and weight coming together rent the air. You could hear their loud breathing and the crunching of their hooves on rocks and gravel as they made their swift charge; then all hell broke loose.

''Come, we'll rock that black bugger out of the country,'' Dad excitedly said to Al and Agnes.

''Me, I'll go too,'' I said, overcome by the excitement.

''No, you won't, you're too little. You stay on the porch and watch,'' he instructed.

They took off in a run, crossed the creek, and armed themselves with rocks as they drew near the fighting animals. It was apparent that despite Pitt's size and determination, he was a poor match for the agile black one with his long, keen-pointed horns which were made for fighting. Pitt was of a short-horn breed, and his small horns were proving poor defense for him.

It was just as the black one had forced Pitt through a bush and over a log, and knocked him off his feet in a pile of rocks, that the folks drew within throwing distance. They began a simultaneous barrage of rocks, thumping hard against the black's ribs and head. This had little effect upon the maddened bull. It looked as if he would kill Pitt, as he gored him to the hollow and Pitt screamed in agony.

Thoroughly hating him for the way he was butchering Pitt alive, I took off the porch and crossed the creek, arming myself with rocks as I went. I'd get a few good licks myself, having no doubts of being big enough to do it. As I came up out of the creek bed, I could see Pitt was up and they were again fighting. They were on the fartherest side of the flat again, and all three of the folks were still raining rocks onto the black's head and ribs.

I was past the center of the flat when our bull made a charge, hitting the other bull about midship, knocking him down with such force that he went spinning and half rolling across the ground. Dazed, he began getting to his feet, when Dad threw a rock as large as a baseball. When it struck, it sounded like the crack of a pistol shot. It landed squarely on one of the big horns and broke it loose from the bull's skull. That was the turn in the battle. With a bawl of defeat and agony, he began running. Pitt, sensing victory, came after him, hooking, racking, and ripping the black's hind end at every jump.

It was not till then that the folks saw me standing in the middle of the flat with a rock in each hand, braced to deal the black bull some more punishment when he came by me. Over the roar and thundering of the bull's running feet, I could hear Dad yell, "Get the hell out of the way, or they will kill you!"

In headlong flight, I ran towards the creek directly in the path of the running bulls. I could hear their snorts and breathing. They were almost upon me. Then, of a sudden, Agnes grabbed me by the arm and began guiding me to one side. We were really moving on. She could run like an antelope. I was pulled off my feet and she was dragging me. When we gained safety, down in the gulch, there was very little skin left on my legs, from my knees down.

"I'm gonna blister your little bottom, simply blister you!" she exclaimed, as she yanked me to my feet and shook me hard. "Should have let the bulls run over you for not stayin on the porch like you was told," she shrieked. She turned me over her knee and got in a few blistering blows when I squirmed out of her grasp. I ran a few yards, and she was about to nail me again. I stood my ground and eyed her sharply, and swore at her.

"Damn you, old Hell," I yelled at her, and picked up a rock and stood waiting for her next move. She stopped; she was a little afraid of my rock-throwing. "I'll tell Dad what you done," I shrieked. I seen him coming into the gulch, and dropped my rock and went yelling and bawling, and told him, "Agnes is tryin to kill me, Dad."

"You're all right now, Honey, don't cry. I'll carry you to the house," he said, as he gently picked me up and quieted my sobbing. Then he turned to Agnes. "I don't understand why you and your brother wants to beat on 'the Scrub' all the time. She's only a baby."

As we crossed the creek, Dad carrying me, I felt much better. As Agnes and Al came following along, I stuck out my tongue and made a gruesome face at them. I heard Agnes calling me a brat under her breath. When we reached the house, I was feeling smug over the fact that Dad had taken my side and defended me from Agnes' wrath, as always he had done.

Suddenly, there was a dour change in his attitude toward me, as he held me by my coat collar and hung me on the porch wall. My collar he hooked over a spike drove into the wall. I thought this a big joke.

"What you got her hangin there fer, Att?" Mom asked, coming from the garden.

"She don't mind a damn word I say, so I put her there so I know where she is," his sober voice said.

"What about her eatin and sleepin?" Al asked, with a titter in his voice.

"Oh, I'll take her down to eat and she can sleep there; hang a blanket over her, she'll be all right," Dad nonchalantly answered.

He means it, I thought, and began kicking and crying so loud the cats all shot under the house. Al and Agnes looked at me hanging there with a gloating expression on their faces. "Hurray," Al said, and Agnes added, "The place for the spoiled brat." Al seemed overjoyed, and pulled my legs far out from the wall and let me fly back.

"Now watch yourself, young man, you ain't too big for me to finish the job on you that I started a long time back fer throwin rocks on the barn roof," Dad sternly said. This ended Al's pestering me.

It seemed that when he was a small child, he had a yen for bombarding the barn roof. Dad tried to correct this by explaining that Al was breaking the shakes, and the roof would have to be torn away and a new one put on. Al promised he wouldn't throw rocks again, but as soon as Dad's back was turned, he began slamming rocks harder than before.

Dad, seeing him, slipped up, grasped him by the seat of his

pants and took him to the woodshed, placed his neck across the chopping block and held it there with his foot, and picked up the axe.

"What are you fixin to do with him?" Mom asked.

"Cut his damn head off. He won't mind a word I say, so I think it best to chop his head off and get rid of him."

Al pleaded for his life and said he would mind anything Dad said. Finally, Dad let him up, but with the understanding that one more time, and off would come his head.

This had meant about as much as hanging me on the wall forever. But at the time, I knew no better, and was sincere in believing every word he spoke.

2

OLD THAD

ABOUT THE TIME of the bullfight, an interesting visitor came to our hills. His likes I had never seen before. He was somewhat like Tom Moore [see page xxix] only perhaps a bit gentler. He had come into the country in a rather mysterious way; at least he kept it a secret as to where he was from and what led him to be content to live in the secluded shack he had built in a brush cove back on the mountain. He was about fifty years old.

I can't remember ever seeing him without his pistol. It was a long-barreled forty-four, its handles badly worn and scarred. Protruding from one boot top was the handle of a knife, which looked as if it was made by hand, and in a crude manner. He hunted a lot. It was said he lived on deer meat and beans.

He was a tall, lanky individual. His loose-jointed body made you think of another Abe Lincoln. His face spoiled this thought, although it had the same long shape. His well-developed chin stuck out, defying the world. He wore a handlebar mustache. His nose was what you would describe as long and large, but it was chiseled in a shape that you only thought of as "hawk-nosed.'' The skin on it was thick and wax-like, resembling the peel of a banana. His eyes were greenish-gray, and you felt as if they were seeing right through you. One drooped slightly, because of a scar which showed on an upper lid — as if maybe a knife had slashed it. His forehead was straight and square, the eyebrows upturned at their outer ends, which, to my young but observing eyes, made me think, ''Tom Cat.'' Without this joint-by-joint, feature-by-feature description of ''Old Thad,'' it would be impossible for you to see him as he really was.

The first time we seen him was the day he came by Hardscrabble afoot. Dad was out past the front gate shoeing a horse, and ''Old Thad'' stopped to talk to him. Mom called dinner, so Dad asked the man in to eat. He was quite talkative to Agnes and Mom. It was plain to see he had taken a shine to Agnes' young beauty. After that time, he came often. It seemed he was usually always around. His greatest desire, it seemed, was to show how agile and nimble he could be in performing some athletic stunt in Agnes' presence.

He didn't disclose to us what his name was. Said it was just Thad, so we referred to him as ''Old Thad.''

His hanging around irritated Dad. One day I heard him talking to Mom about ''Old Thad.'' ''He ain't no damn good to have hangin around a young girl, Sadie. You may think I'm a crank, but I'm gonna put a burr under his tail and it ain't fer off. He's a no-good bastard. The next time he comes he's gonna get it.''

Agnes and Al, like all young people in the backwoods, amused themselves in unusual ways. They competed in feats of skill. The games they played, they made up themselves.

The day was Sunday, the day set aside for rest. Agnes and Al (and, of course, I was along) were engrossed in seeing which one could jump the ditch in the widest place — that is, jump backwards. "Old Thad" arrived at the height of this contest. As was his habit, he began bragging of his unmatchable ability in such a stunt. True to his boast, he could jump the ditch backwards at its widest place, as nimble as a rabbit. Being outdid by the old codger, we lost interest in the game.

"Beat you over the fence," Al challenged, looking at Agnes.

They ran and leaped the fence, which wasn't very high. It was made of pickets and kept the orchard pigs away from the house. "Old Thad," not wanting to be left out, sprinted along just behind the two, and leaped the fence.

"That ain't nothin," he said. "From a standstill, I can jump it backwards. Watch me, my dear," he said to Sis with a smile.

Up went his bony, lean body for the backward jump. It looked like he had made it, but one boot caught on a picket and down he came astride the fence.

"Haw, ripped your britches, didn't you? You're too old to cut the mustard," Al said, laughing.

"Ah — shut up," "Old Thad" said in an undertone. "I'm gettin sick of you and that pesky little sister, always bein around and in the way. Damn kids like you don't know nothin no how."

Nosey brat I was, I seen and heard everything that happened. I hated "Old Thad." Dad had said he was no damn good. "Old Thad, you shut your own mouth!" I bristled at him with all the childish spite within me, as I picked up a rock to throw at him. "You ain't no damn good! Do you know what's gonna happen to you? Dad said he's gonna put a burr under your tail and it ain't fer off. You're a no-good bastard!" I shouted, picking up another rock and saying, "I'll bust you one."

"Babe, Babe, what are you saying, put those rocks down," Agnes scolded. She grabbed my arm and near yanked me off my feet.

"It's true," I defended. "He said it and it's not very fer off."

"She's only a child. I understand. Why don't you and I go for a walk by the creek, my dear?" "Old Thad" said to Sister wanting to smooth the little episode over. He touched her elbow in a gentle way, as if it was settled and she was going with him.

"Naw, I don't want to walk, you go if you want to walk. I'm goin in the house and help Mom. She's cookin a larrupin supper," she said, pulling her arm away.

She ran to the house to escape. Refusing to be eluded, "Old Thad" followed and spent the afternoon setting in the kitchen talking to her and Mom.

Our kitchen, to me, was the nicest part of our house. It was spotlessly clean, the floors were boards scrubbed white, and the walls were covered with a blue oilcloth. The furniture was homemade, with the exception of the chairs. They were boughten, but their bottoms had given away, and Mom had fixed them by lacing and weaving rawhide in a loose basket weave, which made them look unique. Best of all, I loved the tantalizing odors of homemade bread, cakes, pies, cooked meats, and coffee that was a part of this room.

Suppertime came, and all the goodies were heaped upon the table. "Old Thad" began his usual bragging on Mom's cooking and, greedy-like, took big helpings of everything on the table. He directed all his conversation to Agnes and Mom. His manner gentle, for he was endeavoring to charm the women with his smiles and beguiling ways.

Al looked sullen and Dad was finding nothing to say to the "Prince Charming." I was sure he must be getting set to place the burr under the old codger's tail, and this I didn't want to miss.

About the middle of the meal, "Old Thad's" manners took a noticeable change. He became serious of face and fidgeted in his chair, occasionally acting as if he intended to rise from his seat

12

and leave the table — but he never did. He was not eating anything, only pretending to do so.

Dad's place at the table was on the end. I refused to set any other place but directly beside him.

"He's gettin scared, he figures he's about to get it," I whispered to Dad.

"Huh? Get what?" he asked.

"The burr. I want to see you fix him. I told him today you was figurin to do it when he acted so smarty. He thinks you're about to fix him, cause I told him it weren't very fer off," I said, feeling good that I had told "Old Thad" straight from the shoulder what was going to happen to him. Dad looked perplexed, as he did not know about the incident that afternoon.

When supper was finished, "Old Thad" was still acting like a horse with the bellyache. Dad and Al went outside to do some chores, and Agnes and Mom began clearing the dirty dishes away and washing them. "Old Thad" was seated at the table, and I was taking the golden opportunity to bolt down a little more food. He was as fidgety and sick as a cut cat. Every time Mom and Agnes had their backs turned, he reached under his chair with one hand. He did this over and over, his face getting purple, his eyes glistening with pain.

"Oh Lord!" he said.

"What's the matter, 'Old Thad?' " I asked, getting to the floor on my knees and looking up under the chair to see what he was doing under there with his hand. Just then, I heard Dad's footsteps on the front porch.

"Oh, Lord!" again "Old Thad" ejaculated, and began in earnest jabbing and punching at a bit of himself that ran down through one of the diamond-shaped holes made by the rawhide straps. It was toggled securely there. Down came his hand again and he shoved hard with his fingers, and with an anguished moan, he leaped to his feet. He was free. He ran through the living room like a turpentined pup and met Dad head-on at the doorway, almost upsetting him as he rushed past.

"What's eatin that old bastard?" Dad asked.

"I think he's got a burr under his tail, Dad. I wanted to see you fix him, but someone else must have done it, cause I seen it under his chair, and from the look on his face, the burr was stickin his tail bad," I innocently said.

"What in hell are you talkin about, Scrub?"

"I don't know," I answered, not being exactly sure what I was talking about myself.

Nobody exactly knew what caused "Old Thad" to behave like he had, as I was the only one that actually saw the predicament he had been in, and I was too young to know really what I had seen.

3

GHOSTS IN OUR HILLS

WE HAD ANOTHER NEIGHBOR who, like "Old Thad," was a bachelor and lived alone. He had filed a homestead on government land a few miles up the creek from Hardscrabble. His name was Abe. He was talkative but seldom said anything worth listening to. He came often and stayed late into the night. Our whole family was aggravated at seeing him arrive, for he stayed and robbed us of our sleep. We learned, from his conversation, that he was afraid of the dark. He explained that was why he usually carried a lantern wherever he went. He was cautious not to be caught after night without a light.

He was downright comical looking. A bit on the fleshy side, and of an average height. The upper part of his face was round, as was his head; but when it came to his chin, it receded so far back in his face you doubted his having one. But as you followed down to his Adam's apple — which was almost as large as an apple — and it began wobbling up and down in a spasmodic way, as he spoke so quickly, you knew the tiny lump at the center of his jawbone was truly his chin. His eyes were milky blue, and stared in a fixed gaze. They watered badly, and reminded you of a peeled, frozen onion. He walked every place he went, as he had no horse.

Early one morning, as he passed by our house, he was not carrying his lantern. Presumably, he intended on returning home before dark. The possibility of having supper with us caused him to stop by on his return from town. Before the meal was finished, darkness came, and he was terrorized by having no light. He asked if we would loan him one of ours. Being told we had an extra one, he settled back for a long visit. We were disappointed he didn't leave immediately so we could enjoy the evening by ourselves. But everyone knew he would stay far into the night.

It was a stormy night. The rain roared on the roof, and it was black as cats outside. The fire in the stove roared, snapped, and crackled, as if it was trying to outdo the storm.

Conversation centered on bear and panther stories. Dad told of dreadful happenings concerning these animals when driven by hunger or the plain urge to kill.

Abe sat with his butt on the very edge of the chair, his big, watery eyes glowing as they shifted from one face to the other. At the conclusion of each story he would bounce to his feet and say, ''I've got to be gettin up that road.'' But Dad kept the stories going, and it seemed these dreadful things always happened to innocent people who were away from home on a dark, stormy night, such as was Abe's case at the moment. He was either too fascinated by Dad's stories or too afraid to leave. The lantern that he was borrowing had been lighted for two hours or more.

The wind moaned and howled around the corners of the house; the rain roared on the roof and splashed on the window panes. Suddenly, Dad jumped to his feet and exclaimed, ''God, what a night for a murder!''

16

Abe came near falling out of his chair from fright when Dad did this. Finally, he came near leaving. He was standing by the door with the lighted lantern in his hand, and seemed to be bracing himself for the fury of the storm and the darkness out there, when Dad nonchalantly said to him, "Say, I've been meanin to ask you. Did you ever hear any strange noises when you're goin past Nickel Flat after dark?"

Abe's eyes bulged slightly, and the big Adam's apple made a few quick trips up and down his neck. He loudly swallowed, then gasped out in almost a whisper, "No, I can't remember any, why?"

"I just wondered," Dad answered, but said nothing more.

"What kind of noises is it that I might hear up there?" Abe sidled back toward his chair and set down.

"Well, I ain't heard them fer years; in fact, I've not let myself be caught there after dark fer a hell of a while. I can't say fer sure if it goes on any more," Dad informed the curious listener.

"Tell me, what did you hear?" Abe sputtered.

"Well, I guess you've got the right to know about it, bein's how you live up that way and pass by the place so often after dark. Even if it maybe don't happen any longer, you have the right to know, I think," Dad said, and then went on with his story.

"Away back, long time ago, and about midnight, and on certain nights when the moon is full, there was some damn strange things would go on around there. The noises came from near where the old cabin used to stand, kinda between those fireplace stones and where that old broke-down wagon is now. I'll tell you the story, and you can take it fer what you think it's worth." And Dad cleared his throat as if preparing for a long speech.

"Long years ago, some folks by the name of Andrews lived

17

fer a time in the old Nickel cabin. Mrs. Andrews' brother, Les Bibble, came to stay with them fer a spell one spring. Les was said to have a heap of money and t'was told he carried it on his person at all times.

"This Andrews pair was a kinda tough and a skinflint outfit. They were always in some scrape or other, and fought and quarreled amongst themselves sompin awful. The story goes that these Andrewses wanted Les to lend them money and he wouldn't give up nary a damn cent to them.

"One night, they got in a hell of a row, and Andrews and his wife jumped on Les, and beat him to death fer his money. The Andrewses skedaddled out of the country that night — just took their horses and Les' money, and weren't heard of since.

"Frank Boyce was just a kid then, and the next day after it happened, he found Les beat all to hell and dead, layin there in the yard. The neck yoke to the wagon, still there, was layin beside him, all smeared with blood. Looked like that's what they had killed him with. It was a gory sight."

"Oh, Good Lord!" exclaimed Abe at this disclosure.

Then Dad went on. "It was some years after that, before anyone moved into the cabin. An old codger by the name of Blue and his old lady moved in there and lived fer about two months and moved out," Dad nonchalantly said. "They claimed the place was haunted. I heard all this talk, but didn't put no stock in it. Then, finally, Bill, my brother, took it into his head to move up there and make shakes. I took the team and moved his plunder up there one evenin and, by Christ, by sunup next mornin, he was down here scared to death, and wantin me to move his things back out.

"He told me of some of the derndest things about what he'd heard there. I told him there ain't nothin to it, nothin but your imagination.

" 'Imagination, hell. By goodness, I tell you it actually happened!' Bill said.

"Well, I decided I'd go up there and stay a night with him, and prove there weren't nothin to it, t'was all a bunch of hogwash. That night, we'd had our supper and had been playin cards fer quite a while, when all at once, we heard talkin in the yard. I says to Bill, 'Someone's come,' and I got up and went to the door.

" 'It ain't no one come,' Bill tells me. 'Wait, it's startin just like it did last night.'

"I looked outside anyhow, and the yard was empty as could be. I could see just like day out there, the moon was so big and bright. I turned to Bill and admits maybe he's right. The hair on the back of my neck was gettin kinda crawly feelin. He was pourin himself a cup of coffee, his hands shakin to beat hell."

I had never heard Dad tell this story before, and I was setting bolt upright on his lap, catching every word. I was plain jumpy.

Abe sat as if transfixed, his mouth slightly ajar. His big onion eyes never blinked, as if he was afraid to wink an eye, afraid he would miss seeing something.

Then Dad went on with the story. "Well, I set back down to the table and told Bill to come on, it was his deal, tryin to act like it was nothin. He fetched his coffee over and sat the cup down and was shufflin the cards fer our next hand, when the damndest fight you ever heard started not more than twenty feet from the shack.

"I jumped up and run to the winder and looked out, but I couldn't see a blessed thing out there. By this time, there's several voices, all in mad arguin tones, but I couldn't make out what none of them were sayin.

"There was a terrible thrashin sound then, sounded like somethin bein beat with a neck yoke. I could hear the rings

19

arattlin, and a man yelled like he's bein killed, then some more thumpin and rattlin noises, a long, pleadin, agonized yell, a long, low moan — and all was still. Nothin but the chirp of the katydids and the croak of the frogs at the spring could be heard.

"I looked at Bill. He was still settin at the table, hadn't moved a muscle. He was as white as a sheet and, by God, I couldn't say a word neither. I'd never believed in such things before, but I'll confess, I ain't got caught up there any more after dark."

The story finished, Dad told me to go to bed, it was late. Abe set slumped in his chair, his mouth still open. The knuckles on his hands showed white, he was grasping the arms of the chair so tightly; and as yet, I had not seen him bat an eye. The wall clock struck the hour of midnight.

"Twelve o'clock," exclaimed Dad. "Hell, it's away beyond my bed time. You'll have to excuse me, I've got to hit the hay, got a big day tomorrow," he said, yawning.

Abe came out of his trance and quickly got to his feet, picked up the still-lighted lantern and, hesitating, walked to the door.

"Do you suppose that still happens up there after all these years?" he asked.

Dad, engrossed in the act of unlacing his shoes, and without looking up, said, "Damned if I could tell you. You'll just have to take the story for what it's worth." Then, carrying his shoes in his hand, he went into the bedroom and closed the door.

Abe departed, and as soon as he was outside our yard gate, he began running.

"Blow the light out, he will be back and we'll have to put up the darn fool all night," Dad ordered, as he came out of the bedroom, laughing. Through the kitchen window, we watched the light of the lantern bob up and down.

"I loaned him that old lantern that flickers out so easy if you don't handle it careful," Al said.

"What I'm wantin to see is how fast he can go if that old sow and pigs jumps out of their bed in the hoghouse, there by the willers," Agnes added.

"Yeah, douse the lights and we'll all watch," Dad said. "No tellin how much noise those hogs will make gettin out of the shed. I'd like to be up there and give a hell of a yell about the time they come foggin out," he added with a chuckle.

"There it goes out," Mom said, and you could tell by the tone of her voice she was enjoying the happening.

We all pressed our faces to the window, but the blackness outside kept us from seeing anything. In minutes, the dogs barked and the clatter of footsteps on the porch sent us scurrying to a hiding place.

The front door burst open. "Mister Aldridge! I heard the deadly yell!" Abe exclaimed. We could hear his breath coming in gasps.

All was quiet for a few seconds, and then we heard him cautiously raise the squeaky bracket on the lantern and light a match to its wick. Silently, he crept through the door and was gone.

"Goin fer the hay mow, I'll bet you," anticipated Dad, as he tiptoed to a front window and peered out. "No, by thunder, he's hoofin it down the road towards town. Maybe I shouldn't have told him that story, but I figure he should know."

"Maybe we can get some rest if he ain't down here every night," Mama remarked, satisfaction in her voice.

Thus our neighbor, Abe, walked out of our lives forever, as he did not return to our hills.

4

SAN FRANCISCO BY TRAIN

AN FRANCISCO was a place I had heard a few people speak about, but had no idea where it was. Anyway, despite my early years, I had a vague idea it was a big town. Having an imaginative mind, I thought it was as far away as the end of the earth, and must be far larger than Anderson, where Grandma Parker lived. One thing was certain: I would soon find out, as Dad and Mom and I were going there on a business trip. We were going by train.

Mom had a timber claim up in the big pine country, on Bear Creek Ridge.[5] A buyer for a lumber company came, offering to buy her land. The timber was cruised by this man, Cuttingham, and he set a price on Mom's claim. It was later discovered there was a small legal error in Mom's papers, which, to clarify, she would have to go to San Francisco. She was to be at their main office in this place, San Francisco, in a few weeks.

Our house buzzed with talk of this unexpected trip. Dad had never rode on a train, and had an awesome idea what it would be

_____
5. Sadie's timber claim consisted of forty acres of excellent forest on Camp Creek. The land had been homesteaded by her father.

like. The only thing he said favoring a train was it looked to him like they ran along "slicker than an eel."

Long before, when Mom was a girl, she had ridden on a train one time. "They travel along at a terrific speed, but don't flop ends like you think, Att. They're smooth ridin and have good seats. I think they are 'stem winders' to go on," she said, by way of consoling.

Her words did not console me. I had a feeling that this train would surely "do me up." The sight of one, as it went clanging past Granny's house in Anderson, set my heart fluttering like a fish flopping in a wet sack.

About four days before we were to go to Anderson to catch the train, Dad suddenly decided he was not going. This was brought about because Mom told him he would hafta buy a suit of clothes to wear down there. "You'd look awful tacky in your overalls, and you can't wear your old hog-runnin shoes," she said.

"I ain't goin a step, then, Sadie. If I ain't good enough to go amongst those city folks like I am, I ain't goin," he said in a decided tone. "You can take Scrub and go down by yourself. By the time I'd buy a suit and shoes and we'd pay to go on the train and pay to put up in a hotel, it would cost me too much. You're the only one has to sign those papers anyhow, and there's no sense in me goin," he snorted.

Mom's black eyes smoldered like a mule's when he's going to balk. "If that's the way you feel about it, I'll just let sellin my claim go, cause I ain't gonna be shoved out by myself fer no money. I'll write and tell those fellers down there to not be lookin fer me, cause I ain't comin," she said in a low, even tone, and went on putting a patch on the seat of one of Al's pants.

The money she had been offered for her timber was a considerable amount. Her taking this "don't care" attitude set Dad thinking. Losing this sale was an unthinkable thing: a dollar in hand was worth two in the bush to him. He began bargaining with Mom to get her to go.

"This may be the last chance you'll have to sell out, Sadie, so think we orta kinda make an effort to go and do it. I wouldn't have to buy a suit, would I? A feller looks purty damn good with new overalls and a short jumper on. I've got good ridin boots and hat. That way, I wouldn't be buyin somethin I won't be wearin never again," he told Mom. "You can buy a hat or somethin you gotta have, maybe a new dress if you hafta," he offered.

"Oh, I've got several dresses, but my Sunday shoes are kinda run over and scuffed up. I'd hafta get me a pair, maybe, but that's about all," Mom told him, and then happened to think of the suit he had when they were married. She put her patching aside and hurriedly went into their bedroom, saying, "I wonder if you couldn't wear the suit your brother gave you when we was married. I've got it here in the trunk. I'll get it out and you try it on. We'll see how it looks. I thought you looked powerful good in it, then."

"That was a long time ago, Sadie. The damn coat was skintight when I wore it then; but I'll try it on, if that's what you want," he said, as he went into the bedroom to put it on.

As he had said, the coat was tight. It had only one button, and he had to pull himself in pretty far to get it buttoned. The front of the coat was cut short in a circular way, which gave it a look, in front, like a cut-off vest. In the back, the tail ran to some length and hung as a sort of a flounce. In the center of the back, it was puckered slightly, and two small decorative buttons were on each side of the gathered place. The sleeves were too short and lacked three inches of reaching his wrists. The pants seemed a better fit, only the legs were somewhat short and tight; they

25

came several inches above his ankles. As Dad struggled to get the coat buttoned, he proudly looked down at himself.

"This thing is sure good cloth. I think it's all wool," he said, and run his hand up and down a sleeve. "But damned if I don't hate like the devil to think of wearin it fer four or five days. I always did feel like a dressed-up monkey in a suit, the few times I've had to wear one," he lamented. Mom told him she thought she could set the button out a little, and clean and press the coat, and he would look all right.

The day came for us to start to Anderson to catch the train. We left home early with the team and buggy. We were planning to stay the night with Grandmaw Parker and leave the team at her place while we were gone. Charlie, one of our neighbors, was also selling his timber claim, and to the same company that was buying Mom's. He was to meet us at Granny's and go with us to the City. He arrived, and Dad informed him there was no reason to rent a room at the hotel; he could spend the night with us at Granny's.

Dad went to the station that evening to buy our tickets and learn the time the morning train came through. It was scheduled at nine fifty-five. Mom and I went to the dry goods store, where she bought she and I each a pair of shoes, and a straw suitcase to carry our things in on the trip.

Charlie and Dad had to shave next morning. Between the two of them, in front of Granny's mirror, it took them two hours. Neither of them shaved often, and by lamplight it was near a catastrophe as they slashed away with their straight razors. They lost considerable blood, but neither was cut very deep, or often.

We had been waiting at the station for some time when we heard the whistle blowing and could see the train come racing along. I had a feeling to act like our horse, Prince, when he seen a traction engine.

"Have you bought your ticket yet, Charlie?" Mom inquired.

"Naw, do you hafta get it before you get on the train?" he asked.

"Sure, Att bought ours last night. You'd better hurry, I see it comin," Mom instructed.

"Where do you get em, Att?" Charlie quickly asked.

"In there from that feller, behind that cage kinda place," instructed Dad. Charlie took off in a trot to get his ticket.

The train came charging into town about then. It reminded me of a big, black snake as it came gliding along the track. With the hissing of steam and the grinding and squealing of brakes, it came to a stop. We climbed up the metal steps into the train and went ahead into a car. Most of the seats were taken, but there was two vacant ones next to each other.

"You and Scrub set in this seat, and Charlie and me, we'll set here behind you," Dad said. "Say, where is Charlie? He's gonna get left if he don't hurry."

At Dad's words, we all bent to the window trying to see where Charlie was. He was standing out there looking ever which way fer us. You could hear the engine away up front, clanging and sputtering steam like a nervous horse chomping the bit to go. A man someplace outside called, "All Aboard!"

"I'd better go tell Charlie to get in here. We're almost ready to go, ain't we, Sadie?" Mom's one trip on a train before this put her in the know on train travel, in Dad's estimation.

"Sure, Att, we'll go any minute now. Go get Charlie," she said hurriedly.

Dad ran to the door and called so loudly we could hear him back in the car. "Come on, Charlie, hurry. Sadie says the train's gonna start anytime now."

"Aboard," the man called again. The engine began puffing, there was some short toots of the whistle, and we began moving along.

27

"I didn'get no ticket. I found that cage in there, but there weren't no feller in it, like you said there would be," Charlie explained, as the two men came to their seat. They set down behind Mom and I.

"Oh, I think you can pay one of the fellers on the train, bein's there was no one in there to sell you one," Mom said.

We were gaining speed, the engine blowing its whistle ever little ways. Black smoke bellowed past our window, and the wheels went clickity-clack.

"I'm askeered of this thing, Mom," I said, and I truly was.

"It's all right, Babe, sit still," she comforted me. I had a desire to go back and set on Dad's lap, but Mom had said "sit still," so I'd have to halfway mind her. In a few minutes, I did venture to get on my knees in the seat and look back at Dad and Charlie. They were busy gabbing to each other. Neither one noticed the man standing by their seat, holding his hand out to Dad. He was seated next to the outerside of the seat. Dad finally seen this man and jumped to his feet, grasped his outstretched hand, and vigorously began shaking it up and down.

"Well, howdy, Mister. Blamed if you ain't got me stumped, who you are. I don't seem to recollect you, but you must know me, offerin to pump my hand and all." Dad beamed at the idea of this man offering to shake hands with him.

"I want to see your ticket," he said, as he pried his hand out of Dad's firm grasp.

"Huh? I don't hear too good," Dad said, and held a cupped hand to his ear to catch the man's words.

"I'm the conductor," the man loudly said, and extended his hand once more.

"I'm right proud to meet you, Mister Conductor," Charlie said, as he rose to his feet and, reaching past Dad, grasped the conductor's hand and shook it. "Whar you headin fer?" he asked. "Me and Att and his missus and the kid there are all strikin out fer San Francisco to sell our timber claims this mornin."

"I'm not traveling like you people. I work for the railroad company and my name is not 'Conductor.' I'm the conductor of this train. I want to see your tickets," the man explained, looking from Charlie to Dad with an amused expression. Dad and Charlie were speechless over the fool mistake they had made.

"Hell, yes, I've got the tickets. Bought them just last night," Dad said, as if to himself, searching through his pockets.

"I expect you're the guy I orter see about gettin my ticket. I didn't get one back thar in Anderson," Charlie said, climbing over Dad's legs. Meantime, he had whipped out his purse and had money in his hand.

"I couldn't sell you a ticket to San Francisco, but you can pay me for your fare from Anderson to Red Bluff," the conductor said, and took the offered money. "You will have to get off at our next stop, Red Bluff, and purchase your ticket."

People seated in our end of the car were showing considerable interest in the way we were acting, but none of us felt badly about it, as we knew no different. Settled in our seats, we rode in silence for a time, until Charlie broke the spell. "That feller, the conductor, said I'd have to get off the train in Red Bluff to get a ticket. How in heck am I gonna know when we're there? I ain't never been in that place," he added, with deep concern.

"Oh, you'll know. They come walkin through the train every town we'll come to, yellin out its name," Mom answered in a knowing way. Then she offered Charlie a bit of advice. "You'll have to be quick and get off and get your ticket, cause a train waits fer nobody."

The train sped along, flying across bridges and through cuts, its wheels click-clacking in rhythm as we scooted over the miles.

"Apples, oranges, bananas, fresh-roasted peanuts," a man called out, as he came through the car with a basket filled with fruit and a lot of other things I had never seen before.

"Get me some of that dope he's got, Mom, I'm hungry."

"We got lots of grub in the lunch box, Honey. Tell your Dad to get you somethin out of the grub box," she instructed.

"I don't want none of that. I want some of that stuff that man's got," I whined. All I had to do to get what I wanted was raise a big fuss and, if it was possible, Dad would get it for me. I turned in the seat and said to him in a choked, injured tone of voice, "Mom won't get me none of that stuff that feller's got."

"What you wantin? We've got apples, oranges, boiled eggs, fried chicken and a lot of sandwiches in the grub box. Why don't you have a boiled egg?" he coaxed.

"No, I don't want no egg. I want some of those 'banners,' " I wheedled.

"The kid here wants some of your bananas," Dad said to the man, who was returning past where we sat.

"How many?" he asked.

"Oh, two or three, I reckon," answered Dad.

"That will be thirty cents," he said, and handed me three bananas.

Dad had to look fer more money, as he had only one dime in his hand, in expectancy to pay with it. I began on the bananas at once. I crouched behind Mom, hiding from people. The bananas were gone almost before I knew it. I straightened in the seat, wishing there had been more.

"What did you do with your 'banners,' Babe? You ain't got all of them down already, have you?" inquired Mom. In the seat beside me lay the three empty peels. "I never in my life saw a child that could eat stuff down as fast as you can. You can hold as much as a hog, I do believe!'' she scolded in a shocked and angry tone of voice.

''Your little girl surely loves bananas. I love to see a child eat with a zest. I have a granddaughter around your girl's age, and my daughter simply has to coax her into eating anything,'' a gray-haired lady in the seat opposite ours, smiling at me, said to Mom.

''This kid don't have to be coaxed to eat. I don't see how she can hold so much. Her Dad says he thinks her legs are holler,'' Mom proudly told the lady, as she brushed a few stray locks of my hair out of my eyes.

About then a man, one of the trainmen, came through our car. ''Red Bluff, we are entering Red Bluff,'' he called out in a musical voice.

''We're there, Charlie. You'll have to run, they won't wait for you,'' Mom said, quickly turning to Charlie. He jumped Dad's legs and went up the car, staggering this way and that from the sway of the train.

When we had dressed in our best at Granny's that morning, there was no doubt in our minds but that our garb was in the best of taste, as clothes are clothes with hill people. Now, seeing Charlie hurrying along, everyone's eyes upon him, it was plain our getups was lacking in comparison to the other passengers'. Charlie's suit was old and wrinkled and baggy. The coat and trousers did not match in color. The coat was black, the trousers navy blue, the coattail so short his pants tops showed in back.

He was rawboned and several inches over six foot tall. Charlie had a very nervous disposition and a number of nervous habits, one of which he was enacting as he went hastily along. With one hand he grasped the top of his pants in front, with the other, the back, and gave them a violent jerk upwards; then he

31

switched hands from front to back, pulling up again. You got the impression he slightly jerked himself off the ground when he did this. His tie was only half under his high, celluloid collar, and was knotted in a ponderous way so it came out even with his chin.

He went flying into the depot. He was inside several minutes, and then we heard the man call, "All Aboard!"

Dad jumped as if he had been shot, and went running to the door. "Hey, Charlie, we're leavin, come quick!" we heard him call to Charlie in a loud, excited voice.

Out of the depot raced Charlie, with his ticket in his hand. He and Dad came inside just as the train began to move. "Those darn fellers that gives you the tickets are hard critters to find. This'un here was outside jawin with another feller and I likes to of not got my ticket," he told Dad.

The train sped on towards San Francisco, with the two men talking about the good fortune of selling the timber claim. Both of them were somewhat hard of hearing and were talking in loud voices. Soon, it became apparent that everybody seated anyplace near us was listening to them, as they gabbed away in their backwoods lingo.

We came to a station and the trainman said we were scheduled for a thirty-minute stop. Some of the passengers got off the train and went into a dining room near the station.

"By gosh, I guess they're gonna eat in there," Charlie said. "It ain't noon yet, is it Att?" he asked.

Dad looked at his watch and said, "Hell, yes, it's half past already. We might as well get the grub box out and eat, hadn't we, Sadie?"

At the mention of eating, I came to attention and could hardly wait fer them to open the grub box and begin passing the food out. We had just opened the box when a young man who had been sitting in the seat directly across from Dad said to him, "If you gentlemen will pardon my intrusion, I would like to show you how to turn your seats facing each other to make it convenient to eat your lunch," and he smiled at Mom. "If you and the little girl will stand a second, I will arrange it for you, Madam," he addressed her.

We stood while he deftly reversed our seat so it faced Dad's and Charlie's. Mom thanked him and said, "Would you like a piece of chicken, Mister — "

"Jones, Madam, yes, Ed Jones. The chicken looks delicious. If you are sure you have a piece to spare, I would be delighted," and smiled at her again. "I have been wishing I might talk with you people. I overheard some of you gentlemen's conversation, and I must say I am intrigued."

Mom interrupted his conversation long enough to address Dad. "Att, why can't you set here with Babe and I and let Mister Jones set by Charlie while he eats his chicken?"

Dad moved over by us, and our new friend settled down by Charlie. Between bites from half a breast of chicken, he went on. "You see, I'm what you might call a novelist. I am collecting material for a book, which is based, more or less, on the pioneer side of life. I find your conversation very interesting. I could, perhaps, use you as main characters in my novel." At that, he picked up a ham sandwich and cracked a boiled egg.

Mom had put two or three fruit jars of coffee in our lunch.

"Say, Sadie, maybe Mister Jones would go fer a slug of coffee," said Dad, and then went on, "I hate a dry lunch, gotta have something to wash it down with."

"I don't care if I do, if you're sure you have plenty for everyone," Mr. Jones answered, and then added, "Just call me Ed, like all my friends do. My, this is the best food I ever tasted. You are an excellent cook, Madam, reminds me of my dear mother, bless her soul.'' By that time, his sandwich and egg were gone, and Mom invited him to have another piece of chicken.

''Oh, my dear lady, I am ashamed of the way I have been devouring your lunch, but it isn't every day that I have such delicious food before me, so I am tempted to eat just one more small piece of chicken,'' and took another half a breast. ''Now, to get back to my novel. I have traveled from east to west and north to south in quest of material for this story. I am striving to make it as true as possible and would like to make my main characters someone who are actual people. That's where I thought you would fit in nicely.'' Without looking at any of us, he took himself another sandwich and a pickle. ''The thing I must do is get an accounting of your entire lives. Your experiences, hopes, and successes — fit all these things together in my book. Speaking of success,'' he went on to Mom, ''I think you are one of the most successful cooks I have ever seen.''

''That's what Att here tells me all the time, but I never figured I was so good that a feller who has been all over the world would go fer it like you do.'' Mom was proud of herself. Her face glowed with pride.

''She don't believe me when I tell her she's the best damn cook in our county. She can fix the best darn bear roast you ever flipped a lip over,'' Dad boasted.

Charlie had been silently eating up to this point, but he had to brag on Mom's cooking also. ''I ain't sayin her roast bear ain't no good, but I tell you somethin she can cook better than anythin I ever tasted, and that is deer steak. When she fixes deer meat like she can and has biled spuds with the jackets on and gravy, I likes to bust myself eatin,'' he concluded.

''Now, that's what I mean I want in my story,'' Jones spoke up. ''If you will consent for me to write about you, there is a fortune in it for all of us.''

34

Dad's eyes gleamed at the mention of a fortune, and he asked, "How much do you figure you can get fer a book like that'un?"

"It's hard to say, but I dare say enough to make us all independent of financial worries our entire lives." At that, he cracked and shelled another egg, picked up a sandwich, and eyed the cream cake Mom had stored in the corner of the big grub box. "My, that's a beautiful cake, I'll bet it's tasty. If there should be a wee piece of it left over, I would love to sample it," Ed said, with an expression in his eyes like he was looking at some sacred object.

"There'll be lots of it left. Whack Ed a big hunk, Sadie," Dad told Mom. To Mr. Jones, he said, "Damn, she can sure make cakes that are a ringtailed dandy ever shot."

Mom whacked a piece of the cake for Ed, and said, "Won't you have some coffee? It's cold, but good, Mr. Jones."

"Yes, please, but just call me Ed. It seems I have known you good people all my life."

"All right, Ed. A good thing to write about in your novel is Att's experiences he can tell you about. He's caught wild hogs out of the woods up home and killed bear and panthers; he's the darndest feller you ever saw. He's took one catchin claw offin every panther he's killed. I was countin them just the other day, and he's got two hundred and sixty-three," Mom boasted.

Ed was now examining a big red apple. "This is my lucky day, accidentally crossing paths with you people," he said. "Do you grow these apples on your farm, Att?"

"Yep, we sure do," Dad answered.

"I want to see your farm some day, and perhaps go with you on a hunting trip. An experience like that would be priceless to me." And friend Ed had a faraway, dreamy gleam in his eyes from merely talking of such an adventure.

"We'd be tickled pink to have you. We're goin to San Francisco to sell Sadie's timber claim, and as soon as we get that

35

fixed up, we'll be headin home. Charlie here is sellin his claim too,'' Dad explained, then went on talking. ''Say, why don't you go home with us? And you can get goin on your story. Charlie's got a darn good place too. He raises a few head of cows and makes shakes to sell in the summer and runs a trapline in the winter. By cripes, that's sumpin you could put in your book, about Charlie's trappin. Folks in the hills nicknamed him 'Coyote Charlie,' on account of him catchin so many of those varmints. Ain't no one in those hills can outsmart those crafty devils like Charlie can,'' Dad said.

It was plain to see Charlie was more than pleased with the short account Dad had given of his activities. ''Yep, Ed, I'd sure like to have you come up and spend this winter with me, I batch and I sure would like fer you to come. Be a good place fer you to write,'' invited Charlie.

''I'll do it! I'll do it!'' excitedly exclaimed our friend. Suddenly he sobered; a troubled look clouded his face. ''I'm not sure I can get around to going with you at this time. You see, I've had the misfortune of running a bit low, financially. When I bought my ticket in Seattle, I found that I had only enough money to take me to Sacramento, and as much as I would like to continue the trip with you to San Francisco, I'm afraid it's impossible. Really, my home town is San Francisco, and there is where I'm bound, but I'm going to be compelled to wire collect to my sister, who lives there, and have her wire money to take me home. I'm afraid you will have completed your business and gone home by the time I will be reaching there. If I knew someone I could borrow a small sum from, I could repay them with interest when I reach San Francisco,'' he wistfully said. He seemed glum and disheartened at his misfortune.

The trainman came through our car. ''Sacramento! All out for Sacramento,'' he called. ''There will be a thirty-minute stopover here.''

"This is where I must leave you," sorrowfully said Ed. "I have a feeling it's the parting of our ways. I would give anything if my ticket would take me to the city with you. The saying is, 'opportunity knocks but once upon your door,' and if you are unable to grasp it then, it's lost to you forever," he lamented, as he prepared to leave the train. He carefully put on his hat, straightened his tie and hung his topcoat over one arm, slowly removed his one small bag from the rack, and was ready to go.

"I want to thank you, my friends, for the wonderful lunch. The thoughts of you and it will always linger in my memory." He gently shook Mom's hand, saying, "I have enjoyed meeting you, my dear."

"Well, I can say the same to you. I think you're a nice young feller," Mom brightly said.

Ed shook Dad's hand. "Old timer, I'll do my utmost to call on you in the near future, as I must hear about those hunting adventures of yours. Until then, I will regretfully tell you good-by."

Charlie had arose to his feet and he and Ed clapped hands. "I'll be seeing you, Charlie," Ed said, and began stretching one leg. "I'm afraid I set too long, that seat is a bit cramping, don't you find it so?"

"Ain't noticed it, but now that you've said it, I do feel a might stiff in my knee joints."

"You should come outside and stretch your legs," Ed said.

"Guess I will go out a spell." And Charlie and Ed walked out of the car together. After a few minutes, we seen Ed with his luggage, hurriedly entering the station.

"There goes Ed into the station. He sure seems like a smart young feller, don't he Att?" Mom asked.

"Yeah. I wish I had the educated gumption he's got in that head of his. I'd write that book myself and get all the money," Dad confessed.

37

We could see Charlie standing a little distance from the train, nervously pulling his trousers up every few minutes, and spitting great streamers of tobacco juice.

It had been a long time since I'd been to a restroom, and I whisperingly told Mom I had to go.

"Where you gonna take her, Sadie?" Dad asked.

"They got a back house right on the train," she answered. "Come on, Babe," and we went along, I hanging to the back of her dress, keeping hidden from people.

"The durn thing's locked," Mom told me; then muttered, as if to herself, "What do you suppose they got it locked fer? Do you have to go terrible bad, Honey?"

"Yeah, awful bad," I told her. I was finding it hard to restrain myself when we went back to our seat. The trainman outside called, "All Aboard." People began filing in, and among them was Charlie. He sat down, then began watching out the window with a worried expression on his face.

"If Ed don't hurry, he's gonna get left. I gave him money to buy his ticket and he hurried off to get it and phone his sister to meet him when we get to San Francisco, so as she could bring the money to pay me back when we get there. I guess that's what he was meanin when he said he would reimburse me at that time."

"Maybe he's having trouble gettin his ticket, like you did in Red Bluff," anticipated Dad.

"That's about what's holdin him. Those fellers don't act like they care a hoot iffin they sell you a ticket or not. I'm just wonderin if it would do any good fer me to go holler out the door to him that we're about to go. I gave him twenty dollars. He asked me fer fifteen, said that was enough, but I only had two ten dollar gold pieces, so I gave him both of them. I sure wish he'd hurry up. Do you reckon he got turned around and climbed on

38

another one of the cars?'' Charlie rambled on. The train was sliding from the station, leaving our friend Ed someplace behind.

''He might done like you said, Charlie, got on the wrong car. Darned if I know which one was which, look alike so much, same color and such,'' Dad reasoned. Charlie fidgeted like a hen on a hot skillet. Twenty dollars was no minor sum to Charlie; he was overwrought with worry about how he was going to find Ed and get it back.

''If he did miss the car, he'll look till he finds you, Charlie. If he's on one of the other cars, he'll come lookin fer us, cause that's what he hated so bad, was him not gonna get to ride the rest of the way with us,'' Mom said. ''You'll see, he'll show up pretty quick,'' she predicted.

The conductor came checking tickets. He was almost about to leave our car when, at Mom's insistence, Charlie called to him, ''Hey, Mister Conductor, you're the feller I wanta see a minute,'' as he scrambled to his feet and gave his pants two quick pulls. The man came back to Charlie with a look of inquiry. ''What do you want?'' he asked.

''Do you know if Ed Jones boarded the train back there in Sacramento?''

''I'm sure I don't know,'' the conductor answered in a kind voice.

Charlie, pointing towards Mom, said, ''Sadie, there, she's pretty smart about travelin on a train, and she says, bein's he had to get a new ticket there, that you had maybe noticed him. You see, we met him on the train, and he was such a nice feller, we had him eat lunch with us. He's gettin stuff to write a book about, and he got to listenin to me and Att here spin a few yarns about things we do back in the hills. He said he'd give his front

39

teeth to get us fer main characters in his book, and he wants
Sadie in it, too.''

''If you will describe your friend, I will try to locate him for
you,'' the trainman said.

''You'll know him when you see him, cause the first thing
you'll notice is he's got one gold tooth right here in front,''
Charlie said, pointing to the exact tooth on himself, and went on
explaining. ''He is wearin a fine-lookin gray suit and hat, and
sorta reddish shoes.'' With this description, the conductor went
looking for Jones.

Mom had not taken me to the lavatory, and every minute was
an eternity. I was almost out of control as we reached the door. If
that door was still locked, what then? I thought. But it was
unlocked. I breathed a sigh of relief.

The conductor returned and had not located Ed Jones. ''How
long have you known this chap Jones?''

''Oh, a little after noon today,'' answered Dad. ''He seemed
such a nice feller, we asked him to have a piece of chicken with
us, and like Charlie told you, he wanted to write a story about
us. He claimed there'd be a pile of money in it fer him and us
too. I thought it a fine deal to get in on all that money. But damn
it, now it appears he's skipped with Charlie's twenty. Dang me,
I should have knowed he was a deadbeat, cause, to stop and
think it over, he never asked our names nor where we live or
nothin. After he got a taste of our grub, he never stopped eatin
and talkin till he got off the train in Sacramento. Hell, he must
have been as full as a goose when we got there,'' Dad concluded.

''Did you say he has twenty dollars of Charlie's?''

''Yes,'' Charlie answered. ''Soft-headed me, he talked me
into givin him the money, promisin he'd phone his sister to meet
us at the train in San Francisco and pay me back. But now you

can't find hide or hair of him. It looks like he's skedaddled with my twenty.''

''Yes, I'd say you have been cunningly robbed. The world is becoming overrun with imposters and crooks,'' the trainman said, and went on his way.

''I still don't think he missed the train on purpose. He ain't no crook. You just wait, he'll find some way to be at the station to meet us, or his sister will be there and pay Charlie,'' Mom said.

''Fiddle-faddle, Sadie. That feller's got you soft in the head, his braggin on your cookin and all. He's skipped and I knowed he was a wrong doer when he kept gabblin like a goose; but I thought, bein's he had the education, there might be truth about wantin us in his book, and I wanted to be in on the money end of it,'' Dad said.

''I'm scared we ain't got enough grub here fer even another meal,'' Mom said, as she checked the lunch box.

''If that's the case, we'll have to round up some place to eat in town,'' Dad answered.

It was now dark outside. The lights in towns we were passing fascinated us. About here, I fell asleep and knew no more until we were in San Francisco, and I was awakened by Mom shaking me and saying, ''Wake up! We're in San Francisco.''

I was not fully awake until we were outside in the cold wind. It was as if awakening in a new world. Unaccustomed sounds and smells had me as confused as one of the wild animals from back in the hills would have been. A sea of people thronged about the station.

Mom held my hand and was carrying the suitcase. Dad looked as perturbed as I felt, as he stood with the big, red lunch box atop his shoulder, appearing to be wondering what to do next. The lumber company man, Cornelius Cuttingham, had promised he would meet us here and take us to a hotel, where he said he would engage rooms for us in advance.

"I wonder where Cuttingham is? He promised he would be here to meet us and I figured he'd be here or bust a gut tryin," Dad said, looking at people passing by. "You watch sharp for him, Sadie. He may not know us dressed up like we are," he added, and he bit off a chew of tobacco.

"I ain't been lookin fer him as hard as I have fer that Jones, or maybe his sister. I figured he'd be here to meet us," Mom answered. Then she added, "I'm beginnin to believe the conductor, all right, that he is a crook. A person should take a feller like that out and pour hot lead in his ears." This was the most severe punishment she could think of doing to some scamp, and she was making no exceptions of the "nice young feller," Ed Jones.

Charlie pulled his trousers up until the cuffs reached halfway to his knees, spit a long stream of tobacco juice, and said, "I'd like to get my hands on that mealymouthed gink; I'd kick the pants plumb off of him." He meant every word he had spoken.

"What do you reckon we orta do, Charlie?" asked Dad. It don't appear like Cuttingham's gonna keep his word, either."

"Durned if I know. I'd like to find a place to bed down, my feet's killin me," Charlie answered.

"Oh, here you are!" It was Mister Cuttingham. "I'm sorry to have kept you folks waiting, but I had a business engagement that made me a few minutes late. I didn't recognize you at first. I don't know why, but I was looking for you dressed as I saw you in the mountains," said Cuttingham.

"That's what I told Sadie — you'd never know us like this," answered Dad, as he looked down at himself and ran his hand down over a sleeve, as though proud of his finery.

"Your hotel is but a short way up the street. We may as well walk," Cuttingham decided.

42

He walked ahead of the four of us a few feet, leading the way. We came along, knotted into a compact group, acting like a bunch of wild steers being drove through town. We crowded and jostled against one another as we walked along. Mr. Cuttingham stopped at the door of the hotel, looked back at us, then opened it, waiting for us to go ahead of him. We went only far enough to give him room to close the door, and again formed into a huddle as we waited for him to lead the way.

"You folks step right over here and register," he said. Then to the clerk behind the desk, added, "These are the folks I engaged two rooms in behalf of."

"Yes Sir," the clerk said in a bored way, as he turned the ledger for our signatures. Charlie was standing the nearest to the desk, so the clerk offered him the pen. "This line, Sir," the man instructed. Charlie laboriously wrote his name. "Your address also, Mr. Rice."

"It's just Inwood," said Charlie.

"All right, please put it down."

Mom and Dad and I had been standing by. Dad had the grub box upon his shoulders. Mom set our suitcase on the floor and was holding my trembling hand. A thick, soft carpet covered the entire lobby. I had never seen anything like it. It was like walking on the deep moss that covered the ground by our spring.

"This is sure a dinger of a place, ain't it?" Dad said. "A feller mires almost to his hocks on this carpet."

When Dad had finished signing the register, a young man with keys in his hand picked up our suitcase and said, "I will show you to your rooms;" he opened a door, stepped back, and said, "This way."

We crowded through the door and he shut it with a bang. He pressed a button and we began gliding swiftly upward. None of us had been on an elevator before. It is doubtful if the folks had even read about one. We went speeding up and up and eventually came to a stop. The boy stepped out and again said, ''This way.''

''That thing's sure a crackerjack!'' ejaculated Dad. ''I never knowed they had such fancy contraptions.''

Next morning, when I awoke, Mom and Dad were up and dressed. A knock on our door — it was Charlie, and Dad asked him in.

''If Cuttingham's gonna take us to breakfast, I wish he'd hurry. I ain't had no hot coffee since we left Anderson. I gotta have my coffee,'' Dad said.

''Me too, but I'll bet these city folks don't get up early like we do, probably don't budge till after daylight,'' guessed Charlie.

We sat around and waited almost two hours for Mr. Cuttingham. When he arrived, he said, ''I'm giving you a city man's version of a ham and egg breakfast. But I'll warn you, it won't be in any way as fine as those breakfasts you served to me at your ranch. There is a small place just around the corner. I eat there quite often and I think you folks will like it.''

''I hope they got good hot coffee,'' spoke Dad.

''They have excellent coffee. That's one thing I look for in a restaurant,'' Cuttingham answered.

''You had better get the grub box, Att. I've got the grip,'' Ma interrupted.

''Leave your luggage here, you will be back soon. Lock the door and everything will be safe,'' Cuttingham advised.

''I ain't thinkin so much about the stuff bein safe here, but we're headin home as quick as we get our business straight with you. If we'd leave our plunder here, I'd probably have to pay another night fer it being here and I can't see throwin my money around like a drunk Injun,'' Dad explained, as he shouldered the big box and followed Cuttingham towards the elevator. Mom,

44

Charlie, and I followed, with her carrying our one piece of luggage. Out on the street, I felt as if the devil of all times was upon me — the people, the rattle and clang of street cars, and a newsboy calling, ''Get your morning paper, read all about the murder.'' I thought this murder had happened right here. I couldn't keep from looking behind me every few seconds. I was thankful when we entered the restaurant, getting out of the hubbub on the street.

We sat down at a table. Before setting down, Cuttingham placed his hat on a hanger, but Dad and Charlie set down with theirs on. The waiter was a middle-aged, paunchy man. He came to take our order, and he and Cuttingham greeted each other in a friendly way.

''George, meet my business associates from up in the northern tip of our State.'' He introduced us and ordered ham and eggs for everybody. Mom buttoned my coat to the very top button, without saying why she was doing so.

''What you buttonin her up so tight for, Sadie,'' Dad asked; ''tain't cold in here.''

''She's so blamed bad to fling grease and egg when she eats, is why. I'd rather have it on her coat than her dress, it won't show so bad,'' she explained. ''Ain't you and Charlie gonna take your hats off?''

They looked foolishly at each other and then at Cuttingham. ''Yeah, I guess we should,'' answered Dad and swept his big hat off and placed it on the floor under his chair, and Charlie did likewise.

While we were eating, Mom asked, ''How long should it take to get our business done?''

''I have the details on your transaction pretty well completed. It shouldn't take too long to get it finished. Charlie will have to go with me to the government recording building on a small matter,'' Cuttingham confided, and then went on to explain, ''I will drop you by our office and you can go up and wait for Charlie and I there.''

After breakfast we walked to Mr. Cuttingham's office building. He stopped near the foot of a stairway that went upward from the sidewalk, and said, ''Our office is on the first floor, and four doors to your right. You can't miss it; our company name is on the door. Just go in and make yourselves at home. I'll phone Barker when I get to the record office and instruct —''

Just then, there was a loud clatter of horses' feet and the rattle of wagon wheels from around the corner. In sight came a ponderous, long, low-slung wagon, drawn by three sleek, gray horses. They were galloping at full speed. To us, it had the appearance of being a runaway.

''Look there!'' exclaimed Dad. ''It's a runaway. Whoops! See em go.''

The driver of the wagon was holding a frazzled, short whip in one hand, manipulating the lines deftly with the other. He seemed unconcerned that the horses were traveling at such a reckless speed. Over the back wheels of the long wagon, another man was setting, turning a steering wheel. He expertly guided the back wheels out in almost the exact path the front ones had gone, as they came sharply around the street corner.

We were watching in popeyed wonder. Other people were uninterestedly going about their business, and I could not see why they weren't seeming to grasp the excitement of the moment.

''They're sure gonna have a hell of a crackup if that feller don't get them stopped pretty quick!'' Charlie exclaimed excitedly.

''That darn fool driver ain't even tryin to stop them,'' Dad said in astonishment.

"It isn't a runaway," Cuttingham put in by way of explanation. "That is one of the many dray wagons of the City. They hurry from place to place like that all the time."

"Well, I'll be damned," ejaculated Dad, still excited over the novelty of the thing. "Looks like that would be rough on horses, goin like that all the time. I never in my born days seen a pair of back wheels steered from behind. It's kinda like a picture I seen one time of a ladder contraption on a fire wagon."

"Similar," admitted Cuttingham. He picked up his interrupted conversation. "As I was about to tell you, I will telephone our man, Barker, and tell him to drop all other procedures and begin with your papers at once, as I know you are anxious to get started on the next train for home." He and Charlie went down the street. They were so unalike. Cuttingham was at ease as he strode along at Charlie's side. Charlie's long legs were carrying him in an awkward, overbalanced manner, resembling the gait of a crane.

We found the lumber company's office and entered. Several people were waiting in the outer office. All the seats were taken, except a wicker settee. We took possession of that, our bag and lunch box at our feet. A man came from the inner office and addressed Mom. "You are Mrs. Sarah Aldridge, I presume?"

"Yes, that's me," admitted Mom.

"Come in," he said to her, as he held the door open for her to enter his office.

"Ain't you comin with me, Att?" Mom asked.

"Guess I orta," he answered. Turning to me, he went on, "You stay here, Scrub, and watch the grip and lunch box. Your Maw and I will be back in a little while. Now, don't move one inch," he cautioned, as he set the suitcase at my side on the settee.

To be left alone like this was as near a calamity as anything

47

could possibly be. I hugged the suitcase closely to my side and placed my feet upon the lunch box. A man and woman with a little girl about my size entered the office immediately after Mom and Dad had left me. This couple eyed me, seated in the very center of the settee, possessively clutching the suitcase to my side.

"Would you like to move over to the end of the seat, Dear?" the lady asked.

"No," I said in a choked tone, and suddenly became intensely interested in my feet. The lady gave a grunt of disgust, and looked at me in a way I was afraid she might do me bodily harm.

"If this child refuses to move over, you and Dollie will have to set on the other side of her," the lady acidly said, as she plopped herself down on my left.

Little Dollie perched upon the father's knee. It didn't take her long to begin work on me. "Your shoes are not pretty like mine," she said, in a small, smirking voice. "I have a nicer coat than you have," she went on.

I hung my head in shame, and was afraid to say one word to her. "Can't you talk?" she chirped, as she swung her foot and cracked me a stinging blow on the shin.

"Behave, Dollie, don't swing your feet," the father scolded half-heartedly.

I didn't move one inch or say a word, but I was thinking. I wished with all my heart I could get this smarty up to Hardscrabble. I'd bust her with a rock, kick her, knock her down and roll her in the ditch and hold her under, that's what I'd do, I angrily thought.

Mr. Cuttingham and Charlie came in the room and passed into the inner office. Charlie grinned broadly at me when he passed by.

"I wonder where *that* came from?" the lady at my side asked her husband. "Did you notice those old-fashioned clothes?" she went on. She had a smirk you could have knocked off with a stick. I prayed these people would leave the place before Mom and Dad came back. I knew their clothes were as old-fashioned as Charlie's, and didn't want these people to make fun of them like they had Charlie.

After twenty minutes or so of insulting questions and remarks from the little she-devil, the inner door opened and Mom, Dad, Charlie and Mr. Cuttingham strode into the room. They were all smiles, happy to have, at last, received the money for their timberland. Cuttingham seemed pleased, too.

"I guess we're about ready to hit the grit fer home," stated Dad. "Do you reckon you'd have time to show us the railroad station?" asked Dad. "I ain't sure we could find our way back there."

"Oh, surely, I'd be happy to," Cuttingham said pleasantly. "But first, I would love for you to be my guests at a seafood dinner. I haven't forgotten the hospitality you showed me when I was up at your ranch," he said.

The restaurant was large and beautiful. Waiters were dressed in black trousers with white shirts and jackets. Our friend escorted us past many tables at which people were dining. He spoke briefly to one of the waiters, then took us to a booth, and we sat down.

"I have promised my good friends a seafood lunch," he informed the waiter. "I would suggest bringing them your seafood special, and see that they get anything they want," he added.

"Yes sir, and you? Shall I order the special for you?"

"No, I have a very tight schedule, so I must be running along.

I'll catch the tab on their lunch when I return,'' Cuttingham told the man, and to us said, "I'll be back to show you to the station," and was gone.

I was beginning to admire the splendor of the compartment — the velvet curtains which draped about us, the shadowed, bracketed lights, and most of all, the gleaming silver. It was a thing of wonder, for at home we had black wooden-handled knives, forks, and spoons, and until I seen these, I thought that was the only kind there was.

The curtains softly parted, and the waiter came in with three glasses of wine, and a glass of orange juice for me. When he departed, Dad asked, "I wonder if we're supposed to drink this stuff now, Sadie?"

"I guess so," Mom decided.

"That's sure good wine," said Charlie.

"Good drink," agreed Dad.

The waiter returned and brought our soup. We made quick work of that. The salad was fetched, the waiter had gone, and Dad asked, "I wonder if this is all we're gonna git? It must not take very damn much to fill these city folks up. I think they bring it on in little dribs, so a feller can't see just how little you're gettin. Didn't bring a darn bit of meat," Dad observed.

Our salad finished, we thought that was the entire meal, and were preparing to go and wait outside for Cuttingham. The curtains slid back and the waiter came, pushing a fancy cart to our table. On it was a large silver tray. In its center were several, covered, silver serving dishes and plates. The waiter arranged everything before us, then asked, "What do you wish to drink?"

"For myself, I want black coffee," Dad promptly answered. Everybody had coffee except me. Mom ordered a glass of milk for me. The waiter returned with coffee and the milk, also a bucket sort of container with two large bottles embedded in cracked ice. Opening one big bottle, he filled glasses with a sparkling beverage. "If you should wish anything more, ring for me," he said, and with a smile, he was gone.

"I wonder what this is?" Mom asked, as she explored through the food in the steaming hot, silver containers.

"Uhm, uhm, sure smells larrupin," ejaculated Dad. "Ain't those pots silver, Sadie?" he asked.

"They look like silver, and the ladle too," she said.

We began on the different foods and Charlie and Dad drank one glass after the other from the big bottle.

"Know sumpin, I bet this stuff's champagne," guessed Charlie.

"It's darn larrupin stuff, whatever it is," approved Dad. "Snap the top offen that other bottle, Charlie," he instructed, as he poured the last drop from the first bottle.

"Now, Att, you be careful how much of that booze you're drinkin. First thing you'll know, you'll be hooched up and hollerin and yellin around like you do sometimes and everyone in town'll know you're soused," Mom scolded.

Finally, the dishes empty, likewise the bottles, we settled back in our seats. "I'm as full as a toad. That was some meal," Dad commented.

Cuttingham came and took us to the station. It was thronged with people again. From someplace, a droning but loud man's voice was calling off the schedules of arriving and departing trains. Our friend, Cuttingham, told us good-by.

"There's a darn fine feller, and honest as the day is long," admired Charlie, as we watched Cuttingham mingle with the crowd at the station.

When Dad bought our tickets, he asked the ticket agent, "Say, how are we gonna know which train to get on?"

"Your train leaves in exactly twenty-five minutes, on track eight. If you will give one of the boys with the caps fifty cents, he will put you on the right train," the man told him.

"Oh, that's the way to do it," Dad said.

After a few minutes, a young man wearing a cap came by. Dad rushed up to him and asked, "Are you one of these guys that puts a person on the right train for fifty cents?"

"Yes, I could, if I knew where you are departing for," the young man hesitatingly answered.

"Well, here's fifty cents. The feller that sells tickets told me any of you boys wearin caps would show us our train." The boy took the money and walked away without a backward look at Dad. We relaxed, as we had the problem solved of catching our train when it arrived. We listened to the drone of the man's voice over the loudspeaker. Very little of what he said could I understand.

"Did you tell that young man you gave the money to where we are goin?" Mom asked.

"Naw, I never. He didn't ask me, and I didn't think to tell him, I figured he knowed," Dad said.

"He couldn't have knowed. I think you gave the money to the wrong boy," she said.

"I've been watchin fer him and I ain't seen hide ner hair of him since he took your four bits and went out that door," Charlie chimed in.

"Do you reckon that wasn't one of the boys that puts you on your right train?" Dad asked. "By God, he took the fifty cents as if he knowed all about it," he said, after thinking a few seconds.

The train caller voice was rambling on. At the end of his spiel we heard, "Track eight. All points north."

"Say, that man just said something about 'All points north.'

That's the way we're headin, I'll bet that's it,'' Mom said excitedly, as she got to her feet. ''I'll go ask the ticket man.'' There was a crowd of people waiting in line at the window, but Mom excitedly shoved her way past them and asked the agent, ''Could you tell me if that's our train that's leavin now?''

''What train are you departing on, Madam?''

''I don't know, but we're goin up to Anderson,'' she answered.

''Oh yes, it's on track eight at this moment, and is scheduled to depart almost immediately,'' he informed her. As we neared the train, the by-now familiar call of ''All Aboard'' sounded off.

Dad ran up to this man and asked, ''Is this the right train to Anderson?''

''I'm not sure, Sir, but this train is going north. This is it if you are going in that direction,'' he added.

We scrambled up the steps and into the car as the train began moving on. The happenings of the last two days had been almost too much for me. I was exhausted and fell asleep as soon as we pulled away from the station, and slept the entire trip to Anderson.

As we went walking along from the Anderson depot, we were glad we were almost home.

''You know, it's been a darn bad trip on all of us. I wouldn't do it again if somebody would offer me twice the money I got for my timber. I figured it would be an education to a feller like me, but all the education I got was twenty dollars' worth, when that damn Jones robbed me in broad daylight. It makes me so mad every time I think of that, I'd like to track him down and get twenty bucks' worth of his hide,'' Charlie said. His eyes shone grim and mad.

''The way I got it figured is that most everyone you meet in

53

the cities is after nothin but your money. Look what that bastard with the cap done to me, took my four bits and skipped,'' lamented Dad.

For years, after our adventure in San Francisco, the folks would tell of our experiences on this trip and was thankful they lived in our hills.

5

THE MOVE

THE YEAR I WAS SEVEN, Agnes was married to Jack and went to live in her new home at Millville. It wasn't until the next year that I started going to school. Mom had taught me to read and write the best she could. Hardscrabble was eight miles from the nearest school at Inwood, and this was too far for me to go horseback by myself. Arrangements were made to board me out with a family who lived near the school. The thought of being away from home frightened me.

Too soon the day came, and Mom took me to school to explain to the teacher why I was starting school at this age. After she talked with the teacher, she mounted her horse and went home. I felt as if I was being deserted forever. Youngsters began arriving, and before I realized it they were every place you looked. They were strangers to me and I shrank from their inquisitive eyes.

My clothes were new, but homemade. My dress was of brown flannelette with a narrow yellow stripe. It was made straight, with no waistline nor belt, and had a foot-long gathered flounce at the bottom. It was much too large and long for my bony body.

The sleeves, which had been made with the intentions of reaching to my wrists, actually stopped a short distance below my elbows, and were so tight it was almost impossible to bend my arms. My shoes were boy's shoes with tops inches above my ankles, and they sported copper-tipped toes. These were the only kind that would ''hold me,'' so the folks said. My stockings were heavy-ribbed black cotton. My hair, which was a yellowish, straw-like color, was long enough that I could set on it when out of its braids. It was parted in the center and braided in two big pig-tails. At the end of each, red ribbons were braided in, then brought up and tied in bows at the base of the braids.

Mom had told my teacher of her teaching me at home: that I knew the alphabet, could count and write, and that I read the weekly newspaper a little.

That first morning, Teacher said, ''First grade, come to my desk. We will select a reading book for you.'' Bashfully, I stumbled to her desk in company with a boy, the only other person in my class.

''Anita, your Mother told me that you read quite well. Therefore, I am not going to start you in the first grade Primer. Will you read Joe and I this story about an apple tree?''

I took the book. At the same time, I looked down at the roomful of grinning faces. Throat dry and tongue paralyzed, I stared at the page before me, but no words came.

''The tree is an apple tree,'' she prompted. I knew what was written there but, stupid-like, stood fidgeting, and occasionally whispered, ''Aha.'' I could hear giggling from down front. The kids were making fun of me.

''That's all right, we will have Joe read to you and I,'' she kindly said. Gently, she put her arm around my shoulders and gave me a reassuring hug. I shall never forget her for this kind act at such a dark hour.

Joe read to us. He had gone to school the year before, and at the near end of the term had taken sick and had not been promoted to the second grade.

I loved the teacher. She was beautiful in my eyes. Her clothes were like no other clothes I had ever seen. When she walked, there was the rustle of silk and satin. Her perfume was sweeter smelling than Mom's flower garden. I wanted to stand near her so I could enjoy its fragrance all the time. Her hair was black and shiny like the wing of a blackbird, and she combed it in a fashion far beyond my imagination. She was from San Francisco. I knew no one in our hills as sweet and frilly as she.

Before the term was half over, both Joe and I had been promoted to the second grade, and at the end of the year we were ready for the third grade the following term. This first year in school had been nerve-wracking for a child as unprepared as I to cope with the world in general.

Soon after the end of my first term of school, Dad heard of a man that wanted to sell his lease on a ranch, which was situated near school. He seen this man and bought the lease, also his livestock and farming implements. This place, called the Schearer ranch, was located across the mountain from Hardscrabble, about four miles east of Whitmore. It was but one mile distance from the Mountain Grove School.[6]

I was elated over moving to this new place, but on the other hand it made me sad leaving all the loved things at Hardscrab-

6. The new ranch, known as the Schearer farm, had been leased by Att's brother, Ethan Allen Aldridge, from the Red River Lumber Company. Ethan Allen, or "Ace," as he was known, leased it to Att for $150 per year. The company allowed Att to use their extensive holdings as rangeland for his cattle, horses, and hogs. Earlier, the Schearer farm had been famous for its hops, which were sold to the thriving brewing industry at Whitmore.

ble. Nothing would be the same.

Our house was a shamble, with boxes of our belongings being packed. Dad was impatient and kept nagging at Mom to hurry with this task. ''You'll have to hurry, Sadie, you can't fiddle around at this packin. I've gotta get over there and plant a garden and irrigate the alfalfa.''

Wore out from packing and lifting heavy boxes, she lost patience and exploded at him. ''If you're so all-fired of a hurry, get yourself around and do somethin yourself. Your hands ain't tied. All you want to do is drag empty boxes in here fer me to fall over and say, 'Fill this one, Sadie, and fill that one, Sadie, hurry Sadie; haven't you got that one done yet, Sadie?' Did it ever occur to you that you talk too much and do too little? Sadie's tired of your faunchin and bellerin like a bull. If you want the junk in these boxes any faster than Ol' Sadie is gettin it, just roll up your sleeves and pitch into it,'' she concluded.

''Me pack stuff? You know good and well I never packed nothin in my whole life. You're as unreasonable as a buffalo cow,'' he answered.

While he had been talking, Mom had seated herself in the rocker and was idly rocking back and forth, her eyes smoldering and her arms folded loosely, as if they were finished with work for evermore. She sat like this for some time, and he just stood there grinning, neither saying anything.

She finally said, ''If you ain't figurin on helpin me none around here, why don't you take a load over there every day? You've got plenty to move, with farmin things and all. Then, when I've got the things I'm takin over there packed, you'll have almost everythin moved.''

''You just leave that part to me. I'll get it over there,'' he promised.

She went back to packing, and he didn't set any more boxes in her way. The only helping he did was carry the filled boxes out on the front porch, where they waited to be loaded, come the day of the move.

The day before we moved, we learned of his plan to move everything in one trip. We had two big wagons, and they were loaded with enough different things to fill a menagerie. The front wagon was piled high with our household things. The second one had plows, cultivators, and a horde of other kinds of ranch tools. There was no less than two hundred chickens in coops, and in a big crate on the tail-end was "Snow Ball," a big white sow, and her litter of pigs. Behind this, the buggy was hitched. Its front was full of Mama's dishes, securely lashed on with rope. In the back was a coop, with my six prized ducks.

We harnessed six horses and got them hitched. Dad was as important as a king. He was showing off by moving everything at one time. Mom began stewing and fretting whether he could handle that many horses and wagons over such a rough, steep, and narrow road. True, it was no great lot better than a cow trail.

"I just don't think you're man enough to do it. I just don't," she said with a worried tone.

"Don't worry, Sadie, I drove more horses and bigger wagons over a worser road than this when I was a young feller. Guess I can do it now," he assured her.

Amongst these six horses was one mean runaway, and a saddle horse that had never had a harness on before. The other four were good, gentle horses, especially the wheelers. By ten that morning, we had everything ready to go. Mom and Dad climbed to the high seat, and Dad gathered the lines in his hand as if he truly was a teamster. He released the brake and yelled "Hi-yah," and they began moving out. The runaway went in buck jumps, and the unbroke horse did some fancy stepping; her eyes popped out in wonder at this thing that was happening to her. Mounted on my pony, I rode along, imagining myself in the same category as a scout back in the times of the covered wagons.

Above the rumble of the wagon wheels, I heard Mom say, "You watch out, Att, they don't get away from you. We'd go to hell in a handbasket quick, if they do." She was holding to the seat with both hands.

He spit a stream of tobacco juice. "Quit worryin, Sadie. You seem to think I'm just cuttin a monkeyshine, drivin these horses, but by God, I ain't," he informed her.

Everything went along fine. We made it up Alder Spring grade without any incident worth mentioning. Contrary to my imagination, this was an eventless trip, so far. From my position, riding behind the wagons, I could keep a watch on the livestock aboard. The ducks had their heads stuck up through the cracks of their coop's cover, continuously setting up a din with their quacks. A hen occasionally cackled, and the sow gave forth with grunts of dissatisfaction. The wagon wheels went bumping over and sliding off the many rocks in the road.

We topped the ridge and descended the other side around the narrow turns on Jackknife Gulch without mishap. Everything was riding fine. We came to where Garden Gulch cut across the road. Here the road was devilish steep. Dad began having trouble controlling everything. His foot on the brake lever, he set the brakes on the front wagon. Mom was seated sorta sideways on the seat, pulling with all her strength on the long rope attached to the brake staff on the second wagon. The back wheels on both wagons were set and sliding, the brakes squealing and grinding. Despite this, the wheel horses were being crowded ahead.

At this moment, the chain which fastened the buggy to the big wagon broke. It gave a lurch forward and collided into the back of the big wagon, driving its frail dashboard back into Mom's boxes of dishes. The horses were galloping by the time they reached the bottom of the hill. The impact had been so hard it threw the coop of ducks into the road, it landing upside down. When I turned it over, two of my ducks' necks were broken and hanging limp through the cracks of the coop. There was almost bloodshed when Mom seen what had happened to her dishes.

From my position up front, holding the runaway by the bit, I could hear the folks arguing and quarreling as they patched up the broken chain in preparation of getting the buggy hitched on again.

I heard Dad say, "It's no use of you claimin it's my fault. I can't help it if your damn dishes got busted."

"It is your fault fer not takin one wagon at a time," she argued, as they were trying to pull the buggy forward to hitch it on. "Dilly-dally is all you've done since I've been packin. Simply dilly-dallyin," she snorted.

"Now, Sadie, don't get so all-fired shook up," he said, with a choked voice.

"Shook up! Huh! I ain't just shook up, I'm mad!" she yelled. She dropped the buggy tongue and sat down on a log, refusing to help him any further. "The only thing in that front box that wasn't busted to smithereens is your fancy shavin mug. It just makes me sick. Those were my fancy dishes," she lamented, acting as if she was talking only to herself.

"Come on, Sadie, and help me get this thing pulled up and hitched on," Dad coaxed, then added, "You're settin there lookin like a mad bull, and bellerin like one too." And he laughed at his own joke. Mom still sat, mad and blowed up like a toad frog. All expression had left her face; it was hard to tell what she was thinking.

He managed to hitch the buggy on by himself. Then he

walked to where she sat on the log and, with a broad grin, swept off his hat to her; then he helped her from the log and gallantly assisted her up the wagon wheel onto the high seat; then seated himself. He gathered the lines, and I let the runaway go, and with a loud "Ha-chaa" from Dad, they moved out again.

"I don't want to see you cuttin any monkeyshines, Att. We could get killed with this old outfit if you ain't careful," Mom told him, as they started on.

"I ain't monkeyshinin, I'm usin all the horse sense I've got," he said in a serious tone of voice, and bit off a big chunk of tobacco.

The road was level now, with few rocks. We were in the pine timber country, and everything smelled of the pines. The ground was covered with devil carpet, which was in bloom. Perfume of those millions of lavender blossoms filled the air, along with the scent of pine. I wished Mom would come out of her sulking over the broken dishes. What the heck — I'd gotten two ducks killed, and I wasn't mad.

We came to the top of Cow Creek grade and started the descent into the big canyon. Again, the wagon brakes squealed and ground, and I prayed that nothing would break and the horses could hold the wagons back. We were almost to the steepest part of the grade when I heard Shep begin yipping on the hill above the road. He was chasing after something, and there, tearing out of the brush, came a deer. It almost jumped amongst the horses as it came bouncing across the road. Shep, hot on its heels, came yipping by.

The startled horses quickened their pace. The smell of brimstone filled the air. The fire-colored sorrel runaway seen his chance to get in his devil work, and began jumping up and down, fighting the bit and crowding this way and that against and into the horse at his side. They began tightening their tugs, and the wheelers couldn't hold back against this force and began trotting to keep out of the way of the wagons. Dad made frantic efforts to slow them down, but they kept going faster and faster. The only thing he could now do was keep the wagons on the grade by guiding the horses in the right position on the turns. They took a curve a little wide, and a low-hanging limb caught and ripped a hole in a feather tick. Feathers began flying so thick, I was riding blindly as I came racing behind on my little horse.

There was a two-way turn at the bottom of the grade and onto the bridge across Cow Creek. They would never make it, I thought. As they neared the bottom, every horse was at top speed, the wagons swaying this way and that. They reached the two-way turn and the bridge.

The horses and the first wagon got on the bridge all right, but the turns was so sharp that the second wagon jammed into the bannister of the bridge, and it and the buggy tipped on their sides over the bank. They didn't break loose from the front wagon, despite the violent jerk. This brought everything to a sliding stop. How Mom and Dad stayed on the wagon seat, I'll never know.

The runaway sorrel was down, floundering on the bridge. When he got to his feet, I seen he had a broken leg. Speechless, the folks got out of the wagon and unhitched the horses. Dad went to the wagon and got his rifle, stripped the harness from the runaway, and led him from the bridge and up the creek out of sight, the horse hobbling along in agony on three legs. A few minutes, and there was the crack of the rifle. No more runaway horse.

Dad came back with a downcast expression on his face, and quietly said, ''I've been intendin to do that fer some time, but it kinda got next to my hide to have to down him. I sorta forgot the ornery things he's done, seein him standin there, that leg danglin, and lookin me straight in the eye. That trigger pulled pretty damn hard,'' he concluded, brushing his hand over his face, as if trying to obliterate the vision of the horse.

"I know, Att, I feel the same way,'' Mom said, and then went on with a faraway look in her eyes. "I haven't forgot what a pretty little stinker he was when I fed him every three hours after his mother died. But damn a runaway horse!''

Chickens were running everywhere, cackling in fright. The white sow and pigs were going at a trot back up the grade; they were headed back to Hardscrabble. I thought about my ducks and dashed back to where the buggy lay. The coop lay down the hill, almost at the water's edge. It had been broken open, and not a duck was in sight. Going down to the edge of the creek, I seen all four of them floating along with the current of the stream. That was the last of them I ever saw, as they went quacking and floating around a bend.

It took us parts of three days and nights to capture all the chickens. We run them down by day and caught them out of the trees at night. Eventually, we got the wreckage home. I never heard one more word of bickering from Mom and Dad over the breaking of her dishes, or whether he had been monkeyshining or using horse sense when it happened. Perhaps they considered themselves soldiers of misfortune in the thing, alike, and dismissed it from their minds.

6

THE HOLE HOUSE

UR NEW HOME was all and more than I had expected it to be. School was still in session here, as the snow fell deep in winter (because of the altitude being high), and I was enrolled the week following our move.[7]

This entire county had, at one time, been a German colony. Even now, our neighbors were German people. I found the kids a bit clannish. At play, they spoke in German, and I felt that they were talking about me.[8] I came home in tears my first day and had to be forced to continue going to school. Dad thought if our family could get acquainted with everyone here, it would help our relationship with the neighbors. He and Mom began thinking how this could be done, and came up with plans for a barbecue, come Fourth of July.

7. The elevation at Hardscrabble was about 2,000 feet, while that at the Schearer farm was approximately 2,600 feet.

8. Whitmore, first known as Tamarac, was founded by a German immigrant, Simon Whitmore, in 1863. The settlement grew slowly until the Eudora Colony brought many German Lutherans to the community during the 1880s. The German influence remained significant until the era of World War I.

A poster was made and posted in town announcing the affair. It said, "COME ONE, COME ALL." A beef was butchered, wrapped, and cooked in a pit. Mom baked cakes, pies, and all sorts of goodies. As early as nine o'clock the morning of the Fourth, people began arriving. They came in buggies, spring wagons, and farm wagons, and on horseback and on foot. The arrival of one family in a Model T Ford was a big deal with me; it also put every cow and horse on the place in flight.

Everyone was friendly, and we got acquainted with these strangers. The men were playing horseshoes. Mom's face was flushed from bustling around, getting the goodies on the long tables. She was being helped by a score or more of women. They were all talking at once. The big hunks of beef were got out of the pit and were cut in serving-size pieces. Uum, it smelled good! All us kids stood around watching this, eagerly wanting to get our little fangs into it. Our noses were twitching like a fox's. Everyone ate until they could eat no more, then settled around in groups, talking. Musical instruments began being produced, and the place vibrated with music from a banjo, accordion, and guitar. Some of the people sang.

The one place on the ranch that I believe everyone found that day was our little backhouse. There was a continual stream of people coming and going. They completely used one big catalog that day. But there was one lady that did not know where it was. She was a big, fat, German lady. When the music and singing was at its best, she came up to me and said in a whisper, "Where is your 'Hole House'?" And I pointed it out to her.

In a little while, we heard a loud scream from out that way. Out of the house shot the fat lady, holding her dress above her waist, running towards us as fast as she could waddle and yelling, "Oh, mine gott! Mine gott! I've been snock bit! Mine gott!" and holding her behind with one hand. This brought everyone to their feet in a state of excitement.

Mom and some other women helped the poor lady into the house and had her lay face-down across a bed. They began inspection to determine exactly where the snake had bit her. One of the women raised up, shaking her head and said, "It's bad! But I know what to do. Get your man's razor, Mrs. Aldridge, I'll have to cut where the fangs went in and suck the poison out. Find someone who ain't got holler teeth," she instructed.

Mom sent me for the razor and when I got back into the bedroom they had the poor, suffering soul jackknifed in a ridiculous predicament on her head and knees. They were paying no heed to her posture, just serious as to the exact spot to make the incision. The dying woman was trembling and moaning and talking as if in delirium. "Oh, mine gott in heaven, have mercy. Have mercy, oh hamuel"! I could stand no more, so I hurried outdoors. The men were out at the little house trying to locate the rattler. I seen them coming towards the house in a crowded group, all talking and laughing at once. How could they act so, when that poor woman was in there, dying?

One of the men came on ahead of the others and, laughing, told me to run in the house and tell the woman not to worry, that it was a chicken hen that had pecked her and not a snake. It was a hen that had crawled down under the seat to lay, and resented being disturbed.

I ran back into the bedroom just in time to save the victim from the razor. Two women were in a hot argument over where the fangs had penetrated, and stood ready to plunge the razor in when I told the news, that it was not a snake that had bit her, that she had only been pecked by a hen.

The poor woman slid quickly from the bed and to her feet, exclaiming, "Oh, mine gott, I thought it was a snock!!"

7

MODEL T

I F WE JUST HAD AN AUTOMOBILE. It don't take all day to go places in a car. If a person had an auto, you could do that. Not like chuggin over the road with a dang horse.'' Such refrains echoed in our house, as persistent as the mew of a cat. Mom and Al wanted Dad to buy an automobile.

''I'll buy one of those iron contraptions, but dang me I don't want to hear no more jawin from either of you,'' Dad said unexpectedly.

The storeman at Whitmore had a second-hand Model T Ford for sale, a 1914 model. We went to town, and Dad bought this black beauty. None of our family had driven a car, with the exception of him.

''You drove one once, Att, you take it home,'' Mom said.

''Oh, not on your life. I'm afeared to ride in it, let alone drive the contraption. It's quick as a mink, Sadie. I'll stick to the team and buggy,'' he added.

A jeweler from Redding had taken him for a ride from Redding to Anderson, not long past. He insisted that Dad drive, to get the feel of what a wonder a car was. There was no paved or oiled roads at that time. He fed it the gas and went speeding along until he came to a sandy spot in the road. The front wheels jackknifed, and Dad and the jeweler upset in a ditch. Dad had decided a car was a no-good contraption from this experience.

The storekeeper showed Al how to start and stop it, and how to use the hand-operated gas and spark levers. He took out for the ranch and we followed in the buggy. I wanted to go with him, but Dad said, "No! Hell, no! He no doubt will wrap it around a tree before he gets there. She's a damn dangerous thing, Scrub."

When we reached home, Al had the "prize" parked down by the watering trough, had washed it, and was shining the brass radiator with baking soda.

That evening, after the chores were finished and supper over, Al suggested, "What you say, let's start the automobile and go for a ride." He gave the crank a few turns; the motor sputtered into a mighty roar. We climbed in, Dad and Al in front, Mom and I in the back seat. We went rolling along, kicking up a billowing cloud of dust behind us. The roadway was narrow, with trees growing at its very edges. Dad was riding with his door open and his foot on the running board.

"Better shut your door, Att, you'll fall out," Mom told him.

"Fall out, be damned! I've got it open to jump, if it goes to tanglefootin'," he exclaimed. In spite of his fear, when we got home he remarked, "Seems to be a ringtailed dandy, but it cost me a heap of money. How much does tires fer an automobile cost?" His question went unanswered, because none of us knew. Long after I had gone to bed that night, I could hear Mom and Al in the living room, talking about the wonder of an automobile.

The cans of cream were taken to town every other day. The

mail stage took them to Redding to the railroad. From there, they went to Cottonwood to the creamery. The next day after we bought the Model T was one of these days. Bright and early the cans were loaded in the car. We were all going for the ride.

Dad, Mom, and I got into our respective seats, and Al began cranking. He cranked for several minutes, but it did not start. It was apparent something was wrong. We all got out. He lifted the hood and looked at the motor, with a perplexed look on his face. Having had no previous experience with a motor, he had no idea what was wrong. He knew what the fan and spark plugs were, which was about the best of his knowledge. He shook several things on the motor, then brightly said, ''Don't seem to be nothin loose. The damn thing should start.''

''I've heard tell they fill the radiator with boilin water when they get stubborn. I'll run to the house and heat some,'' Mom said, starting towards the house.

Dad looked under the back seat, picked out the largest wrench there, and went over and tried it for fit on the nut on the buggy's wheel. It was far too small. He tossed it back in the car with a look of disgust and muttered to himself, ''Ain't nothin about the thing worth a tinker's damn.'' He bit off a chew of tobacco, still eyeing the car, then picked up his shovel and marched away to the alfalfa field to regulate the water.

Mom panted up with two buckets of hot water. She drained the radiator and filled it from the buckets. She and Al took turns cranking. He was not sure that he remembered which way to turn the key to ''on.'' They cranked a while with it turned one way, then turned it the other and cranked again. Nothing persuaded the ''black monster'' to belch, even one time. Their enthusiasm wasn't dampened by the fact that it wouldn't respond. The miracle of the automobile was the topic of their conversation.

Dad came back from irrigating and asked, "Ain't you got her goin yet?"

"Nope, I think the spark plugs are dirty. I'm goin to clean em," Al knowingly said.

"Do you know how to do that?" Dad asked.

"Yeah, any damn fool can clean a spark plug," answered Al.

"Well, I don't know about that, I wouldn't know where to begin," Dad admitted. "What's that thing?" he asked, pointing to the oil cap.

"I'm not sure. It's some kind of a doodad that makes it run," Al guessed, not knowing it was where oil was put in the motor. "Just a few days ago, I was listenin to that new feller that moved over across the hill. He was tellin about cars, and he said a motor is made up of a lot of movin parts. Before it will start, they all have to click. I think that may be what's ailin this. I ain't heard anythin click," Al told, then went on, "He must know what he's talkin about, cause he was tellin he's awful good fixin cars."

"Ain't you gonna be late gettin the cream to town?" Dad asked. "The stage will be gone," he reminded.

"Naw, won't take but a few minutes to buzz down there in this. Ain't like goin with a horse," Al nonchalantly said.

Dad hitched the harness team to the buggy, moved the cans of cream into it, and, without a word, drove away toward town.

Getting the car started lasted for three days. Gallons of hot water went into the radiator. The spark plugs shined — they had been cleaned so many times they looked new. Dad still hauled the cream to town in the buggy. He didn't go near the car anymore. He shied away from it as if it had the plague. He had been so busy doing most of the work, since Mom and Al had thought of nothing but starting the car, that the irrigating of the meadow had been neglected at Hardscrabble, so he left to do that.

As soon as he was out of sight, Al and Mom hitched the team to the Model T. They towed it up and down the lane, the team in a gallop; but the little car refused to cooperate.

Al called the new man in the country on the telephone to ask his advice on what to do to start it. He said he would come over and see what the trouble was. He eyed our car with an air of importance, and asked, "Have you cleaned the plugs?"

"Clean as a whistle," Al assured him.

"Now, it could be your coils are out of adjustment, or they might be damp. It's best to take them out when you're not usin the machine and put them in a dry, warm place," he advised. "It could be your magneto post is dirty, or it might be she's got a loose wire. Have you checked for gasoline?" he rambled on. "Have you jacked up a hind wheel, and tried to start her, after fillin the radiator with hot water?" he asked.

"We've filled her with hot water fer three days. Didn't know about jackin a wheel up," Al told him.

"Well, jackin a wheel up is a sure way to start a car, after you pour boilin water on the manifold," he importantly told Al. "There's a good possibility your wiring is shot, or maybe your mag is gone." Mom and Al looked at the man in wide-eyed wonder at what he was saying.

"Maybe we have bought a lemon," Mom said. "I didn't know there was so many things a feller has to know to run a car." She spoke in a worried tone.

"We've pulled it up and down the lane till the team's wore out," Al informed him.

"Turn the switch on. I'll turn her over and see what's the trouble," the man instructed. "Got it on," Al answered. The man gave the crank a spin; the motor chuck-chucked, and started with a rattling roar. It had happened so unexpected, Mom jumped to one side. Al stood there, red-faced and grinning. "I'll be damned. How did you do it?" he asked.

"Choked her," the genius said, smiling.

"How you mean, choked it?" Mom inquired, looking at the little greasy man as if he might be a tin god.

"See this balin wire stickin out here in front?" he asked. "As you turn her over, pull that out as far as it will pull just once, then let it fly back. That's the sure way to start a machine," he boasted, and strutted around like a greasy and dirty bantam rooster. He shut the motor off, explaining he would tune it up. Mom and Al watched him as he unscrewed the magneto post and held it to the light for them to see. "Look at that gob of lint! It's a wonder she started a'tall!" he exclaimed.

"It must have took you a long time to 'get on' to all this stuff about a car," Mom said in admiration.

"No, it didn't. I'm quick at reasonin things out. What I'm really trying to say is, my mother had no foolish children." He laughed loud, with a self-satisfied air and a smile on his face. "A motor is made up of a lot of movin parts and they have to all function together before it will start," he continued. "I've got to be runnin along home, now. If you get stalled again, give me a ring and I'll fix it for you."

After he had gone, we cranked the car to see if we could start it. We went racing out the lane and back, around and around the barn lot, and through the lane some more. It was far past chore time when Dad returned. We hadn't as much as thought about them. We were busy enjoying this miracle, the little "black beauty."

"I see you got it goin," Dad said, as we stopped beside him.

"Yeah," Al answered, with a smile.

"Had to pull it with the team I see, from the tracks. I figured you'd do that, soon's I weren't lookin," he sour-voiced said.

"Pulled it with them, but didn't do no good," Al admitted.

"What got it goin, then?" Dad asked.

"Choked it," Al answered in a way you could tell he was trying to impress Dad and let him believe he was the mastermind, and wouldn't tell about the way it had really been started.

"That's what I'd done to the bastardly thing a long time ago if I figured it had any life in it," Dad laughed. "What did you do? Grab it by the guzzler and just hang on till it quit kickin?" Dad asked, laughing again. He was taking this choking thing as a big joke.

"No, no, you don't understand, Dad. There is a heap more to a car than you think. First, all the movin parts have to function together. Your mag post has to have all the lint and grease off it, your coils adjusted and dry, plugs clean and wires tight, hot water in the radiator, one hind wheel jacked up, boilin water poured on the manifold and choke it. She'll start every shot," Al concluded, proud of his burst of knowledge about a car.

"Hell, that's about like tryin to go with a horse that got bots, the thumps, and ring bone all at one time. He ain't no good that way, but if you doctor him up fer a while, he'd go," Dad said. "I just figure I've threw away that money, buyin that worthless piece of tin," he added. "What about that click you was listenin fer the other day? Did you hear that before it started?" He laughed again, scratching his head, and squirted tobacco juice to one side.

"No, the way I get it now, all those parts merely have to function together," Al explained.

"Oh, hogwash, you don't know any more about that contraption's innards than a jaybird, and you just as well admit it," Dad said. "But what I can't figger, after crankin fer three days and it hadn't started, how did you find out how to do it?" Dad wondered.

"Just simple deduction, Dad."

Anita and her dog Fanny at Hardscrabble in 1911,
when she was four years old.

Att and Sarah around 1912,
resting in front of
Hardscrabble.

Anita at age seventeen.
The picture was taken by
Poke on an afternoon's outing
near the Schearer ranch.

Anita in 1925, a few weeks before she moved
from the Schearer ranch to Dunsmuir.

Anita and Poke's wedding picture,
Christmastime 1925.

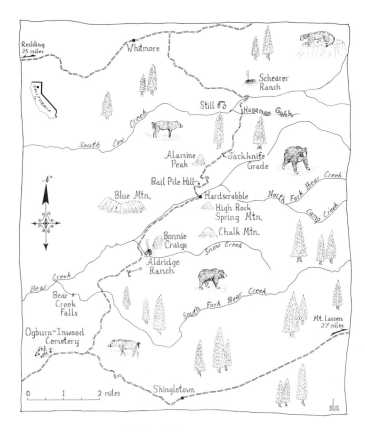

Hardscrabble country.

The old road in front of Hardscrabble, where Anita once played (picture taken in 1973).

Looking down on Hardscrabble from Rail Pile Hill.
The house was located about thirty yards east of the present barn
(picture taken in 1975).

The Schearer ranch house in 1973.

The site of the Schearer ranch house in 1975.

8

WORLD WAR ONE

AL ALWAYS HAD BEEN a little shy of women, but after Dad bought the used 1914 Model T, Al suddenly began chasing around the country with the girls. He stopped chewing tobacco, and shaved every day, and polished his gold tooth until it gleamed like the sun. Overnight, it seemed, he blossomed into a dandy, his hair slicked down with goose grease, and not a trace of the smell of skunk or stinky trap-bait about him. He had pulled up his trapline shortly after he began sprucing up. Saturday nights he dressed up in his new suit, boiled shirt and all, and — plus the grooming he gave himself — it made him, to use the word loosely, a genuine "Don Juan."

In a few short weeks, he was engaged to Ivy, and they had set the wedding date. She was small of stature, quick-acting, and a vivid girl. They were married in Redding, and the whole family went to the wedding. Al and Ivy moved their belongings to Hardscrabble and temporarily made their home there.

There was much talk of war in the newspapers. Words of war fell from the lips of people in our hills. They feared the United States would be compelled to join forces with our Allies oversees and fight in the war that was being fought over there. True to this fear, war was declared in the spring of '17.

Al was in the age group that must register for induction in the Service. Soon after this, I was in Whitmore to get the mail. There was an official letter addressed to him, and I let no grass grow under my horse's feet to get it home to him. He was in the upper field, plowing, and I rode up to where he was working. The letter was notification for him to be in Redding on a certain date for a physical. As he read this notification, standing there in silence, the only thing that appeared to live on was the wild geese passing overhead in flight to their nesting grounds far to the north. The sky was full of them. Their honks were loud and seemed to chime in many tones as they winged their way over our heads. The call of the wild goose had always stirred my soul into excitement and an unexplainable feeling of something akin to lonesomeness.

"Do you think you will have to go?" I asked.

"I reckon so. Yeah, I expect I will," he answered, as he began unhitching the team and quietly singing.

> Good-by, Maw, Good-by, Paw,
> Good-by mule with your old Hee-Haa,
> I may not know what this war's about,
> But you bet, by golly, I'll soon find out.

Watching, I visioned him in some faraway place, wounded and dying and not even Mom there to doctor him.

Al took his examination, and Uncle Sam said, "You're the kind of a boy I'm looking for." It would be but a matter of time until he would be whisked away to the battle.

Dad was deeply worried how he was going to take care of the ranches and cattle with Al gone. Mom began learning to drive the car, being sure Al would be gone in a short while. She learned by herself, as no one would ride with her. After she had ran through several gates, hit a tree, and killed a hog, she declared she could drive as well as anyone, and began buzzing around everyplace. Horse and buggy days were past, as far as she was concerned. What she lacked in know-how, she made up for in speed.

The folks learned that Dad could claim exemptions for Al, since he was needed so badly at home. We went to Redding to fill out these papers, and Mom drove. When we came to the main road, it had been recently repaired with a liberal covering of coarsely crushed rock. We went charging along this road with the gas lever pulled to wide open. Rocks from the size of a marble to as large as an egg showered each side of the road for thirty feet or more. Dad sat upright in the seat, his door open, one foot on the running board so he could bail out if things got any rougher. I hung to the top's bow in the back seat, fighting to keep his tobacco juice out of my eyes. He was spitting every few seconds, he was so excited.

We rounded a turn in Basin Hollow, took the turn too wide, ran into a fence, and drove a fender back tight against a tire. It happened so quick, Dad had no time to jump. He sat as if transfixed, and rode until the car stopped.

"By damn, Sadie!" he ejaculated. "Can't you drive this tin contraption slower?"

"Ain't no good, Att, goin slow. You just jostle along and feel every rock in the road," she matter-of-fact said, as she pried the crushed fender away from the tire. "You get up a little speed and it's as smooth as a ribbon. You shoot up little hills like they ain't there," she went on in a confident tone. She patted the wheel she had raised the fender off of, and went on talking with a smile on her face. "These wheels are made round to roll and I'm made to roll them," she said, as she began cranking the motor, still smiling as she cranked.

"But, Sadie, you're gonna kill the whole shebang of us if you keep it up. By the jumped-up-billy-bedamned, I ain't ridin a bit further if you keep whippin it up like you've been doin. Besides that, look what you've done to it in not more than two months. When thisun's gone, I ain't buyin any more cars fer you to tear to thunder," he finished, with a vexed look on his face.

Mom's smile vanished. She stepped up close beside him so he could hear what she was about to say above the roar of the motor. "Bein's your tellin what you'll do and what you won't do, let me tell you somethin, Mister Aldridge. If I can't have a car, I ain't havin nothin. I'm not goin back to chuggin around in a darn buggy no more. I'm sick of settin up behind a dang horse, it fartin in my face all the time!" she ejaculated, and climbed into the car, saying, "You put that in your pipe and smoke it, Mister."

We went helter-skelter down the road, skidding around turns, rocks flying further than before. Mom's back looked bowed up as she bent over the wheel. Dad sat sideways in the seat, both feet on the running board, with a look on his face like a young robin preparing to take its first flight from its nest. We raced through the one street of the little towns of Millville and Palo Cedro. The car panted along, steam whistling from around the brass radiator cap, as it labored up little hills along the way. Nothing had been said since we had left Basin Hollow.

After crossing Free Bridge and nearing town, Mom broke the silence by saying, "I ain't gonna drive right up town. Not bein use to so many people, I might just bungle and hit somethin."

"Head up this back street," Dad said with authority. We parked under a tree, in its shade.

"Come on, let's get up to the courthouse and get those papers fixed and get started back," Dad said.

"I don't want to go, everyone will look at me," I complained.

Dad looked inquiring at me, cleared his throat, and said, "Scrub, I don't know what's wrong with you, always afraid of somebody seein you. That's what you're fer, child, is to look at. I think you're a pretty little kid," he said, with admiration.

"But I'm sick, and want to stay here till you get back," I argued.

"All right, but stay in the car," he instructed. "It's about a mile to the courthouse and your Mom and me will be gone quite a spell," he warned.

After they had gone, I laid down on the floor of the back and fell asleep. Mom woke me, saying, "Ain't your Dad here yet, honey? I went in a store to buy some thread and he just up and disappeared."

We waited for what seemed hours before we seen him coming down the walk, his hat pushed back on his head. He was stepping lively.

"Well, here you are Sadie, old dear. I plum lost you, honey. Just stopped a minute to say 'Hello' to a feller I know and you got away from me. He asked me in the saloon to have a drink, and just as quick as I could get away from there, I flew here to you. Heck," he hiccupped in a drunken fashion, and began stepping around Mom in a silly and uncertain way, and started shadow boxing.

"You're soused, Att! Get away from me. Climb in the car and quit actin like somethin with no more sense than a scarecrow," Mom scolded, and pushed him toward the car.

"So you think I'm drunk, huh?" he bristled. "I only had one or two little snorts. It weren't hardly enough to wet my whistler. I feel like kadoodlin around, Sadie."

Mom cranked the car as she muttered something about a darn man always tryin to run a shenanigan on a woman. She had a woebegone expression as she climbed behind the wheel. She

81

drove out of town with her back bowed and not saying a word. Dad rocked back and forth in the seat, whistling and singing.

> Oh, did you ever look into an Irishman's shanty
> With the dirt so thick and the whiskey so plenty,
> A two-legged stool and a table to match,
> And the door of the shanty was locked with a latch.

He kept time to the song's lively jig tune by stomping his feet on the floorboard. "Ain't this contraption got any more speed than this?" he asked. "Shove the lines at her and give her the bit. I want to get home! Whoopie!! Let her ramble, Sadie!"

9

LYNX AND BEAR

I T WAS MY BIRTHDAY, the fall I was fourteen. The sun had just peeped over yonder hills and was setting the ranch aglitter with the frost on everything. A million diamonds sparkled in the garden outside the kitchen window.

"I'm glad you two are not goin anyplace today," Mom said. "Maybe you'll get that fence fixed."

"Yeh, I've been fixin to lay off and help you get that done," Dad said with a sigh.

"That's the trouble with you, Att, you're always helpin me. You never take the bull by the horns and fix a fence or build as much as a chicken coop unless I'm right there workin harder than you are and proddin you along," Mom said in a nagging voice. "I'm surprised you got the material out there. But that was three weeks ago. Since that, you've just dilly-dallied and ain't thought of settin a post or nothin," she complained.

The telephone rang and she answered, listened to the caller for a few seconds, and then said, "I'll tell him, Edd. He's out busy fixin fence now. I doubt if he'll leave that, at least not this mornin. Maybe later he can go down. I'll tell him," she said, and hung up the receiver.

"What's this you're gonna tell me?" Dad asked, laughing.

"It was Edd. Somethin killed one of his sheep last night. He is wantin you to bring your dogs and catch what did it," she explained.

"What did he say did it?" Dad asked.

"Didn't know, said you'd know. I told him you was makin fence, which you're gonna be doin as soon as I can get you to budge," she said in a decided way.

"Hell, Sadie, I think we'd better get down there. Tracks will be cold if we don't," he said. "Get the horses saddled, Scrub. We'll just gallop down there and have a look," he told me. "Edd's a good feller, I can't let him down. Won't take long to see," he said, with a ring of excitement in his voice, which was always there when the possibility of a hunt showed up.

We took out for Edd's ranch, with Mom looking scornful at us. The air was crisp and cold, frost still showing where the sun had not hit. The leaves from the oaks lazily drifted down any direction you might look.

Edd and his sister Marie were in the barn lot when we arrived, inspecting the carcass of a ewe. "Sure glad you could come. Look here. What do you think killed her, a panther?" Edd asked.

The ground was padded with tracks around the partly eaten dead sheep. Dad got down from his horse and surveyed these tracks. "No panther. Was a cat, all right. Look there," he said, pointing to a faint imprint. "Big lynx, I'd say, from the size of his track."

Shep began sniffing, and slowly tracked here and there, trying to untangle the tracks to find which way the cat had gone. He showed signs he had hit the right trail as he slid between the rails of the fence across the gulch from the sheep pen, and began tracking toward a patch of small cedars.

"Yahha!" Dad yelled, and Shep stopped and turned, waiting for the next command. When we reached the spot where he waited, he began slowly tracking again, and we followed. Besides Shep, we had three young, untrained dogs. Trump and Deuce were black-and-tan hounds, and Gip was a leggy, brown-and-white shepherd.

"Get off and couple the two hounds together, and I'll give Gip a lesson on stayin back, not botherin a slow tracker," said Dad.

I snapped the coupler on the hounds, which was merely a slim, steel rod about two feet long with a snap on each end. The snaps are fastened into the rings on each dog's collar.

"We'll jump him out of his bed about over in 'Skunk Holler,' or he may hit the other way and be holdin up in the cliffs on the canyon rim," Dad guessed.

The frost of the night had made the trail cold, considering the lynx had gone there but a few hours before. Shep tracked slow, and it was a couple of hours before we jumped the cat. He had not bedded down where Dad had guessed he would. We jumped him from the sunny side of Greenhorn Gulch. Shep became anxious and acted as if he was trying to say, "He's right close here, Dad. Shall I get him?" Our quarry was just ahead.

"Want me to uncouple the hounds?" I asked.

"Yeah, before Shep jumps him."

I looked back for the hounds. They were away behind, Trump on one side of a sapling and Deuce on the other. They were mutely seesawing back and forth, trying to free themselves from the predicament they had gotten themselves in. Being coupled together was a new experience to them. Dad, seeing what had happened, said, "Leave the damn fools alone. They'll get loose in a second. It's the only way to teach young dogs."

One staggered over to the right side of the tree, and they came

trotting up to me with eager eyes, their tails high. I removed the
coupler and, at Dad's low click of his tongue, they streaked out
of sight the way Shep and Gip had gone.

Spurring our horses into a gallop, the fast chase was on. We
kept up this mad dash for more than a half mile, the horses
crashing through the brush. It kept us busy ducking low-hanging
limbs. Coming to a divide of the ridge, we were not sure which
way the cat and dogs had gone. Stopping to listen, the sounds of
the dogs came drifting from the right hand fork. They were
several yards up front, and sounded like they were going strong.

We went on in pursuit, past the brush and timbered country
and came to "Skunk Holler," which was free of either brush or
trees. It was a large, cathedral-shaped depression on the side of
the canyon. It's entire basin was solid lava rock. There, streaking along the upper rim, was the dogs, the cat a little ahead of
them. Shep began pulling to the right, running fast, to reach the
further side of the circular rim. He took this shortcut to be on the
spot when the other dogs chased the cat around.

"Old Shep's a wise devil. Watch him outsmart that lynx,"
Dad said in admiration. He was proud of Shep; they had been on
many hunts together.

The cat kept to the rim, and Shep was there when he came
bounding down the slope within a few feet of the dog before
seeing him. Shep made a rush; the cat gave several, long,
graceful leaps, and was out of our sight on the far side of the
ridge.

Dad turned half around in the saddle with a broad grin on his
face. "Shep's eatin his hind end up now. He'll tree before they
hit the creek."

The other dogs followed the way the cat and Shep had gone.
We hurried to catch up with the chase. Where Shep had surprised the lynx, we stopped to listen. Down near the bottom of

the canyon we could hear the dogs "barkin treed" — Shep and Gip in the regular, even tones of a shepherd, the hounds giving out long, musical-sounding bawls, their voices echoing up and down the canyon walls.

The hillside was rough and steep, but we went straight down it. Our horses slid for twenty feet at times before their feet could find solid footing to stop their slide. Rocks bounced ahead and by us as they were uprooted by the horses' hooves. We came in sight of the dogs. They were on a bench up above the floor of the canyon several yards. The young dogs were milling beneath a sprawling-limbed live oak tree, gazing upward. Shep was standing on top of a huge boulder, which the tree had grew against, his front feet on the tree's trunk and his hind on the big rock. The dogs were setting up an earsplitting roar as they watched the lynx, who was laying on a big, moss-covered limb not too high in the tree.

Leaving our horses back a distance, we approached the tree. Dad began looking around as if in search of something. I thought he was looking for an advantageous place to stand to shoot the cat. But he laid his rifle down, took out his pocket knife, cut a small fir tree off near where it came from the ground, and trimmed its limbs off.

"What are you fixin to do with that pole?" I asked.

"You're young and can climb good. I thought if you can get up above where Shep's standin, and get out on that second big limb, you might pole him out and we could train the pups a little more," he matter-of-fact answered. Surely he couldn't be serious and expect me to go up there! I looked up the tree and said, "I can't climb it, there ain't nothin to get hold of."

"Well, I'll be damned!" he exploded. "I thought you had more guts than that!"

I didn't want him to think I was a coward, knowing what he

thought of anyone who was "yeller." "Give me the pole. I'll try to get up there," I said, trying to keep the shake out of my voice. I gained the top of the rock and looked up to locate the cat's position. He had arose from his reclining position on the limb, his wicked eyes staring intently at me. He stood, back arched, in a half-crouch, growling and hissing, warning me to come no closer. The hair on my head and neck crawled and I suddenly felt sick in my stomach. I jumped from the rock to the ground and tossed the pole down the hill into the brush.

"What's the matter?" Dad asked.

"I'm afraid to go up there, and I ain't goin," I stated flatly.

"By God, as old and crippled up as I am, I can get up and poke that bastard out!" he exclaimed. He picked up a long, dead limb from the ground and went up the boulder and on up the tree. The lynx was showing fight more than when I'd been on the rock, but Dad was paying no mind to that. He reached out with the stick and began pushing at him, and the cat started boxing and biting at the club. He gave a quick jab and the cat began to fall, but caught, hanging to the limb with one foot, clawing to regain the limb again. The longer part of Dad's club broke and came crashing to the ground. This left him with not more than two foot of the club in his hand. He braced himself for the attack the cat was preparing to make. He was standing, his feet wide apart, on two limbs, his back against the body of the tree, the club in his right hand and his old slouch hat in the left, closely watching the cat's every move.

Like lightning, the cat sprang at him; but just as fast, Dad struck the cat in the face with his hat, letting out a rebel yell. This spoiled the animal's aim and knocked him on his belly, across one of the limbs Dad was standing on. Before the cat could regain his footing, Dad brought the club down with force on his head. He balanced across the limb for a few seconds, then limply came tumbling down, his body hitting the earth with a dull thump. The dogs ''nailed'' him as he did this.

Dad came slowly from the tree, taking much more caution than when he had gone up. I expected a lecture on my lack of bravery, but he merely said, ''That was about the maddest damn cat I ever saw. Looked like I was goin belly-side-up when my club broke. When I seen he was hellbent on scratchin my eyes out, I whopped him a mite too hard. I'd like to have jumped him out and trained those pups a little more. They sure than hell need it.'' He was breathing heavy from exertion. ''So you was scared to go up there?''

Ashamed, I turned to the job of tying the cat on behind my saddle and did not answer. We zig-zagged back and forth as we rode up the hill and to the top of the canyon rim. Our horses were streaked with sweat and blowing hard when we got there.

We came to our outside pasture gate. I thought we were going directly home and make the fence. I had opened the gate when Dad said, ''I believe we orta go up to the Beal place and see if we've caught that bear in our trap. Maybe your Ma will fix that fence,'' he laughed, and added, ''You know, I just can't see why she hounds me to do things she knows I'll do sometime.''

''She'll worse than hound the pair of us if we don't get home and help her. The last thing she said when we left was not to dilly-dally around, to get home and fix the fence,'' I reminded him.

He looked at the sun to estimate the time and said, ''Shut the gate and leave the cat here. We won't be gone more'n two hours. Maybe she'll get around and set the posts and it won't take long to slam it up the rest of the way.''

No one lived at the Beal place, and the buildings were tumbled down. Nothing grew there, due to neglect, except apple trees. A bear had been climbing over the rail fence near these trees, and breaking the limbs from the trees to get the apples. We set our bear trap by the fence to stop this destruction.

When we rode in sight of this spot, there was no mistaking we had got him. The rails were flattened to the ground for several rail lengths. The trap had not been anchored — we had fastened a three-foot length of a small fir tree on the end of the chain to serve as a drag. Unless he got this trap and drag tangled in the brush, he was free to go where he liked. His tracks led back towards the mountain. It was not hard to follow; he left a plain trail.

Shep was the only one of the dogs paying attention to the bear's tracks. The young ones came, skulking along behind our horses, with suspicion in their eyes and tails tucked between their legs. To make "bear dogs" of these pups would take a heap of training — they were plain afraid.

The bear changed his course, and we followed his trail down into a little creek. Along its bank, we came to where he had gotten the trap and drag tangled in hazel brush. He had been fastened here for some time. The brush was twisted, broken, and chewed. The trail from here led us downstream for a little way, then turned to the right. Here, we found where he had climbed across a log. There was a smear of dried blood on it.

"That's what I was afraid of when I see he'd been wrapped up in that brush so long. He's about to lose his foot," Dad stated, and continued on. "If he does, he'll be damn rough fer Shep to stop by himself, cause these pups ain't gonna help him, I don't think. I've had young dogs before this would bust themselves to hang up his hide."

We followed along until we were a short distance from Hagamen's pasture fence. Here, Shep winded towards a tangled thicket of small cedars. A fire had burned through here not too many years back, sweeping everything. These small trees were all about the same size, and little taller than your head in most places. Shep stopped, looked at us, and whined as if to say, "He's right there."

"I'll tell you what, Scrub, you take the dogs and go through there, and I'll take your horse with me and circle around to the far side of the thicket. It's open country over there. Maybe I can get a shot at him when you bring him out. I'd bet my bottom dollar he'll tear his foot off gettin out of there. I'd better get him while I have the chance. I think he's a hog-killer," Dad said.

That dark, shadowed thicket took on a forbidding look to me, but I said nothing. I piled off my horse and handed him the lead rope, not letting him as much as suspect that I was about as scared as the young pups. I'd shown a white feather once, and it would never do to not go in there with the dogs.

"How long should I wait for you to get around on the other side?" I asked.

"About fifteen, twenty minutes, I'll be set." He started to leave, then turned and advised, "You be a little careful in there. He'll be out of sorts and may try to get you by the guzzler." He grinned as he said this, and I surmised he suspected the sand was a little thin in my craw.

He went on without another backward look, and I began estimating the passing time to give him the time he asked, so he could get to where it was open country. A million thoughts run through my mind in this time I waited. Why was I forever in such a predicament as I was now? Why didn't Dad let my carry a gun on such trips? It wasn't as if I didn't know how to handle one. I'd killed several bucks and coyotes. Could pick a hawk out of the top of the old deadtopped pine, down by the calf barn, every shot with a rifle.

It was time to go in after the bear. With my heart running wild, I began creeping through the brush and small trees, close behind Shep, the young dogs at my heels. We had gone around four or five hundred yards when Shep bristled and made a lunge into a shadowed hollow. I sicked the pups after him, and in the excitement, they forgot their fear and plunged into the thicket the way Shep had gone, the hounds sounding off with deep-throated bawls, and Gip running silently with them. Trump, one of the hounds, had a voice you could hear five miles away. There was a snort, then a crying, drawn-out bawl like that of a mad bull.

Brush and trees began snapping. I could see the small cedars whipping where the battle was raging. The musty stench of the bear filled the air. Which way they were traveling I couldn't be sure, but it sounded like they were coming my way. I dropped to my knees so as to look beneath the trees. The three young dogs came streaking by me, mutely running for their lives. They did not seem to see me as they went flying by.

My eyes popped out in horror when close behind them came the bear with Shep at his heels, grabbing his hind end every chance he found. Every time he took hold, the bear would bawl and wheel about at him, flattening everything in his path. The trap's chain was clanking and rattling. I suddenly realized I must get out of their way. They were coming directly toward me. If only I had a rifle!

In the thicket there was not a tree large enough to climb. I began running and falling out of there, paying no mind to torn clothes and ripped-out hair. I was on my way to anyplace out of there. It sounded like they were gaining on me. Having no intentions of getting mixed up in their fight, I renewed my efforts, my knees responding as if they were made of rubber as I fought my way along. At the outer edge of the thicket, I saw a pine tree and decided to go up it. The bear and dog were practically upon me. I'd have to climb it, or else. It was twenty feet to its first limbs. I had never been much of a climber, but I pounced upon the tree and shinnied my way up it like an ape. I was almost within reach of the first limb when the bear came beneath me.

Shep grabbed him and turned him around and around. The bear had lost the trap, also his foot, back in the thicket. He was going on the stump of his foot. The blood was pouring from it; the ground was sprinkled red beneath the tree. He took off in a run down the hill. It seemed he was reaching three feet in front of his ears with his back feet as he raced along. Shep was hard put to keep anywhere near him as he went charging along.

I slid from the tree and began running and sicking Shep on, afraid the bear was getting away from him. They went over Hagamen's rail fence and began another circling battle in their strawberry patch. When I was almost to them, they began running again. They went down the road and past Hagamen's house. As they tore along, they raised a great cloud of dust from the road. It was difficult for me to tell just what was happening up front.

Down near these people's barn was a cedar tree which had uprooted and fell into a neighboring oak. It was hanging at an angle. The bear took to this. He could easily go up this incline with his foot off. Shep clawed his way part way up the leaning tree, trying to get the bear, who was black, and much larger than he had looked on the ground. His muzzle was covered with froth. In madness, he looked down at Shep, chomping his teeth and growling. Above the noise of the dog and bear, I heard Dad ''Yoho.'' I hoped he heard me answer and could locate where I was. The bear was restless, showing signs he intended coming down despite Shep's barking and my yelling and firing rocks toward him. In a few minutes, Dad came. He rode up with a clatter of hooves and a fog of dust and, without dismounting, he shot the bear from the tree, its neck broken.

Inspecting it, he said, "Ol sow. No good fer nothin. Tough as whit leather, as strong as a billy goat. Fur's too short fer her hide to be worth peelin her fer. Gotta get her out of here, though."

We hitched our lasso ropes about her neck, and dragged her away by our saddle horns and left her out in the woods. We went back and found the trap. It was almost sundown before we started home.

He seemed in no hurry to get home, so I reminded him, "We better jog along a little faster. Mom's gonna be faunchin with us gone all day."

"Naw, she won't. When we tell her we got the lynx and caught the bear — and a hog-killer at that — she won't say nothin. I've been gone many's the time longer than this, and she never said much, just grumbled a little," he confidently said with a smile. "A feller never wants to run off at the head too much at your Mom when she bows up at you."

"Maybe so, but I've seen times she would loved to have took your hide fer no more than bein gone like today," I reminded him.

When we came in sight of the ranch, we heard her hammering and seen her nailing boards on posts she had set that day. She was working with a flourish, a sure sign she was mad. We rode within a short distance of her and, seemingly, she hadn't seen us. Squaring back to get a better swing at the nail she was driving, she stepped on a hoe laying on the ground with blade up. The handle flew up, whacking her across the head. She came down with the hammer, missed the nail and hit her finger. She threw the hammer away. Looking at her finger, she yelled, "Shit!"

Never had I heard her say such a thing. Dad glanced quickly at me with a shocked expression and quietly said, "Zowie, she's really on the warpath. It's gonna take a heap of sweet talk to get around her on a rampage like she's on.''

She began walking swiftly towards the house, not noticing us yet; but this was just an act, I was sure. We overtook her before she reached the yard gate. Dad began talking to her in a sweet, apologetic tone of voice.

"Well, hello Sadie, my dear," he began. "See you've been fixin fence. You know Sadie, you're a humdinger at fixin a fence, never seen a woman like you. Those posts are as straight as a die, and the boards are as level as if you measured ever one, but I know you just cocked your eye at em, and nailed em on. It ain't every man that's got a good woman like you that can do anythin she sets her hand to. I must admit I never could have fixed it half as good as you have, honey. I'm awful sorry we didn't get home to help you." He paused in speaking for a little while, hoping she would talk to him; but she didn't, just kept hoofing it along, her eyes set straight ahead.

"I thought fer sure when we left this mornin we wouldn't be gone more than two hours, but you see, it was this lynx cat that killed Edd's sheep and it took some doins to track it down and tree him. We had a hell of a time, but we got him. Then after that, Scrub wanted to go see if we'd caught the bear up at the apple orchard, and knowin better, I went with her. Sure enough, we had it in the trap. Had to track it down and was lucky we got it as easy and quick as we did. We didn't skin it fer you to tan fer a rug, and the meat and grease weren't fittin, so we just drug it off and left it. Was a big ol sow, weren't fit fer nothin. She was a bad hog-killer, I think. We rushed right home to help you. Sadie, don't you hear me?''

Drops of blood were dripping from her finger. Without as much as a glance at us, she went through the yard gate and up the path without a word. When she was halfway up the path to the

95

house, he was still trying to talk to her.

He called, ''Sadie, now you go to the house, honey, and put turpentine on your finger. Scrub and I'll do the chores. You don't have to cook, we'll eat anythin. You just rear back in your chair and take it easy,'' he concluded, as she went into the house and shut the door. He knew well that she was apt to be hard to appease, and in his crude way was doing what he called ''sweet talkin'' her. ''You take care of the horses, Scrub, and I'll run get the milk cans and buckets,'' he said.

This was a real turn in events, as it was he that had claimed his fingers were so stiff from rheumatic pains that he simply couldn't milk a cow. When I got down to the cow barn, he had milked one cow and was finishing another. Stiff fingers or not, he was getting things done. Streams of milk were making the bucket sing.

''See your Ma anymore, Scrub?'' he anxiously asked.

''Nope,'' I answered.

''Now that was a damn, sneaky trick on you, me sayin you wanted to go look at the trap, but I lied before I thought. If you can find it in your heart to not tell her different and let bygones be bygones, I'll sure be tickled, Scrub.''

''I ain't gonna tell on you, Dad. Anyway, I don't believe she heard, she was so mad,'' I told him.

Work finished, we went to the house. There sat Mom by the cook stove, slowly rocking in her rocker, with that ''no expression'' look on her face that we were so familiar with. She might be mad enough to try to knife you, or again, she might be as pleasant as an angel when she chose to say something. We knew to keep our mouths shut and out of her way; let her make the first advance. We put the can of cream to cool, and washed. Back in the kitchen, we found she had sat supper on the table. Her smile was friendly and placid as if nothing had been wrong. Her finger was bandaged and the smell of turpentine filled the room.

Dad walked up and threw his arms about her. With a little boy's bashful face, he kissed her.

''You're a darn good ol girl, Sadie. I'm truly sorry about your finger. I'm gonna finish that fence in the mornin, come hell or high water,'' he promised. ''You won't have to lift a hand to help me, neither,'' he told her as he fondly patted her arm.

''Oh, I expect I'd better help you, Att, cause you no doubt will get it crooked, and I couldn't stand that. Remember you told me awhile ago, no one could make a fence like me,'' she said. They both laughed like silly kids.

''I'll consent fer you to come out and just fiddle around and watch that I don't spoil your good work. Yes, Sadie, I'd be tickled to have you out there with me.''

I wondered, is this true love?

I loved Mom too. She had a birthday cake for me. It was elaborately decorated. On its top were these words ''Our baby, Scrub,'' and under this was the number 14.

10

FRIZZED HAIR AND PURPLE SHOES

T HE DANCE HALL at Whitmore held a prominent place in our community. It served not only as a dance hall: the Stockmen's Association held their meetings there, also the Stitch Club. It was the polling place, Socialist meeting spot and, you might say, our Music Hall.[9] When Fourth of July came, the dance hall served as the place of all places of entertainment. It took on the air of a carnival. Ice cream and lemonade stands sprang up in the yard near where the homemade merry-go-round sat, which was powered by a big gray mare. The hall and the yard was gaudily decorated with red, white, and blue crepe paper made into banners and streamers. Firecrackers popped everywhere.

---

9. Whitmore prospered during the 1890s. A large Lutheran church was built in 1895, and during the same decade a school, hotel, and many smaller business buildings were constructed. About 1900, the community became a resort area and advertised itself as having the "coldest water in the state." The region had become a significant producer of potatoes, apples, hops, and beans. After World War I, the town declined rapidly.

The men played horseshoes, Indian-wrestled, and played poker. There was horse races in the town's one, long, dusty street, and someone usually rode a bucking horse there at celebrations. Some of the women sat in groups, gossiping, while others slaved over the hot wood ranges sat out under the trees. They fed everyone. Kids whooped and hollered, rode the merry-go-round, and run foot races. The whole place literally hopped.

The ladies' dressing room was jammed with girls fixing their hair and powdering their noses. The hall's back room was the nicest place about it, or so I thought. It was here the coffee was brewed in five-gallon cans on the wood heater. In one corner was the ladies' dressing room, which was partitioned with a curtain. Its furnishings: a rickety table, a marred and cracked mirror, and five or six new nail kegs for seats. Its light was a candle stuck in a pie tin. It was here the small kids were put to sleep, on pallets of coats and blankets. I'd spent my time here, had my hands and legs stepped on many times by someone trying to get to their "youngen."

The older men had several tables in the back room, where they played cards and complained of their aches and pains. Old Rosco Childers, without fail, occupied one of the nail kegs at a table and did nothing but complain of his lot in life. Every dance night he told about his troubles at home. It made no difference to him whether anyone was listening; he told it anyway. He spoke in a high-pitched, whining voice. You could hear him above the din of the crowd. He lisped badly, and was tongue-tied to boot.

"You take me, for instanth, I ain'th goth no pleasureth no more. Thath old Presidenth Wilson took my whickey away from me, then Mabel, sheth took to sleepin by her selfth. Thath was my lasth pleasureth I had. I alwayth enjoyed sleepin with Mabel when she would concenth to it. Havinth a little nipth of boose now and thenth kepth a man like me on hith toes. A man can'th play a game of poker no more unlessth somebodyth thinkth it's thinful.

"Can'th enjoy dancthin no more, my joinths are so stiffth. Everytime I do try, my ailmenth hitsth me and I've got to pith every minute. A manth be better off ifth he was dead. Yeth he would."

Rosco was withered and skinny, while his wife, Mabel, was tall and rawboned. He only came as high as her shoulder. Her face was round and red as the sun, her hair a fiery red, and she had a tongue as sharp as a whip's lash. She was mean as sin. Most folks felt sorry for the little old man, she treated him so rough.

There was little rivalry among the backwoods folk. At a public gathering they behaved like one big family: all for one and one for all. One exception was amongst the young men, who sometimes battled it out with fists over some girl; or maybe they had dipped too deep in the mountain dew.

Another point of drama lay confined within a group of old ladies, who sat on the benches against the walls of the hall. They sat with their shawls tucked about their shoulders and gossiped about the girls and their love affairs.

"I hear that Luella has left home," said one.

"Yeah, Mamie told me about it, and we think she's pregnant is why, and we decided if'n it's so, and I think it is, the feller responsible fer it is that stepfather of hers," Hettie said.

"Just look!" Sue said, indicating a couple dancing the rag. "If I was that little hussy's mother, I'd jerk her off the floor and beat her butt. I watch my Moranda close. I told her the last time I caught her and the Snow boy out lolly-gaggin in the dark, I'd break her fool neck if'n she does it again. I told her that people don't go much on a girl runnin outside sparkin with a feller in the dark. I ups and told her, and I didn't shield her from the raw facts of life, that girls actin like that will be showin up puffed up like a bloated goat if'n they ain't kerful. In my time, there was no carryin on like that. No siree," she concluded.

"This may just be loose talk, but rumors are that Old Ted is hangin out on the hill above Tabb's house, and everytime Joe leaves, Ted is down there, tomfoolin around with Becky," Mamie said proudly. She admired herself for the stories she started going the rounds in the community. The crux of the whole thing was, all the women believed her and repeated her slandering talk as the truth.

Girls my age had been dancing for some time, and seemed so at ease with their partners. Their dresses were readymade, and their hair was always curled and marcelled as nice as could be done with irons. They had no sun tan, and their hands and nails were clean and white and glittered with rings on their fingers and bracelets on their arms. They did no outside work beyond feeding the chickens.

I was always tanned a deep brown, and usually had an ugly scratch on my face, neck, or arms from tearing through the brush after a cow. Mom still made my dresses, and they did nothing for my gauche figure. The other girls bathed and shampooed before every dance and came smelling like violets. There was never time before a dance for me to bathe and curl my hair like they did. It was sheer luck if I got my face and hands washed and my hair combed. The smell of cow manure and calf slobbers prevailed about my person. So I stuck to watching the old men play cards and listening to the old ladies gossip. Best of all, I listened to the music and watched the dancers do their di-dos.

I loved the music of the violin, banjo, guitar, and the old squeaky organ as they chimed their way through "Red Wing," "Devil's Dream," "Pop Goes The Weasel," and "Over The

Waves.'' Every sixth dance was a square dance, and Dad was the caller. They swung their partners, promenaded, circled, and stomped their feet until the hall vibrated and dust bellowed up from the floor. A feeling of pride came in my heart as Dad stood up there, straight and stately, calling in a loud, clear voice, keeping time to the music with a clap of his hands.

The winter I was fourteen, I began dancing. Dancing and keeping time to the beat of the music came easy, but conversation with my partners came hard. The only things I could think to say was, "How's your cows doin? Sold your hogs yet? Grass is short this winter, we're feedin everything." But after a time I discovered I was looking forward from one dance to the other with anticipation. I was catching on, and could talk almost as frivolous as the other girls.

There was surely some nice boys. They said the nicest things. Handsome was no word for what I saw in some of them. I was getting boy-crazy, or at least that's what the folks said.

Saturday evening, I'd start doing the chores early, rush through feeding the hogs, tending the horses, and milking. This was no small job. We sometimes milked more than twenty head. They were not all gentle bosses. Some of them were bronco cows that kicked you from one end and hooked you with the other, and if they got you down they would run over you, grinding you into the corral dirt. I'd skip supper to begin getting prettied up for the dance. The washtub was our bathtub. Bath water had to be heated on the range and carried into the bedroom. To scrub the last trace of cow manure and calf-slobber smell from me took a lot of soap and time.

I'd not be seen out without my hair curled. You did this with curling irons. Just light the kerosene light and hang the curlers inside its chimney over the flame. When it was hot, you were in business. It was almost impossible to really tell whether the curlers were too hot, too cold, or just right. So you waited a while, plucked them from the light, and wound a lock of hair up tight to your skull. If it was too hot, you knew it almost immediately, as smoke billowed up from your hair and there was a sizzling noise resembling the frying of an egg. It must be done, so you kept up the process until your fingers were blistered, your scalp red-hot and stinging like fire, and your hair crimped and burned until you resembled a Fiji Islander.

I had worn the pages of the mail-order catalog thin, dreaming over a pair of high-heeled, high-topped shoes pictured in it. Mom argued with me about wanting them. In disgust, she finally said, ''Go ahead and get them and shut up about it. They won't be worth two cents, but if they are what you think you want, go ahead and make out the order.''

There was a choice of several colors. I ordered the outlandish color of indelible purple. When they arrived, they were all I had dreamed of, but were so narrow and pointed-toed it was a half-hour struggle to get my feet squeezed into them and lace their high tops. The toe points extended several inches beyond my toes, and it was a cinch they were never meant for anything but to point the way. In the same order with the shoes, I had ordered several new dresses and a pair of silk stockings. One of these dresses I thought heavenly. It was red, with white daisies near its round neckline and a few scattered about its flaring skirt.

Freshly bathed and smelling like a sweetpea, my hair ''frizzed'' and wearing my new purple shoes, my red dress, heart-shaped gold locket, plus five or six glass Chinese bracelets on my arm, I felt dressed like a Lady Astor done up flapper-style.

The second time I wore my new shoes, we came home from a dance, arriving about daybreak. I went to the woodshed to get some kindling and chop a few sticks of wood to make a fire in the heater stove. I placed a manzanita limb on the chopping log and placed one foot on it to hold it steady. The axe glanced from the stick and sliced two inches off the toe of my shoe, just in front of my toes. All that was holding was the sole. I tearfully went to the house to show the folks the dreadful thing that had happened to my beautiful shoe, fully expecting their sympathy and comforting words. They sleepily eyed the flopping toe of my shoe with little concern.

"It's a good thing," said Mom. "The things ain't fit to wear, no-how."

"You had better get your trottin rig off and get down to the barn and feed and water the horses," Dad stated flatly. "I'll feed the hogs while you fix breakfast," he added, speaking to Mom. "We gotta get over to Hardscrabble and feed the cattle and do some ridin today," he said.

"But, Dad," I said, "What am I gonna do about my shoes?"

He said nothing.

Fitting the cut place together, I tried to fathom a way to draw the cut together so it would not be noticed. To buy a new pair was out of the question, as it had taken a month's pay of my chore money to buy these. Something had to be done before the coming dance.

A neighbor boy who had been gone from home for a year or more had returned home. All the girls were buzzing around him like bees after honey, trying to draw his attention to them. Considering myself in the first ranks with him, I couldn't let shoes come in my way now and let the others whisk him away. He had asked me to be his supper partner at the next dance, and I'd be there if I had to wear my gunboots. I hadn't told Mom and Dad about this, but they must have noticed how frantic I was about my shoes because they, too, began talking of ways to fix them.

"Hell, I can sew the damn things up, Scrub, so no one will

105

notice it much," Dad informed me one evening. Later, I found him painstakingly whipstitching the cut together with a small thread of buckskin. With his reading glasses perched far out on his nose, he inspected his handiwork and offered me a view of it, saying, "Ain't no one gonna notice that much, do you think? I'll cover the stitches with some hog lard and black out of the stove, and it will look first-rate. Don't you think she's good?" he asked, with a tone of anxiousness in his voice.

"I guess so," I said, but was doubtful that anything would make it look good.

"She'll hold. Anytime you sew something up with buckskin there ain't much chance of it bustin out," he said with satisfaction.

"It'll never be noticed on a gallopin mare," Mom chimed in, as she passed through the room.

I inwardly groaned, as the stitches plainly showed, and hog lard and soot was not a miracle worker. I wore the shoes despite my misgivings. I guess no one noticed it much; at least, no one said anything about it.

11

WE MADE IT — BUT HOW?

HE DAY FOLLOWING a dance seemed always the time Dad picked to do the hardest, more miserable jobs imaginable. One time stands out above all others. It was Christmas Day, and we had gone to the dance Christmas Eve. Around midnight it began snowing. All the hill folks nodded their heads in a knowing way when it began to heap up fast outside.

"I knowed she was goin to come a blitzer. My old hound laid flat on his back all yesterday. That's a darn sure sign she's gonna come a bad storm," one man said.

"Yeah, that's like our old sow, she did the same durn thing. She carried beddin into her house all day long," told another.

The animals were our weather predictors in the back country. It works out that the animals know about the storms, if you have the knowledge to read them. The only essentiality is to understand how to read their actions correctly.

Everybody wondered how they would be able to drive home in snow so deep, but no one left the party. The fiddles whined on through the old familiar tunes, and people stomped their feet to the beat of the music until broad daylight.

We got "Old Liz" warmed up and the chains on, and began skidding and spinning our way home, the snow becoming deeper all the time. A little hill some distance from home proved too much for the little car, despite Dad and I pushing while Mom fed it the gas. We were shoving snow in front and digging in loose snow with the back wheels. "Old Liz" conked out and could go no further, so we went on foot. I couldn't wear my purple shoes through the snow. I pulled them off and went barefoot. Mom, by habit, kept grumbling as we trudged along.

"This is what a person gits, havin a dang kid when you're as old as you and me," she complained to Dad.

"I know, Sadie, but it ain't Scrub's fault. But it runs a hell of a hardship on old people like us," he answered.

At breakfast, he broke the news to me that we were going down in our lower winter pasture that day to gather all the cattle there and get them into Hardscrabble to feed them. This was a thirty-mile trip, one way. I silently groaned. This was a hell of a day for such a trip.

Bundled in our warmest clothes, plus slickers and chaps, we took off in the storm. The snow was deep and still falling, but was light and powdered, which was easy for the horses to travel through. When we reached the lower pasture, the storm there had turned to a hard rain, driven by a wind that staggered the horses. The snow was no more than a few inches deep, and wet and sloppy here. We searched over a lot of country, from Last Chance through Miller Springs on down to as far as Stone Fence Country. We rounded up the cattle and headed them toward Hardscrabble.

It was mid-afternoon, still pouring rain. The small gulches we had crossed in the morning were running pellmell now, their muddy waters surging over their banks. We came to where the trail flanked along the north side of Bear Creek; and like the gulches, it was high and gaining depth every minute.

Dad took one look at it and said, ''She's sure up and risin. We better cross the cattle here at Mallory Ford. By the time we'd get up to the ranch, that creek's goin to be too high to cross the cattle. Get up in the lead and head them, and we'll cross here,'' he instructed.

With coaxing, yelling, and using the dogs, we crowded the cattle into the swift, muddy water, and they made their way to the opposite bank. The water swept the smaller ones off their feet and they had to swim or sink. The water came high on the horses, but we made it across.

The wind and cloudburst-rain had not let up all day. There was but two dry spots on me now — the top of my head and the seat of my britches — and after that crossing, I was not too positive about the latter.

''We'll have to jog the cattle right along and get back across the creek while we can. It's risin fast,'' Dad observed.

Cattle fed, it was still raining, with a few flakes of snow mixed in. The crossing at Hardscrabble was a raging torrent, and it was almost dark. It did not enter our minds to not try to cross it, as we had to get home, and this ford was the best place to try it.

Above the roar of the water, I heard Dad yell at me, ''Put your horse in just below that riffle up there,'' and pointed upstream. ''Give him his head, he'll come out before you get to the riffle down there,'' and pointed downstream. Looking upstream, then down, it was almost impossible to see where one ended and the other began. The whole creek was heaving and pitching like mad, with an occasional log floundering in its midst.

Again, above the roar of the stream I heard him yell, ''If you see your horse ain't gonna make it with you on him, slide off his rump, get a good hold on his tail, and hang on to beat hell! He'll drag you out!'' he added.

I wildly thought that something had better be capable of dragging me out, or right there I'd be a dead duck. I was riding a horse we had not owned long, and I was not sure of his ability in high water. To make this crossing hinged entirely upon your horse. I headed him into the stream. The water picked him up and swept him along like a cork. He was swimming like he was at home here. His name had been passed on to us when we had bought him. It was ''Steamboat.'' Out in the midst of the stream, with water grabbing at me from all sides, a silly thought flashed through my mind: That's why the name, Steamboat. We were carried downstream, but the game little horse hit solid footing above the lower riffle. We were across.

I looked to see how Dad was faring. He was entering the stream on the other shore. He and his horse were picked up in the rushing water. A small log hit the horse in the side, all but capsizing him. He was exerting every effort to keep his head above water. He began floundering, as the water turned him toward the bank from which they had come. I heard him snort above the roar of the water. Dad and the horse were being carried downstream, the horse still lunging as they went over the lower riffle. There was a small chance of either Dad or the horse surviving being dashed over and against the boulders and tree trunks and the entanglement of wild grapes which lined the creek.

As they were being carried over the riffle, I seen why the horse had not made it like Steamboat had — his feet were tangled in a mat of small wild grape vines which had been floating in the stream. They were hurled into a jam of drift logs which had caught between two alder trees. Dad was half out of the saddle, as he and the horse were dragged under the drift. It was impossible to tell whether they were pressed against the drift or had gone beneath it.

In what seemed like an eternity, I at last caught one glimpse of the horse's head as it showed for a second above the water. He was downstream some distance below the drift. I went running along the bank in search of Dad. The horse had gone under the drift, and there was hopes Dad also had. He could swim good, but with coats, chaps, boots, and spurs on, he might not do so good. There, riding amidst a whirling bunch of driftwood, I saw his hat — but nothing more. I had gone almost to the bend in the creek, but there was no sign of either him or his horse.

Frantic and shaken, I looked upstream and was overjoyed with what my eyes beheld. Standing in a shallow eddy was Dad, holding to an overhanging limb for support. I helped him to the bank and he fell into the snow, coughing and choking, unable to speak. When he was able to talk, he plied me with questions.

"Did the horse get out? Did you see my hat?"

"I seen the horse and your hat goin down the creek before I seen you. I don't know whether he made it out or not," I answered.

"Run and see if you can find him. I'm all right," he said, painfully getting to his feet.

"You don't look all right. Let me help you up the hill," I offered.

"One of my legs seems on the bum. What the hell do you suppose caused that?" he said, as casually as if he had just been for a stroll through the yard. An ugly blue knot showed on his forehead above his right eye and blood from it trickled down his face and dripped off his chin. He limped over beside a big leaning pine tree that offered some protection from the storm. With his clothes dripping water and his wet, white hair clinging tight to his head, he presented a pitiful sight.

111

"Now, you go find my horse. I'll be all right," he said.

I found the horse downstream, standing near the edge of the water. His bridle was gone, blood from a deep gash in his shoulder ran down his leg, and he favored one back leg on which there was marks, caused, no doubt, by the grape vines. I got him up to where Dad was. His eyes fell on the sorrel's shoulder, and he examined the wound.

"He's damn lucky to get out with only that and a strained leg," Dad said.

"I'll say he was. He didn't get out until he was almost to the tater patch," I answered. "I'll make a fire, if you haven't lost your match case, and if I can find some pitch," I volunteered. Using the saddle hatchet, I found kindling and soon had a fire going near the leaning pine. It was snowing hard, and darkness had taken over. It was not a bright outlook to be eight miles from home in this arctic storm, with Dad and his horse crippled.

We were wet and cold and tired through and through. We decided Dad should take my horse and go home and I would follow, leading his. It would be slow going, even doubtful he could make the trip. Dad started on his way. In the darkness and the fast-falling snowflakes, he and the horse were a dark object before me for a part of a minute, and then they vanished.

All that told me they had been at this spot but seconds before, was the horse's trail in the snow. As I followed along, tugging at the horse's lead rope, it seemed that he and I were alone in a mystic world, like being cut off from other existing things by the curtain of swirling snow which obliterated everything. Before we were halfway home, I was wallowing in snow much above my knees, and thankful it was light and dry.

A pack of coyotes set up their "kiyi" up above where I was passing. Their bark and howl always set my hair creeping a little.

By no means did I have the dry spots which, earlier in the day,

I had derived the stupid sense of security and well-being from. I had gave Dad my hat to wear, and crossing the creek had more than dampened the seat of my britches.

When I came to the big timber country, an owl in a tree near the roadway went "hoot-hoot," in a big, coarse voice.

"Hoot-hoot yourself, you old buzzard. I wish I had your wings and you had my wet, blistered feet. I'd fly home," I said aloud, thinking how foolish it was to talk to a hootie owl.

The crippled horse was exhausted but game. He hobbled along at a snail pace. Two more miles and we'd be home.

The sleepiness of the forepart of the day had long passed, but wetness, cold, and hunger prompted me to keep hustling the horse for a little more speed. In my present state of mind, I solemnly resolved to stay home and forget dancing and the boys. How could I have imagined enjoying such things in the first place? Let the other girls have the boys. They had nothing better to do than be charmed by them. I'd stay home and sleep and stay in the house and be warm. I was deep in this resolution when I noticed the reflection of a light some distance away, and I knew it was Mom coming to meet me.

Out of the storm she came, plodding along on Dick, her trusted old horse. She had brought Steamboat back for me to ride.

"I was in hopes I'd meet you way over yonder, and you wouldn't have to walk so far," she said. "Here, take your horse." And I eagerly accepted.

"How was Dad when he got home?" I asked.

"He was almost frozen, and I'm afraid he is a lot worse hurt than he makes out. You know how he is when he is hurt. I doctored him up after he had thawed out and ate. Sent him to bed and gave him a big swig of brandy. He was bound and determined he was comin back after you, but I said, 'No, you ain't in no shape,' " she continued. "He's got a knot as big as a turkey

113

egg on his head. Where in the world is your hat, child? Your hair is covered with snow.''

''Dad wore it home, he lost his in the creek. I'm tellin you, Mom, I thought he was a goner. I never seen that creek as wild in my life as it is tonight.''

''I've been tryin to get that man to make a bridge across there ever since we came to Hardscrabble, but he never listened to me. I don't know whether he is too lazy or never had the time, like he claims. Next summer, me and you will go over there and fall some trees and snake them in with the team and make a bridge,'' she planned.

''Yeah, we should do that, Mom. After today, I'm scared of the thing.''

We could see the light at the house and smell the wood smoke from the stove. Even the crippled horse took new courage and hastened his pace.

I never knew home was as cozy as it was now. Dad was asleep; his deep snores fairly rocked the house. Mom fussed over me, getting me dry clothes and fixing my supper. No one had to coax me to go to bed. As I was climbing into bed, she came with a hot toddy made with brandy.

''Do you know why your Dad is snorin so loud?'' she asked. ''He's been out of bed while I was gone and drank over half of the jug of brandy. He's dead drunk,'' she explained.

''Don't be mad at him Mom, he needed it. You don't know how rough it was out there today. Anyway, we are lucky he is here and alive,'' I told her.

''I know that. Anyhow, that's what the stuff is for, is to drink when you need it,'' she agreed. ''Now, you go to sleep, honey. Good night,'' she called from the other room.

I faintly heard her. Sleep had won. Oh, blissful sleep.

12

RIDING RATTLER

HE BARNYARD was filled with dogs. A man was climbing from a cart drawn by a brown horse. Tied behind the cart was a roan saddle horse.

"Look! Who is that?" I asked.

Dad raised from the couch and looked out the window. "That's old Frank Boyce. Where did that old son of a gun come from?" he said, gladness in his voice. He went down the path to greet his friend.

There was no less than a dozen dogs trotting about in the barnyard, busy irrigating fence posts. Mom looked out the window at them and said, "I sure hope Frank keeps those darn dogs tied up. They run me bugs. Hey, there's a dog fight," she exclaimed. Shep and a lanky hound of Uncle Frank's were fighting to kill. Tip, Bally, and our hound, Trump, shot under the fence and, amidst the circling pack, picked themselves an opponent and began battle.

Dad and Uncle Frank were yelling and hitting at the mad beasts, but it was doing little good. Mom and I ran to help the two men. The racket from the fighting was fierce. We grabbed the dogs by their tails and dragged them apart, only to have them clinch again as quickly as they got back to each other. Shep and the big hound had their fight settled. The hound was running on two feet — Shep had bit the other two feet badly.

"Get a rope! Hurry up! Tip's gonna kill Frank's dog!" Dad yelled as he bent, twisting Tip's collar to choke him loose. I got back with the rope, and Mom was holding Uncle Frank's horse by the bit to keep it from running away with the cart. Dad got the rope on Tip, and between the two men they choked him until he was compelled to loosen his hold on the other dog's throat. Then Dad tied him to the fence. Dad and Uncle Frank went on, yelling, kicking, and yanking at the dogs — but stop one, and two more started. With ever-increasing sound, the fight went on. This was no common dog fight. Both ours and Uncle Frank's dogs were mean and they were tough. They were trained to eat anything up they came to grapple with. Shep jumped on Tip, who was tied to the fence. They were mutual enemies. The only thing that kept them from fighting constantly was they each respected the other's rights about the place. One lived in the front yard and the other in the back. They seldom trespassed on each other's territory, but when they did, they fought to kill.

The barnyard was no-man's land with them, and Shep grasped this opportunity to try to kill Tip while he was tied. But even though he was tied, Tip was no setup. He was bigger than Shep. His main hold was getting his opponent by the throat, and it took force to pry him loose. Shep used the tactics of biting a dog's feet through and through until the dog had not a foot he could stand on. We choked them apart, and also tied Shep to the fence. There was still other fights going.

Trump, our hound, and Uncle Frank's spotted hound, Ben, were in a rolling fight under the cart, and the cart horse was

116

getting more excited all the time. The saddle horse had broke loose from the cart, run down into the cow corral, and was galloping around acting locoed as he put on an exhibition bucking spree.

The dogs fought under the cart horse's belly, startling him into action. Rearing to his full height, he pulled Mom off her feet and threw her to one side, then went stampeding down the hill and through the south lane. A wheel ran over Mom's arm as she momentarily lay on the ground. Getting nimbly to her feet with a wild expression in her eyes, she shook her fist at the fleeing horse, and in a choked voice exclaimed, "Oh, damn a horse, anyhow! Those lousy no-good-fer-nothin dogs, I'd like to kill the whole pack!"

She rolled her sleeve up to examine her injured arm. There was a large bruised place with blood oozing from it and trickling down her arm. Trembling from excitement and athrob with pain, she was fighting to keep her composure. Glancing at the two men, who were stopping the last of the fighting, she pointedly said, "Darn men, that's so bugs to have a pack of dogs around all the time, are plain nuts." Then she began quickly walking up the path to the house.

Fights settled, Uncle Frank and Dad went about their business. Dad tied our dogs, Uncle Frank went to get his cart and horse, and I went down and brought his saddle horse to the horse barn. I was taking the saddle off when Uncle Frank returned with the cart horse.

"Lassie, you best keep shy of that 'cayuse'! He ain't gentle," he warned.

"Oh yeah?" I said, stepping back to look more closely at the roan. He was the most superb looking horse I'd seen. "He's a fine looker. What's his name?" I asked.

"Haint had him long, but I've been callin him Rattler, bein's he sometimes acts like one. He's the skeerdest critter ever I seed of a bear. I'm gettin shed of him, first chance I get. He ain't no good fer the likes of me, cause I can't get on him, he won't stand.''

After supper, just before dark, I seen a campfire down in the barnyard, and went to see what Uncle Frank was doing. He was squatted by the fire, holding an outsized, extra-long-handled frying pan over the flames. In it was a big, thick hot cake which covered the entire pan. His dogs were gathered around, watching him. He tossed the cake out to a side and said, ''You, Jup.'' A big, lanky, battle-scarred hound jumped forward and took possession of the hotcake, turning it this way and that with his paw, anxiously waiting for it to cool enough to be eaten.

The other dogs stood waiting for the next cake, each listening for their names to be called. ''You, Bell,'' came in a low tone of voice from Uncle Frank. Old Bell stepped forward like a queen and stood by her supper. She was old and the mother of many pups, and she was expecting another litter soon. Her ears hung in ribbons from battles she had been through with big cats. She had a scar across her side and hip, where a bear had raked her when she was young.

''Old Bell is gettin pretty old, ain't she?'' I asked, trying to start conversation with the old codger, who hadn't shown any sign of knowing I was present. Just then, one of the fox terriers could not stand the suspense of waiting for his name to be called and began jumping up and down and yipping. ''Cork up,'' Uncle Frank said loudly, giving the little dog a scornful look. The little fellow settled down, with apology in his eyes. Another cake spun out, and the call came, ''You, Flute.''

''Got your dogs trained pretty good, ain't you?'' I ventured to ask.

Without looking up, he mumbled in his beard, ''The damn

critters know who's boss. If I tell one to dry up, they cork up quick." He flipped a cake up and expertly caught it; then looked up at me and said, "You're gettin to be quite a growed-up kid. How old be yuh?"

"I'm past fourteen, almost fifteen. I've got a feller," I boasted.

"A feller. Ain't one of those city fellers be he? What kind of feller you got?" he inquired.

"He's awful nice, Uncle Frank. Just lives down the road a ways," I chattered on, then added, "It's said by some folks he's moonshinin, but it's a lie."

"Well, might be a fittin feller then," he approved with a grin.

Uncle Frank was a true mountain man and hunter. His dogs and hunting was his sole interest in life. Both he and his dogs were as tough as rawhide.

There is always something in a man's early life to set his future on a course which he follows. This had been done to Uncle Frank. When he was in his early teens, Indians had come to their house, while all of the family were away excepting his Mother and a small sister. They struck his Mother into senselessness, and took his sister by her feet and struck her head on the stones of the fireplace, killing her, then took her scalp. His Mother lay in a coma for weeks before she regained her senses.

Uncle had taken a rifle and his dog and went tracking the Indians down. It was told he sent a good number of these people to their happy hunting ground. Life in the mountains appealed to him and, after there was no more hostile Indians, he hunted varmints. He had never been married, not staying any one place long, always wanting to see what was on yonder side of the mountain ahead.

Dad was like that, but he had Mom and us kids, which kept

him anchored. But if he made up his mind to go hunting, he would go regardless of what Mom said or what he was doing.

For instance, this night he and Uncle Frank made plans to go on a hunting trip and be gone two weeks. How he expected to go and be gone that long was a mystery. We were in the middle of gathering beef cattle. They were going into the headwaters of Battle Creek to hunt panther and bear and bobcat. They were going there because, long ago, they had been over there hunting and the woods was "workin with varmints."

Next morning, by daylight, everyone was on the trot getting them ready to leave. Dad made no mention about gathering the cattle until a few minutes before they left.

"Scrub, I guess you'll hafta get in the rest of the cattle," he said in a matter-of-fact way.

"Yes, Dad," I agreed.

"It shouldn't take you too long, orten it?"

"I reckon not," I answered.

"Be sure to get those two old bulls, cause I wanta get shed of them, especially Ben Hur. Be sure to take salt and put it out on the salt logs you git to. You'll have to git the mail pretty often, cause the cattle buyer, Stewart, is supposed to write and let me know when he's comin to look at the cattle and make his offer on price. Don't ride that black horse while I'm gone," he warned me.

"Well, you're takin Dixie and Smut with you. That leaves me with Toby that's shod, and his shoes need settin; they're plumb loose now. They will be off before I get all the cattle in," I remonstrated.

"Well, couldn't you sorta tack them back, if they do?" he asked, in a tone of voice so that I knew he was wheedling me. "Sadie, did you hear what I told the kid about not ridin Eagle when I'm gone?" he asked.

''No, I don't hear half what you say. You say so much and all of it 'Do this, don't do that,' when you're runnin off and leavin us to do all the work,'' she answered. Her voice sounded flat with disgust at his leaving.

''Well, I told her she couldn't ride him when I'm not with her,'' he repeated.

Mom was busy packing eggs in wheat chaff to go on the trip.

''Did you hear me, Sadie?''

''I heard, but if she takes it into her head to do somethin when you're gone, she does it, come hell or high water. She's just like you, another bull-headed Aldridge,'' Mom told him.

''I'm awful sorry to have to run away now, in the midst of things, but this may be the last chance me and Frank will have to go on another huntin trip,'' he apologetically said.

''I'll bet you are. Yes, you might bust out and cry, you're so sorry,'' she said sourly. It was debatable whether Mom meant all she said to him when she was angry.

When they were ready to leave, the two men rode in the cart. They had a broad smile on their faces. There was a wide contrast in their appearance. Dad was tall and lean; thin-faced, with a bit of a hook to his nose; sharp, gray eyes; and long white hair that lay in tight curls against the brim of his old slouch hat. His mustache was white and the old-time handlebar type. His hair and mustache were so clean they glistened in the light of the rising sun. His shirt, pants, and jacket were clean and ironed.

Uncle Frank was taller than Dad, a giant of a man. He had an untrimmed, untrained beard and mustache, which pointed in all directions. It appeared as if he slept on his chin was what caused his beard to separate and every hair to stick out at rakish angles. His eyes were black; he had a flat stub nose. His hair was long and untamed, like his beard. It and his beard was streaked with gray and looked as if they were moldy. His clothes were soiled and wrinkled, and he wore leggings, from which a butcher-knife handle protruded from the tops. This, on occasions, he had used on bear and panther, to help his dogs escape from close encounter.

Like Dad, he stood back from nothing when his dogs' life was in danger. He was taking all his dogs with him, excepting Bell. She was staying at the ranch. Her pups would be born any day. Dad was taking two of ours, Tip and Trump, leaving Shep and Bally to help me with the cattle.

Mom still was grumbling about Dad's going hunting.

"He's run off like this ever since we've been married, expectin me and you kids to get things done, while he was out galavantin with his darn dogs," she complained. "When you get old enough, Babe, to get married, don't get a feller that's crazy on dogs. They ain't got a lick of sense," she advised.

"I don't see much wrong in runnin things with dogs. It's lots of fun, Mom. Your soul would have to be a goner if you didn't go fer hearin a bunch of dogs hot on the heels of somethin," I answered.

"Dogs are all right in their place, but I never will be able to see how your Dad and Frank just want to live with them," she answered.

The following week, I gathered cattle and found the ones we wanted to sell. The last day, my horse lost some shoes. I felt lucky I was finished riding.

Early in the morning, two days later, the cattle buyer came to the ranch and looked at the cattle. He made an offer per pound for them, delivered to the railroad. His offer was half a cent below what Dad had expected to get. Mom told him that she would send me over to tell Dad, and the buyer could drop by the ranch next day, on his return from Burney, and get his answer.

A thought flew into my mind as she told the buyer this. Now was my chance to ride Rattler.

"I guess I'll have to ride Uncle Frank's horse," I began. "He's the only horse on the ranch that's shod, exceptin Eagle," I added.

"Frank wouldn't care, I'm sure, but is he safe? I've noticed, leadin him to water, he's snorty," Mom said.

"He's bound to be gentle fer an old feller like Uncle Frank to ride," I reasoned with her, hoping she hadn't heard him say the roan was almost an outlaw.

"Well, all right. Get him saddled while I fix you a lunch. It's a long way over there and back," she agreed.

I flew into the barn and put my saddle on him before she changed her mind. Leading him from the stable, I noticed he had a hump in his back and was taking short steps, as if he was cinch-bound or had bucking in his mind. I took him in the corral behind the barn so Mom could not see the way he was acting. Tightening the cinch a little tighter, I turned him around a few times and he seemed to straighten up, but his chin was tight and his tail clamped. I swung into the saddle and took around the corral at a gallop. Three times around, and I headed him through the gate and around the barn.

Remembering to take salt to put on the salt log I'd be passing, I got off and went into the grain shed and got it and tied it behind my saddle. As Mom was coming down the path with my lunch, done up in a flour sack, I swung into the saddle again. The horse tried to bolt, but I held him back and brought him around to where she stood, holding the lunch sack up toward me. As I got it in my hand, he jumped high and wildly to one side, almost losing me. He began bucking down the hill and I could not get control of his head and get it up. He had gone "hog wild," twisting and bucking and bawling in a hoarse tone. One foot out of the stirrup, I was doing everything I could to stay aboard. As we reached the bottom of the incline, he gave an extra twist, which sent me flying through the air, landing on my head and shoulders. Birdies tweeted in my ears and the whole world looked afire, and I thought, "God, he's killed me!" I was half on my feet when Mom got to where I had fallen.

"How bad did he hurt you, Babe?" she anxiously asked.

"Not bad, I'm all right, didn't hurt me a bit," I glibly lied, as I began walking to where Rattler stood, ears forward, innocently watching my approach. He stood and let me catch him.

"You ain't gettin back on that devil, Babe?" she asked in frightened tones. "You ride Eagle, he won't buck," she continued.

"You know what Dad told you and me about that," I reminded her.

"If he gives you the devil about ridin him, just tell him I said you could, and if he wants to get his back up at someone to just come see me about it," she said, with a fight glistening in her eyes.

I had a burning desire to ride Rattler, this magnificent animal. Uncle Frank had said he was a Tennessee Walker. I had never seen one before, let alone ridden one. This was my one chance. With determination, I quickly mounted.

"You get off that devil," Mom sputtered. "A darn horse will be the means of your end," she predicted.

"I'll be all right, Mom, never been hurt very bad by one yet," I consoled her; but I was fighting to keep my composure and the tears out of my eyes. My shoulder and neck hurt as if they were broken.

"You're a stubborn and bull-headed girl. It's your neck if somethin bad comes of your not mindin a word I say," she both advised and warned me.

Rattler and I took off on our long trek. He was acting as docile as a lamb until we came to the big canyon. It was different as we started down the steep trail. His hind end seemed light and it was plain he wanted to buck again. I eased him down the hill, keeping him under control to the bottom. As we started up the other side, I spurred him into a run. By the time we gained the top, he was breathing hard and athrob from the run, satisfied to settle down. He was a good traveler. His color was outstanding — a blue roan with a spider-web veiling of pink over the blue.

We were at porcupine salt log almost before I realized it. I began calling cattle before reaching the log. Cattle back on the mountain's side began bawling in answer. I could hear the clang of their bells as they started down the mountain to the log. Reaching there before they arrived, I poured the salt on the log in the chopped-out places made for that purpose. It was then that I seen small spatters of blood on the ground near the log. I began tracking about to find what had done this. I found two horse tracks, which were perhaps two days old. Knowing who the horses belonged to from the tracks, I wondered what these people had been doing here, as they had but a few cattle and kept them in their field. Dad had taught me to observe and know every horse's or man's track in the country.

Being in a hurry, I dismissed the spatters of blood and the horse tracks, got on my horse, and had gone but a few feet when Rattler shied to a side with a snort. There, laying near the trail, was the head, hide, intestines, and feet of a yearling. I seen by the ear mark it was one of ours. It had been butchered here.

The cattle came trotting down the hill, stopped at the offals of the yearling, and began circling and bellowing like cattle do when they smell blood or find a dead critter. I had seen this ritual many times before, but it is so fascinating it is not to be ignored, so I stayed and observed. The fantastic ceremony went on and on. Some of them were on their knees, neck and heads swaying back and forth in the blood and dust. Others, their bodies bent in a rainbow-shape, tromped over the heads of the others. Their wild crying and off-key bawls rent the silence of the hills. The choking dust they stirred enveloped the spot. They seemed gripped by a holy spirit, or perhaps an unholy one, and were denuded of all their common senses.

Rattler seemed caught up in the thing, was nervous and prancing to be gone. I had just started on when an imaginary spook caused him to jump sideways, almost unseating me. A spur accidently dug his shoulder, which fired him off. He bucked through a patch of small cedar and fir trees and on under bigger trees with low-hanging limbs, which caught my braided hair, almost tearing my head off. He raked me from his back despite my frantic efforts to hang on.

I was not actually hurt, outside of my hair being partly pulled out, but I was mad and my pride was damaged. He did the amazing thing of trotting back to me, and began nuzzling my arm as if to say he was sorry for this thing he had done. I was half afraid to get back on, but it was too far to where I was going to walk, so I swung on and he dutifully traveled along in his smooth, mile-eating gait.

I laughingly thought: If Dad finds out I've been bucked off twice this day, he will throw a fit to behold. I could hear him roar and rant in my mind, and knew all he would say. I must remember to caution Mom to keep mum about being thrown off at the ranch. I wasn't planning to tell even her about this last mix-up.

Arriving at their camp in the afternoon, I could see the men were there, although I could see neither of them. Smut, Dixie, and the cart horse were there in a little enclosure, and everyplace you looked about the camp, some of the dogs were tied to trees, while others trotted about. The pelts of three large panthers and one very small one hung from a pole, and beside them was the hide of a deer. The men had been busy, I wondered where they could be. Riding around a bit of brush just beyond camp, I came upon them. They were busy skinning a small bear they had hanging from one hind foot. I happily greeted them by saying, "Hi, you old hunters, I see . . . "

I'd forgotten what Uncle Frank had told me about Rattler being afraid of a bear. He stiffened; then reared in the air, coming down facing the opposite direction; then went plunging through camp. I was keeping his head up and preventing him from bucking. I got one look at Dad as the horse reared and went charging away. Dad was standing by the hanging bear with a knife in his hand, swinging his arms about, and I heard him yell, "Get the hell off that blue bastard!! Get off!" He drew the word "off" out, long and shrill.

There was a swamp near the camp, and the horse went sashaying through that, miring deeper every jump, and was going faster and faster until his front feet went into a seemingly bottomless spot. His hind end came up, overthrowing him on his back.

I had been caught in this kind of scrape a few times before, and was expecting this to happen. Unconsciously, I threw myself to one side to escape the fall of his body. In an uncontrolled manner, I came to earth on my head, burying myself to the neck in the slimy, black mud. I wished I could keep my head buried here and not have to face Dad and listen to all he would say. Getting up, I thought I'd just bluff my way through this, like I had so often when I was small; I'd work on his sympathy. I fought to scrape the black stuff out of my eyes. I could see nothing. I could hear the horse getting to his feet, and when I

127

could see a little, he was miring almost to his belly, buck-jumping through the swamp. He and my saddle was covered with mud.

Uncle Frank was running around the far side of the swamp to catch him when he came out.

Dad? He was standing by me, looking down upon me with a hump to his neck and shoulders like a wrathful bear about to do battle. In a whining, small voice, I said, ''Dad, I think I'm a goner. I was almost killed.''

''You ain't dead yet,'' he bawled. ''What the hell are you doin up here? What are you ridin that damn outlaw fer?'' Giving me no opportunity to answer, he stormed on, ''Can't you remember a damn thing I tell you? I never in my born days seed one kid that could get herself in so many scrapes as you.''

Rattler turned away from Uncle Frank at that moment, and he yelled at Dad, ''Head him off, Att.'' And Dad took across the mire to comply.

''Now's my chance to get away and let his temper cool,'' I thought. I hurried down to the creek, peeled off my boots, and dived into the creek to wash the mud away. The ice coldness of the water made me do a quick job, and I set on a log in the sunshine to warm up and let the water drip away. I could hear Dad's and Uncle Frank's voices, but could not understand what they were saying above the babble of the creek. I had an ace up my sleeve. I knew it would settle his wrath at me when I told him about the slaughtered yearling — he would forget all else.

I walked silently into camp. Dad was kneeling by my saddle, scraping the mud from it. His back toward me, he didn't know I was there. ''Frank, you're damn lucky you ain't got no kid. Just look at that saddle — it's new and look what care she takes of it. She had a saddle, kind of a battered-up one. So what does an old simp like me do? I puts out a heap of money and buys her thisun. It's the best that money can buy.'' Uncle Frank winks at me and held a finger up for me to keep quiet. "But, you know Frank," he concluded, "I've got to admire the darn kid fer the way she got out from under that horse when he fell. Take another kid her age and they wouldn't of knowed what the hell to do."

"That's right, Att. I'd be right proud to have a youngun like she be, by goodness if I wouldn't."

Dad turned, seeing me standing, listening. He looked me up and down for a time, then, smiling, said, "What you so damn wet fer? Fall into somethin?" Things were like they had been when I was a little shaver. My system of getting his sympathy might be considered a dirty shame, but it still worked.

I told him about my horse losing his shoes, that I had got the beef gathered, and about the buyer's offer; why I had rode Rattler, and about the butchered yearling, and about the horse tracks at this spot, and who the horses belonged to; told him everything but that I had been bucked off twice before the episode he had witnessed.

"I'll go in the mornin and track those horses. I can tell if they're carryin it. I'll make you some coffee and a bite," he said. I had eaten my lunch on the way, but I'd be foolish to say so and miss some of his tasty camp grub.

"You tell Sadie to tell that buyer I'll split the half cent difference in his and my price on the cattle," he instructed.

"What if he won't?" I asked.

"He can take it or leave it," Dad decisively said. "I think he will, he liked the ones he saw; but of course, he didn't go over to Hardscrabble to see the bunch there. But I told him they were about the same grade of stock. He said he'd take my word fer it." While he poured the coffee and put the food out to be eaten, he said, "I'm tellin you one thing fer sure, Scrub, you're not ridin Frank's horse home. Take Dixie, she'll get you home safe."

He made me disgusted, treating me like a baby, but I knew

this was no time to argue; so as quickly as I had eaten, I went to get her. She was lame. She could put but the point of her toe to the ground on one hind foot. Her ankle was swollen twice its size. I called to Dad, and when he cleaned the dirt out of her foot, there was a stob as large as a pencil in her heel just back of the frog. It took all his strength to pull it out with pliers.

"I'll be damned if I know when she got it. She's in bad shape," he said. "You may have to ride the roan horse after all. I've got to have Smut tomorrow to track those thieves down, and be damned if I think I can get on a horse anymore that won't stand. My leg's too stiff since I had my knee busted."

"He's all right fer me, Dad. He was just scared of that bear," I answered.

"Well, I reckon you got up here without a bobble, you can make it home on him, but mind you, use a little sense with him," he cautioned. "Without a bobble," he had said — when at this instant my shoulder and neck screamed with pain, and my scalp smarted where the hair had been pulled out.

After I had followed the trail for a ways from camp, I took across country, as this would be the shortest way home; but most of all, I went this way to see the beautiful country I would travel through. I wanted to see and hear all the wild creatures and birds which lived in this high-altitude country. There was a hint of fall in the air. A sprinkle of red and gold leaves showed here and there, and the velvety red seeds on the dogwood made the whole country like a fairyland. All this was enhanced by the majestic background of gray and red cliffs, with towering spirals, deep chasms, and narrow crevices.

Eagles sailed overhead, screaming at me, a stranger in their territory. Ravens cawed their disapproval as they dipped and circled overhead. Squirrels swore at me as I passed through their kingdom. Catbirds fluttered from bush to bush, clicking their surprise at my intrusion. Mountain quail ran in front of me; the males whistled their call of danger to their flock. Then, there was the little katy birds, perched in the tops of the tallest trees. In a small, forlorn voice, they seemed to call, "Sweet Katy, Sweet Katy." They were everywhere I rode.

The magnitude of the woods in a primitive country such as this never failed to entrance me. I wanted to linger here and drink in the picturesqueness of this land of magic I was passing through. To perhaps set on some high spot and merely listen to the many sounds that come to you, magnified by the clearness of the air. This was the deeper part of my soul. But I was still wet from the dip in the creek. The breeze was chilly, as it was nearing sundown. I quickened Rattler's gait and we went scooting toward home.

It was long past dark when I arrived there. Mom was waiting for me to return, and bubbling over with questions of what had happened and all I'd seen. Uppermost, she wanted to know when Dad was coming home and what he had said about the price of the cattle. I told her everything that had happened, and that Dad would be home next day. I told her about the mixup I got in with Rattler on account of the bear, omitting what had happened at porcupine log; but I didn't forget to caution her against telling Dad what the horse had done to me that morning.

"I expect I should tell him, but he would go on fer hours about it," she said. "But I'll tell you one thing, young lady — if you ever go ahead and do somethin again with me yellin at you not to do it, I'll sure gab on you," she threatened.

"Yes, Mom, I don't blame you, but if I'd listened to you this mornin, you would have had me walkin over there. Anyway, look at all the fun I'd missed." And I laughed, thinking how much fun I'd really had.

Next evening, Dad returned home. By habit, I took his horse, unsaddled her, and put her in the stable for him. I hurried to the house to find out what he had learned concerning the butchered yearling.

"Do you think the ones on the horses were the ones that killed it?"

"Hell, yes, I tracked them to their front gate," Dad answered. "The old man had it on his horse. He walked and led the horse all the way home. The bastard was in the yard hoein, and when he looked up and seen me, he looked sheepish-like and says, 'Hello, neighbor, I'd ask you to light and come in, but the old lady's havin one of her spells and I daren't ask a soul inside.' The old lady was, no doubt, boilin up a pot of 'old Att's' beef right then. That's the brazenest bunch I ever had the misfortune of runnin up against," he concluded.

"Couldn't we have them arrested?" Mom asked.

"Not a chance, we couldn't prove the meat was ours," he answered. "It's best we forget about it, but keep our eyes peeled fer them next time," he added.

I had not fed the hogs, so I left the house to do that. When I got home, Dad said, "So you got bucked off Frank's horse twice yesterday."

I looked quickly at Mom: she had gabbed when she promised she wouldn't. She was slicing bread and didn't look up. It was impossible to read from her stone-like face whether she had or had not.

"Must have been a pretty good show, I'd say, from the way he tore up those little trees and run on through those low limbs," he said. I should have known his eagle eyes wouldn't miss Rattler's tracks where he had tore up things at the salt log. Mom wasn't guilty, after all, and I was ashamed of the hot anger I had felt for her a few minutes before.

"Yeah," I admitted, "he got scared of the cattle's ceremony

over the dead yearlin, and I did some tall ridin and hangin on, but I didn't make it.'' So the subject was dropped and we began talking of the things to be done.

The cattle buyer wanted the cattle delivered five days from this day.

''I'm goin to have to find someone to help me take the cattle down. I can't think of a man I could get that would be worth a damn,'' Dad said. It had been my fondest hopes since I was big enough to set in a saddle to go on a cattle drive to the railroad. Maybe Dad would be forced to take me this time.

''Why can't I go with you?'' I asked brightly.

''Ah, you couldn't go, you wouldn't know what to do. Anyhow, I never seen any of the other girls in the country go on a beef drive,'' he quickly answered.

Mom unexpectedly came to my rescue by saying, ''I don't see any real reason she can't go, Att. You know she wants to go bad. You say she wouldn't know what to do? I noticed she knew enough how to gather the cattle off the range while you went scalawaggin over the hills with Frank and that bunch of dogs.'' Mom had that look in her eyes again that buffaloed Dad. ''I say she goes,'' she added in a rather stern voice.

''We'll see, we'll see. Maybe she can go if I can't find someone else,'' he concluded. My heart done a double flip, just thinking of going.

13

CATTLE DRIVE

W E'LL HAVE TO GO over to Hardscrabble in the mornin and drive that bunch of beef over here,'' Dad planned. ''We've gotta start out of here early, day after tomorrow, for the railroad. We gotta have plenty of time to take them in. I don't wanta knock the flesh off of them by hazin too far in a day,'' he added.

Next morning, he discovered he was low on chewing tobacco. He had left his surplus up at camp. ''You can finish doin the chores, and I'll go around by town and get some tobacco and cut across Blue Ridge and meet you at Hardscrabble,'' he told me. After breakfast, he mounted Smut and started for town. ''I'll see you. I should be there by the time you get there,'' he said.

I arrived at the ranch. He was not there. I pottered around the house, content to idle and wait. The only worry I had was that he might see someone in town that he could persuade to go on the cattle drive and I would have to stay home. I read part of a book as I lay on the old cot on the porch. My stomach told me it was past dinner time. Looking at the sun to estimate the time of day,

I thought it must be around two o'clock. I decided to start the cattle home, figuring that Dad would overtake me on the way.

"Where is your Dad?" Mom asked, as I drove the stock into the pasture.

"I don't know. He never showed up at Hardscrabble, and I figured he'd overtake me before I got here," I answered.

"Do you suppose his horse could have fallen on him?" she wondered, with a worried expression on her face.

"I don't see how, that's not bad country. Maybe he's just talkin to somebody downtown," I reasoned.

"I'll get on the phone and call and see," Mom said, going to the telephone and ringing the store. "That you, Lidie? How long ago did Att leave town?" she asked. I could hear Lidie's voice coming over the telephone, but couldn't understand what she was saying. "I see," Mom said flatly. "Thank you, Lidie," she added, and hung the receiver on the hook. "He ain't even left there yet. Him and old Jake's been in the back room all day, and that means one thing — him and Jake are gettin boozed. He makes me so mad, I'm plain bugs when he swills himself on that slop," she stormed in disgust.

Later that evening, I was out by the horse barn when I heard a horse running up the north lane. When it came in sight I saw Dad. He was bent over the saddle horn, fanning Smut's ears with his hat, and loudly yelling, "Whoop-pie." The mare was neither a fractious or high-spirited horse by nature, but as she raced on toward where I stood her appearance was that of a devil horse — eyes wild, nostrils flared and showing red, ears pinned back, and great flakes of white lather specking her black body. She slid to a stop at the stable door with Dad swinging drunkenly forward, almost falling.[10]

---

10. As Att grew older he became hard of hearing, and began to

He gazed down at me through half-seeing eyes, and yelled "Yah-hah!" and fanned Smut's ears with his hat again. She capered about, not standing for him to dismount. I caught her bit and held her steadfast while he stepped down. He almost toppled when he attempted to stand. He staggered to the yard gate and held to it, red-faced and grinning. This was a good show, and I laughed as I watched him perform.

"You needn't laugh at me like that. I may be a little disfigured, but I'm still in the ring," he mumbled in a jerky, drunken voice. Still holding to the gate, he made a bad attempt at dancing a jig, and laughed, ending the laugh with an ear splitting "Yah! Hah!" Then, "Whar's your Ma?" he loudly asked, as he went through the gate and zigzagged up the path to the house.

I had the crazy mare to unsaddle, and lost some of the show while doing this. In her stall she struck at me, got both front feet in the manger, fell down, then jumped to her feet and reared, hitting her head in the feed rack and crushing me against the side of her stall. I got her out into the horse corral, took her saddle and bridle off, and turned her loose. Old Jake had "high-lifed" her, thinking it a huge joke on Dad. She went running, tail over back, and you could have heard her snort a mile away.

I hurried back to the house to see what was happening there. Mom was seated in her rocking chair, her eyes focused on the rug. Dad was standing in the center of the room talking to her.

"You're a purty good ol gal, Sadie, I'm plum stuck on you, yes I am."

"If you're so all fired stuck on me, you'd better get out there and feed the hogs. We ain't fed them yet," she answered, with disgust in her voice.

"But baby doll, I was just, ah, fixin to sing you a shong!" he

_____

speak quite loudly. He was well known for his exhibitionism and loud talk when drunk.

137

came back. He seemed genuinely startled that she would not listen to him sing.

"Fiddlesticks! Get out of here and do like I say and quit runnin off at the head," she said, getting up from the chair and brushing him aside as he hugged her. She went to the kitchen, and he turned to me, saying in a wounded tone, "Your Mom sure takes the wind out of my sails. I'd better straighten up and do like she says, or she'll heckle me until I do." He staggered outside with a silly grin, hiccupping slightly at irregular intervals. The clang of the hogs' feed buckets announced the fact he was off to feed the pigs.

By four o'clock next morning, everyone was up and astir. We were mounting our horses when the sky glowed with a rose hue, indicating the near arrival of daylight. We hazed the cattle through the lane and headed them towards the railroad. I was "walking on air" that I, at last, was going on the beef drive. Dad was having little to say as we drove the cattle along. He was pale and shaken, and drank from every creek or ditch we crossed. The dust raised by the herd enveloped and choked us as the cattle strung out down-country.

The first night we rented pasture from a rancher along the way. Also, we arranged to stay all night with these people. They were what Dad called "white-collared ranchers." Their house was two-storied and painted white. Surrounding it was the landscaped yard, planted with a big lawn and roses. Near the main house was a guest house where the two daughters and I slept that night. Dad had a room upstairs in the big house.

I was self-conscious and shy in the presence of these semi-strangers, and did not eat but little at the evening meal. Being with strangers did not seem to bother Dad. He ate a lot, and drank almost an entire pitcher of water and scads of coffee.

In the night, I awoke hungry and couldn't fall back to sleep. All I could think of was the sandwiches, boiled eggs, and deer jerky in my saddle bags, which were down by the barn on my saddle. Slipping from bed, I dressed and eased out the door. I was going to the barn and get something to eat, and maybe could find a drink of water. As I passed through the yard, something tall and white showed up almost in front of me. I recognized Dad standing there in his undershirt and long drawers. What was he doing here, dressed like that? Was he also hungry, I wondered?

"Dad," I said quietly, and he whirled about, facing me. He didn't even have on shoes. "What you doin?" I asked when I was beside him.

"S-h-u-s-h, they'll hear you," he whispered. "I fell out of that winder yonder. Liked to caved my damn ribs in when I hit on that rose trellis."

"How on earth did you fall out?" I asked in amazement.

"Never you mind how I fell out. I tried to get back in the house, but they've got the damn doors locked. I've been out here for two hours or more. What time do you reckon it is?" he asked.

"I don't know, but must be toward mornin," I guessed.

"By God, it'd better be. Undoubtedly this is the worst picklement I've been mixed up in in my whole life," he whispered.

"Just how did you fall out a window in the middle of the night?" I again quizzed.

"Just — slipped. I'll tell you someday," he answered. He was so concerned with himself, he seemed not wondering what I was doing out there. Just then, a light came on in the house and Dad jumped like he'd been shot and hid behind a rose bush and beckoned me to follow.

"They're up!" he whispered loudly. "Now, Scrub, you go knock on the door and ask to go upstairs and wake me up. Tell them you think I should go tend our horses. Don't bungle things by actin like anythin's wrong," he continued.

The Mister came in answer to my knock. "Well, good morning, young lady. Come in, you're up early. I'm just finishing dressing," he said, as if surprised at my early intrusion. He had one shoe on and the other in his hand.

"Can — may I go up and wake Dad up?" I asked.

"Surely. He is at the end of the hallway, the room to the right," he instructed.

Finding the room, I gathered clothes and boots, tied them in a bundle, and dropped them to Dad out the window. Early dawn was lightening the outside, enabling me to catch his look of relief as he caught the bundle. I had a mental vision of his plight if I had not been on hand to help him. He was so right and proper; to be seen as he was dressed would have been a major calamity. I shuddered as I looked down at the fall he had taken. He was stopped, untangling his clothes.

There was footsteps off the porch, and the rancher stepped into the yard. "Mercy! What are you doing out here?" he exclaimed.

"Er — er, had a little accident," Dad came back with a gulp.

"Accident. What happened?" he asked. The moment of truth was upon Dad, and I stood at the window to hear.

"I was hopin you wouldn't find out about it. I fell out the winder. You see, my kidneys are bum and I had to go. I opened my door, figurin I'd slip downstairs and out, but I seen that girl in the room across from me, and she had her door open and a light goin, so I just figured I'd let it fly out the winder. I can't fer the life of me figure out how it happened. I must have been reared over too fer and the rug slipped on the floor coverin, and I was out before I knowed it. I hit on that trellis and it kinda buckled me up," Dad confessed.

"Mercy, I should have told you that our little nephew was in that room. He is sick and my wife leaves a light for him. What made you believe he was a girl?" the rancher inquired.

"Well, I don't know. I seen a shock of yeller hair, and it looked like a girl to me," Dad answered.

"It's all my fault, Att. I should have explained about the boy and shown you where our water closet is. Come in when you finish dressing and I'll have my wife put something on those rose thorn scratches," said the man.

"Hell, no!" ejaculated Dad. "It's bad enough you seen me, let alone anybody else. Everyone will be waggin their tongues and makin light of me if this gets around."

Down at the barn, I raided the saddle bags for food and quenched my thirst at the water trough. Dad led our horses out to the trough. He looked bedraggled and battered.

"You sure got a beaut of a black eye," I ventured to say.

"Hell, no!" he denied. "Hell, no," he repeated, putting his hand up to feel of the swollen knot on his cheekbone. "Hurts to beat hell," he said. "I'll tell you one thing fer sure, it will be a cold day in hell before I stay all night at a place like this again. I hate to go back in there and eat breakfast, and havin this shiner makes it worser. I wouldn't go in if I didn't have to have my coffee," he concluded.

"Well, there is one thing fer sure, I ain't goin in. You can tell them I don't feel good," I said.

"But Scrub, you gotta eat. She's a long drag till night," he reminded.

"I'm full. Ate three sandwiches and two hardboiled eggs and a lot of jerky. There's a lot more if you want to eat it," I offered.

"By God, I never knowed you had all that stuff with you. I'll just eat a bite and to the devil with the coffee. I'll get the grub while you saddle up, and we'll be ready to haze on out of here," he said, with a relieved tone in his voice.

The cattle had been put in a pasture with some of the rancher's the evening before. In getting our cattle cut out from his, it took a little fast maneuvering on the part of our horses. After we got the cattle separated and lined out down-country, Dad began turning his horse one way and then the other and spurring her some, and commented, "This damn mare, I don't know what's got into her. I can't get her to move out this mornin. She ain't got no speed."

He was riding Smut, the horse he had been riding the day when he got drunk, which old Jake had high-lifed. Until now, I had not referred to that incident, afraid he wouldn't take me on this trip. Now, I was safe, and innocently said, "Maybe you should have Jake high-life her again — she had plenty of speed, then. How come you got so drunk that day?"

"Oh, Jake had a gallon of moonshine and him and Peg-leg Willie was nippin at it when I got there, and Jake asked me to sample it, and before I knowed it I was as drunk as a billygoat and it was almost night. Do you suppose that old devil did high-life my horse? Come to think of it, she acted scatterbrained and snorty when I started fer home. I'll get even with that old cuss if it's the last thing I do," he said in an angry tone.

The cattle were driving fine, but going too fast for their own good. "I think I'd better get up front and kinda hold em down," he decided.

By noon, the sun beat down upon us and the dust was choking — that is, for me, back in the drag of the herd. I could see Dad up front. He was slowly riding along out of the dust. The thought came to mind that this, perhaps, was his reason to stay ahead. The cattle were reluctant to move, now, and I kept prodding to keep them moving; but Dad stayed up front. The smell of tarweed and warm cow manure filled the air. This, and the heat and dust, almost sickened me. There was no water along the way. This was not my kind of country. Even the birds here looked rumpled, lazy, and forlorn. Long-tailed magpies, crows, and buzzards were the only kind of birds in this country.

By evening, we had crossed Stillwater Creek and Stillwater Plains, on past Churn Creek. Dad was behind the herd, helping with driving. We could see Redding a distance away. We would soon be to Sacramento River, and across that it was around two miles to the stockyard.

As we approached the Free Bridge, which spanned the river, Dad said, "I'll get ahead again, crossin the bridge to keep them from crossin too fast. We'll let them string out in the lane and I'll get up front and you start a small bunch after me. Then, you come back and ease the main herd onto the bridge. Now remember — don't crowd them; let them cross as slow as they will. If they should start trottin or runnin, they might knock the bridge down," he cautioned.

I knew this was true, from the warning signs on the bridge that it was both dangerous as well as unlawful to trot a team crossing such a bridge. I painstakingly listened to his instructions and began carrying out his orders. Everything worked as he said it would until the drag was upon the approach, which was constructed of timbers and was a quarter of a mile long before it joined onto the steel suspension span crossing over the water.

The leaders of the last group began trotting to catch up with the ones ahead. In seconds, the whole bunch were galloping along. I could feel the bridge tremble under their impact. The rear herd caught up with the leader and pushed the entire bunch into high speed as they went along. They crowded into the bannisters, some slipping and falling on the bridge's decking. Dad was on the suspension section, trying to slow them — but it was useless. He was compelled to speed on or be caught in this mad scramble.

The steel supports on the main span were shaking and clang-

143

ing as I followed behind the cattle. Surely it would give way, as the complete structure felt like it was rolling and swaying under my horse's feet. Across the bridge and in the lane several hundred yards ahead, Dad had made a stand, trying to stop the animals' wild flight. He was wheeling his horse about, yelling and waving his hat to try to stop them, but only succeeded in crowding them through a fence that enclosed a large vineyard.

Every head went stampeding through the poorly constructed wire fence and on through the vineyard. We rode at breakneck speed to catch up with the leaders to turn them in a circle and get them back on the road. Eagle had the speed of a racer, and I was soon up front, flanking the leaders, forcing them to run in a circle. Dad had gone back through the broken place in the fence and was near the end of the bridge to guard them from recrossing. The cattle slowed to a slow trot as they were on the road once more. The last few minutes had been exciting. The herd had poured like a flood through the fence and run with increasing speed and sound, until they were turned about.

I saw a man running towards me, shaking his fists and loudly saying something I could not understand at that distance. I hesitated to leave the spot, as undoubtedly this was the owner of the vineyard, and I wanted to inform him we would pay for any damages our cattle had done. As he came nearer, I seen he was a short, dark man, and guessed he must be Italian. He panted up and began swinging his arms about, acting like a complete scatterbrain.

"You getta him out," he shouted, pointing towards the retreating cattle. "My nicea grapeavine, she's alla bust," he shouted, his mustache abristle.

"I'm sorry, Mister, they stampeded and broke through your fence, but if there is any damage to your vines my father will pay you as soon as we can take the cattle to the stockyard and come back," I promised.

"Thatsa all righta boy. If youra Pa-Pa willa pay, it will bea fine. My nicea grapeavine, I no wanta him bust."

This was no time for me to "fly the coop" on Dad and the cattle and set talking, so I dashed away, jumped Eagle across what remained of the fence, and was on the road once more. It was then I heard the man call, "Goodbye, boy." Evidently, he actually thought I was a boy.

Overtaking Dad and the cattle, who had simmered down to a plodding walk, Dad asked, "Who was that guy, and what was he runnin off at the head about, Scrub?"

"Oh, he wanta my Pa-Pa to, ah, pay fer his nicea grapeavines our cowsa busted," I answered, laughing.

"I had an idea he was a Dago from the way he was beatin his chest and swingin his hands," he said. After riding along for some time in deep thought, he asked, "Did he say how much he wanted?"

"No, but I told him you would come back and see him as soon as we git the cattle to the yard," I answered. To this he made no comment; just took off his hat and held it and the reins in his left hand and scratched his head with the right, which was his habit when deeply concerned.

It was not long until we arrived at Menzel's Stockyard, and began the task of weighing the cattle. The stockyard's scales held about ten head at a time, so this was no small task. Weights figured up, the buyer gave us a check for the cattle.

By the time we had rode the two or so miles to town, darkness had fallen. As we rode along the brightly lighted main street, to me it looked like a metropolis. We rode directly to the feed stable and left the horses. As we were walking towards the main part of town, Dad remarked, "Damned if I know where to grub up. I always go to Jagel's when I'm by myself, but that's a saloon and you can't go there, but it's a good place to eat. I guess we will eat at the Temple Hotel dining room. That's where we'll stay tonight,'' he decided.

The clip-clop sound of my boot heels on the sidewalk was making me self-conscious, as we mingled among the throngs of people on the street. Through the hotel lobby and into the washroom we marched, with Dad leading the way. The washroom was a poorly lighted den of a room, with a long, wooden trough. In it was a number of wash basins. The mirror on the wall revealed to me how dusty and dishevelled I was. When I had finished washing, I looked for a towel, but could not see one.

"Ain't they got no towel?", I asked.

Dad stopped washing and looked about and said, ''I guess they ain't, but they useta have regular roller towels there on the wall. Musta forgot to put one up,'' he guessed, and resumed washing.

A young man, who had just arrived and was starting to wash, said, ''They are right there, Son.'' He pointed to a metal box on the wall.

Looking at this container, I could not see a towel and was beginning to doubt the man's word of one being there. A sign read ''Blot, Do Not Rub.'' I had not, until now, seen a paper towel. It was soon apparent Dad had not either. He finished washing and also began looking for a towel. He examined the tops and sides of the metal box, then tried to wrench it from the wall, but it held firm. He fit his thumb nail into the screwhead-looking slot, where the key inserts to open the box, and began vigorously trying to unscrew it. I was confident he would find the towel if one was there.

The stranger had finished washing and was standing, waiting to get a towel, and watching Dad tackle the job of producing one. He looked amused as he watched Dad wrestle to get the box

146

open. Dad was still trying to turn the key slot around with his thumbnail. The young man, after watching a moment, stepped up, reached past Dad, and pulled out two paper towels. He handed one to me and began drying himself with the other.

Dad looked dumbfounded, and exclaimed, "Well, I'll be damned. Paper, nothin but paper!" He jerked one out, and after swiping his face a few times with it, threw it into the wastebox. "Who in hell could wipe on a paper?" he said, and began drying himself on his bandana.

Mom had fashioned my hair into a neat French Braid before we had left home. My cowboy hat covered this fact entirely. I had not removed my hat while washing, but in wiping my face and neck it accidentally fell to the floor.

The stranger, seeing my hair, looked surprised and exclaimed, "Are you a girl?"

"Yep," I meekly answered.

"You should not be in here. This place is only for men. The ladies' washroom is down the hallway," he said, opening the door and pointing to the sign over a door reading "Ladies Lounge."

Dad was standing, looking over my shoulder, and said in an apologetic way, "Dang bust it, Scrub, I never knowed they had that place. Hell, I thought everyone washed in here." He read the sign over the door: "Washroom, Men Only." He said, "Now that we know, you'll have to do the right and proper thing in the mornin and go in there. Come on, let's go get some chuck." He began leading the way to the dining room. The tables were almost all occupied. He steered me to the nearest vacant one and we sat down.

I wished we had not come to this place to eat. The women and girls wore fancy dresses and appeared so ladylike and at ease. The men wore suits and boiled shirts. I was so ashamed, I slumped down in my chair and hid my hands beneath the folds of the white tablecloth. Dad looked shockingly out of place when compared to the other gentlemen, in his soiled hickory shirt, levis, and bob-tailed jumper. His half-shoulder-length, white hair looked rumpled and unkempt, as we had brought no comb. He had taken his hat off and stowed it under his chair, and I still wore mine. Not having been in a fancy eating place before, I didn't know what to expect or how to behave.

The waitress came to our table, bringing us each a glass of water. Her fingernails gleamed with cleanliness, and she was so neatly dressed. There was no menu to order from. The lady, in a fast and singsong voice, began calling out what they had on the bill of fare. She named off many things in a rapid-fire way, and I was so excited I did not understand a word she said. Dad sat with his hand cupped to an ear, trying to catch what she was saying. From his confused expression, it was obvious he had not heard what she said, either.

"What did she say, Scrub?" he asked, his eyes turning quickly upon me.

"I don't know," I confessed.

The woman repeated the same singsong as before; but again, it was lost to both of us.

"Give me a steak, will yuh?" Dad asked.

"What kind of a steak would you like, Sir?" the waitress asked.

"A beef steak," he answered.

"I understand you are speaking of a beef steak, but do you prefer a T-bone, a round, rib, or sirloin?"

"Oh, that. I don't give a hoot where it's off of, as long as it's off a cow critter," he answered.

That satisfied her that any kind of a steak would do, so she turned to me and asked, "What will you have, young man?" I gulped; no words would come. I motioned towards Dad with my thumb and nodded my head.

"You want a beef steak also?" she asked. I nodded my head, and our order had been given.

We sat waiting for our meal. I shyly watched the people at the tables around us. What did such people do for a living? I decided these must be society folks that I had read about in newspapers. Their lives must be boring, setting around duded up all the time. I'd bet not a one of them could track a bull elephant in a swamp or tell one cow from the other. In my backwoods way of thinking, this was about as dumb as you could get.

After waiting for what seemed like forever, the waitress came with our meals on a large tray. She placed our steaks before us, then began dealing out to each of us a number of small dishes which contained a variety of vegetables.

"What do you wish to drink?" she then asked.

"I'll have coffee, and I don't want nothin in it, just coffee," stated Dad.

She turned to me and I choked out, "Have you got milk in here?"

At this, she smiled "You bet we have!" She hurried away to get our drinks.

I was so self-conscious that it made me awkward at cutting my steak. It slipped about like no steak I had ever attempted to eat. The dishes of vegetables, which were clustered about the platter, were a pain in the neck. The food would spill off my fork before I could get it to my mouth. Dad had dumped his vegetables in the platter with his steak, but I was sure that wasn't the proper way to handle the situation.

"You better fill your hide, Scrub. Quit foolin with your grub and get it down. It will be a long time before breakfast," he warned. "Just dump it all together and whittle up your steak and get goin on it. You ain't ate nothin yet.''

''I ain't hungry,'' I replied, which was the truth at that moment, because I felt that everyone in the establishment was watching the awkward way I had been behaving.

The waitress came to our table and asked, ''What would you like for dessert? We have ——— '' That was all I understood until she ended with ''shortcake.''

''I'll have shortcake,'' I said.

''That's jake with me, I'll have a slug of it too,'' said Dad.

When she arrived with the cake, she looked at me as though seeing me for the first time. ''Well, you are a girl. I thought you was a boy,'' she stated.

''Yah, I'm a girl,'' I answered in a simple manner.

''Do you and your Grandpa live near here?'' she pried.

''He ain't my Grandpa, he's my Dad. We live away back in the hills. We brought the beef cattle to town,'' I explained.

Dad had heard what she said and wished to set the woman right about his being my father. ''She's my kid, all right. She's a change baby. Our other kids were almost grown up when Scrub came along. It was the best thing Sadie and I ever did when we had this youngun. At first, Sadie was a little spooked at havin a kid at her age, but I was pawin the air about it. A feller my age gits kinda busted up, and havin a kid like Scrub here saves an old geezer like me a heap of steps.''

The lady's face had become red, as if she was embarrassed, and she hurried back to the kitchen. ''Wonder what I said that shook her up so?'' Dad asked. Not knowing, I said nothing.

We went upstairs to our rooms and I was glad to be out of sight of all those prying eyes. Dad came in my room after a while, and told me, ''I've done some scoutin around to get the lay of the land in here. If you want to go to the privy tonight, it's just down the hall. The door says 'Ladies.' ''

"Thanks, Dad, but what about you? Don't go fallin out of any winders here, or you'll go 'kersplash,' " I said, laughing.

"Now hush, I don't want you tellin anybody about that, not even your Ma," he scolded.

Strange noises kept me awake long after I had gone to bed. The trains thundered through town, blowing their mournful whistles and clanging their bells. How anyone could sleep in such a place was beyond me.

Morning came, and we were the only customers in the dining room at this early hour. We chose a table and the waitress came with our water and a friendly smile. She seemed nicer than the one the evening before. She didn't start a speech on all the things they had to offer to eat. She merely said, "Good morning, folks. What would you like for breakfast?"

"I believe I'll have ham and eggs," Dad said.

"We have cooked cereal, if you would care for some," she offered.

He studied over this a few seconds, then replied, "No, I don't think I'd like it."

"Would you like cereal?" she inquired of me.

"No, I want some mush. Have you got mush?" I asked.

She smiled sweetly and said, "Yes, I think I could find you some."

Dad had cautioned me before we came to breakfast to eat a lot, as it was a long ride home. I'd best order more than mush. "I'll have ham and eggs too," I hastily said.

"How do you like your eggs?" she was asking Dad.

"Oh, I like them fine," he answered.

"I understand you like your eggs, but how do you like them cooked?" she asked patiently.

"Cooked? Sure, that's the only way I can eat them is cooked. I'm not like my brother, I've got to have mine cooked. That feller is worser than a blasted weasel, he'll eat every egg he can find, raw. But not me, I just gotta have mine cooked,'' he concluded.

She did not bother to ask any further concerning our breakfast. She went to the serving window and gave our orders. When our ham and eggs were served, the eggs were sunnyside up, like both of us liked them.

Dad wanted to deposit the check for the cattle in the bank before we went home. After leaving the dining room, he said he was going down to the bank and see if the banker was in yet, and that if he was, Dad could get him to take the check and deposit it.

''Why can't I go back to my room and wait there until you get your business attended to?'' I asked.

''Naw, I don't think you'd better. You've left the room and ate breakfast now. I think if you would show up there again they would charge me another day's rent. You'd better come with me,'' he decided.

We went down to the bank, and despite the early hour the banker was at his desk. Dad held the check to the plate glass window, the banker let us in, and Dad deposited the check. Dad had done business with this bank for many years, and the banker was a personal friend of his.

We were a short distance from the stable where our horses were when I heard, in the distance, what sounded like team bells. I must be mistaken, as I hadn't seen one of these teams since the big teams had stopped hauling lumber from the Leture sawmill. But closer came the sound, and there was no mistaking the beautiful music the chiming of these brass bells could render.

''I hear team bells, Dad. Let us wait and see them,'' I said.

''Sure that's what you hear? Ain't many of those guys left.''

Dad stopped and squatted by a tree along the street to await the team's arrival. They came past where we were. There was four, sixteen-horse teams, one following the other. The wagons were loaded with ponderous machinery. The teamsters were a hard-bitten bunch. The fellow on the hindmost wagon was a small man with a gray mustache. ''That's Alex Clark,'' Dad exclaimed. ''I knowed him when we were young fellers. He's as tough as whangleather.'' Clark stopped his team and the two men talked a few minutes to renew old friendships. The machinery was being taken to Trinity County. It was gold-mining equipment, Mr. Clark said.

After he went on his way, we hurried on to get our horses and start the long, hot ride home. After we were mounted, Dad said to a man loitering out front of the stable, ''Say, is there a bridge out north of town?''

''Yes, about a mile out, you'll find it,'' the man answered.

''That's the way I wanta go. Thanks fer tellin me,'' Dad said.

''But Dad, that way won't take us by the man's place at the vineyard. You know I told him you would come by and pay for the damages,'' I reminded him.

''I know, I know. That's the reason we're goin home this way — so the old skinflint won't see us pass.''

14

SIXTEEN

IXTEEN IS IMPORTANT, and the most interesting age in a girl's life. It is fantastic the rapturous thoughts and actions of a girl of that age. I had celebrated my sixteenth birthday herding sheep, when Ivy [Albert's wife] and I were in a mountain camp.[11]

The feeling of inferiority and bashfulness I'd always held within me had somewhat gone. At dances, I didn't sit among the old ladies of the gossip ring or watch the old men play cards anymore. Nor did I set on the sidelines and watch the dancers, for lack of someone asking me to dance. It was wonderful, the self-possession I held. I enjoyed the boys' company and was almost as glib as the other girls when in their presence. At one time, I'd think I liked one the best; and next, I liked another better. The truth was, I liked them all but was serious about none

---

11. Anita's brother, Albert Carl, had married Ivy Billings in 1916. The couple ran sheep camps in the mountains during the summer, and in the Sacramento Valley during the winter. Anita lived with them for long periods of time and helped herd sheep, cook, wash clothes, and perform other chores at the camp.

of these. Lloyd, a boy I had known all my life, filled my thoughts.[12]

A day or so before New Year's Eve, I went to town to mail letters and get the mail. Town was usually a busy place around mailtime, and I hoped Lloyd would be there and maybe I could talk to him. The long line of hitching racks on each side of the store was crowded with horses tied there. I looked at these animals to see who was in town. Sure enough, tied to the far end of the furtherest rack was a lanky-built bay that I knew belonged to Lloyd.

Inside the store, a glance told me there was something unusual taking place, as everybody was facing toward the back of the store. I discovered their attention was being held by an argument between Lidie, the lady of the store, and Old Percy, a feisty little man who had a hot temper and wanted everything his way. In a loud, quarrelsome tone, he was saying, ''Yes, I know, but you stood right there by that sack of onions the other day and told me you would give me fifty cents fer my nuts.''

''Oh, the devil with your nuts,'' Lidie shot back. ''Take your stinkin old nuts and go home with them. I don't want nothin to do with your nuts or you,'' she said.

''But the other day you told me you would take my nuts,'' he argued. ''Get out!'' she said loudly, with menace in her voice,

---

12. The young man was Lloyd Kunkler. His father, Joseph Kunkler, had a ranch about six miles from the Schearer farm. Joseph's parents, Guilliam and Maria Kunkler, both from Alsace-Lorraine, had immigrated to Missouri during the era of the Franco-Prussian War. Joseph had pushed on west, married a girl named Jennie, and settled near Whitmore. Lloyd was eight years old when his father died in 1912. Jennie, with her eight young sons and two daughters, operated a large ranch.

and brandished the old cheese knife at him as if she intended slicing him with its long blade.

Percy argued no further. He quickly shouldered a filled grain sack, and with his little black eyes smoldering with anger he forced his way through us spectators, a few walnuts spilling from the sack as he hurried along. There was a chorus of laughter as he closed the door behind him.

"That old devil thought he was pullin a fast di-do on me, sayin I promised to buy his nuts," Lidie said, and then with a short laugh added, "He had me so danged mad there for a second, I'd've grabbed him by the guzzler and hung on till he quit kickin if he hadn't gone." There was an undertone of loose talk and giggles from some of the fellows, who lacked the wisdom to keep their minds out of the gutter. This was short-lived, as Lidie scrutinized them sharply and said, "Hush up, you scatterbrains, before I nail onto you." Red-faced with shame, they went outside.

A woman, a stranger to me, entered the store and stood waiting at the front counter. She held an egg carton in one hand. She set the carton on the counter and pulled the lid back, revealing that three eggs were missing. "We bought this dozen eggs from you last evening. I opened three of them and they were spoiled," she said in a small voice.

Lidie pursed her lips and said nothing, acting as if she was not surprised by the situation. Reaching under the counter, she produced three eggs, which she carefully placed in the carton, and quickly closed its lid.

"Damn a hen that lays rotten eggs," she stoutly said.

"What about the other nine?" the lady asked, reopening the lid. Lidie did not answer, but walked to the back of the store and began hanging horse collars upon pegs, the egg deal closed with her. The woman lingered briefly, then took the eggs and left.

Lidie came tiptoeing back to the counter, her brogan shoes making hardly a sound. The big, puffy coil of red hair done up on top of her head was not bouncing, as it usually did when she hurried about the store. Peeking through the window, she muttered, "Beats all how people skinflint me. She wanted nine more eggs!"

Lidie was lean of waist, hips, and legs. Above the waist, she ballooned to a gigantic size. Her large, fat breasts filled her dress to its utmost, and her arms and neck were like that of a wrestler. She was also hump-backed.

The stage came and went, and I got the mail and started home. Lloyd had no more than said "howdy" to me. He had been busy talking to the country's most notorious moonshiner.

At the edge of town, I heard a horse coming at a run behind me, its feet splashing loudly on the muddy road. Looking back, I seen it was Lloyd coming, flying toward me. He was standing in the saddle, showing off in a tomfoolery way. He slipped down into the saddle as he overtook me.

"Bet you can't do that," he said.

"Bet I can," I answered.

"How about a race?" he challenged.

"On that?" I asked, pointing at his horse. I had doubts that Steamboat could outrun his bay, but gave no indication of what I thought. "I'll race you to the creek," I said.

"Hell, I said a race, not an endurance test," he answered. "The creek's up there two miles," he added. "I'll race you to Saw Mill Gulch."

"All right, but that ain't far enough to get this nag warmed up," I agreed. I had hoped I could get him to race to the creek. Steamboat was long-winded and no doubt could win if we raced that far.

"Get on the mark, ready, go!" he said.

The horses, sensing the excitement of a race, leaped ahead,

and we went helter-skelter up the muddy road. The bay was fast and before we reached the gulch he was three lengths ahead, and my face and clothes were plastered with red mud. My eyes were so filled with mud the horse and rider ahead was a blurred object.

"You're a hell of a lookin 'mud-in-the-face,' " he said, laughing.

"It ain't funny," I cried, fighting the mud from my eyes.

"Wanta go on to the creek?" he wanted to know.

"Sure, just as soon as I can see," I said.

"You can see good enough," Lloyd said in an unfeeling way.

We raced on, and before long he was ahead and feeding me the mud again. This was simply killing my pride, and I began jocking Steamboat for all the speed that he had. I was gaining, and the bay began running with her head and tail high. I knew she had reached her endurance, and my horse was just warming up to the race.

The creek was just ahead and I was passing Lloyd. He was in the center of the road when we came to a curve and a low place in the road, which was filled with water. This presented a problem, as hidden beneath the muddy water was deep ruts. I'd be compelled to skirt around these or take a gambling chance and keep straight ahead. I chose the latter in a flash decision, as I had to win. About halfway through the pond, the little sorrel stepped into a boggy rut and turned a somersault. I loosed in the saddle and sailed clear of his falling body, coming to earth on my hands and knees in the icy, mud-filled water. My mind flew back to the time that almost the same thing had happened when I rode Rattler into the swamp at Dad's hunting camp on Battle Creek. I was on my feet before Lloyd turned and came back to where I stood.

"You hurt?" he asked.

"Naw, I guess not. But look at me, ain't I a mess? I'm afraid of what Mom and Dad's gonna say,'' I worried. ''They give me the devil fer racin — say I'm goin belly up someday if I don't quit it.''

''Looks like you went belly down, this time,'' he laughed, looking at the mud on my front side. ''I just wouldn't tell them,'' he advised.

''But look at me, the horse and saddle — you don't get this way if you ain't been doin somethin you shouldn't have,'' I reasoned.

''Well, just say you fell off your horse in a muddy place,'' he said, smiling.

''That would be a likely story. They would sure swaller that. I gotta get home, I'm froze,'' I said, and climbed in my saddle without attempting to wipe the mud away.

''I gotta be gettin too, I got to help move cattle this afternoon,'' Lloyd said. ''I'll see you at the masquerade; and don't forget, we are goin to supper together,'' he reminded, as he started to leave.

''Sure thing, I'll be there,'' I agreed.

When I walked into the house, Mom and Dad were cleaning chickens. ''What in hell happened to you?'' Dad exploded, eyeing me.

''I was sorta racin with some kids downtown and that crowbait fell down with me. I wasn't goin hardly at all. I don't see fer the life of me what caused it,'' I lied.

''What do you mean, not hardly goin?'' he bellowed. ''If I know you, you had that mustang stretched out like a greyhound. You ain't never rode a horse like you had any gumption, since you was big enough to get on a cayuse,'' he stormed.

''Get those filthy clothes off. You are completely runnin me bugs, Child,'' Mom scolded.

''Can't help it, Mom, I'm a buggy kid,'' I answered, attempting to be funny.

"It's no jokin matter. I can't see why you and Agnes have both rode a horse like you ain't got a lick of sense, while Albert's always rode like he knew somethin. Both of you are just scatterbrains," she accused.

"Al's never had any fun, either. He rides like an old maid goin to church," I laughingly said. Al was the apple of her eye, and unless you did as he did, you were doing wrong in her eyes.

The evening before the dance at Whitmore, I said, "What do you think I should be, Mom? A witch or an angel, at the dance?"

"An angel! Huh! You'd look more natural in a red suit with horns and a long tail," she scoffed. "Ain't much time fer me to fix you anythin," she lamented.

"Do you know what I'd fix up like, if I was you, Scrub? I'd dress like a cowboy gunslinger. You'd have to dance with the girls, but I'll bet they would never guess who you was," Dad said, looking up from his reading.

The idea pleased me, and Mom thought it would save her a lot of sewing, not making a costume. I strolled into the dance hall that evening like a cowboy in all his splendor. Big hat, flashy shirt and tie, levi pants, leather chaps, cowboy boots — and Dad had buckled his twin .38 pistols on me. The getup was further enhanced by a pair of big, roweled spurs, which chimed like music as I stepped.

The first dance of the evening was in sway as I came in the hall and stood near the front door and admired the different costumes. A Spanish dancer, Goldielocks, a hula dancer, a witch, and the Queen of Hearts were the best costumes among the girls, outside of a big colored girl who was dressed in a yellow dress with outlandishly large black polka-dots. Among the men, the most outstanding was Uncle Sam, a gambler, a minister, a beggar, and Old Father Time, with scythe and all.

161

The musicians struck up a new tune for the next dance and I sashayed over to where the girls sat on the benches, wondering which one I should dance with. My eyes fell upon the large colored girl, and I offered her my crooked arm and she accepted. I almost forgot to dance on the side a man dances, and found it awkward for the first turn about the hall.

At midnight, the floor manager went up on the platform and announced, "Quiet, everyone. The next dance you will unmask. I have prizes for the couple chosen by our judges for the best costumes. Also, to add color to our doins, the partner you have at unmaskin time will also be your supper partner." There was a chorus of disapproval from the crowd.

"Choose your partner for a waltz!" he called.

This was a dirty trick, after I had thought of little else but going to supper with Lloyd the whole week. I would look silly taking one of the girls to supper, and it was certain she would not enjoy it either. First, I thought I would not choose a partner. No, I could not do that, I reasoned. Hurrying over, I asked the colored girl to be my partner. She was smooth at dancing a reverse waltz, I found.

The judges were out looking the couples over, and after they made their decisions, the music stopped and the floor manager made the announcement that the witch and Father Time had been chosen. At this announcement, my colored girl swooned and fainted. The floor manager ran and fetched a dipper of water to revive her. She lay sprawled on the floor, seemingly unconscious, and I fanned her with my hat. It was then I seen her long yellow dress had fallen above her knees, revealing a pair of men's shoes and socks, which were supported by men's garters.

The man returned with the water and was beginning to pour it on my partner. "Hold it, I'm all right, it was just a joke!" My partner exclaimed, as he removed the mask and leaped to his feet, laughing. Of all the luck, this was the best — it was Lloyd.

I removed my mask, and he looked as astonished as I. "You," he exclaimed. "I thought you was Paul Cramer all the time. He is about your size. A two-gun man — don't know if it's safe to have supper with you or not," he laughingly said.

"If you feed me the right grub, I promise not to shoot," I laughed back. The night wore on, and at daybreak everybody headed for home, tired, sleepy, and happy.

Before the next dance, the folks agreed for me to go, unescorted, with Lloyd. When that time arrived, it was storming. Snow lay a foot deep, and it was still falling. He was coming to get me in his car, but with this storm it was impossible to drive to the ranch. In the latter part of the afternoon, Mom called me to the house, saying I was wanted on the telephone.

"I think it's that Kunkler boy," she said in an acid tone, as I picked up the receiver. She was right. He was calling to tell me he was coming to get me on horseback. A sparkle at the good news, I gushed out the plan to Mom.

"Huh, I was in hopes he couldn't come," she said, with disappointment in her voice and manner. "I don't believe I'd get too wrapped up with that boy, Babe. He's too wild. I heard the other day that he's moonshinin. I told your Dad about it, but he doesn't think it's so, he says I ain't got the wisdom of a sow and listen to gossip. But I ain't carin, I don't think he's right and proper," she concluded.

"Infernal Hell, Mom, you're a wet blanket. You listen to old Mamie and a dozen more of those old cacklin hens and take their gossip fer the truth. Sakes alive, Mom, if you listen to all their loose talk, you will go completely bugs," I scoffed.

Only a few people braved the storm that night. No more than a dozen couples were there. Mamie came, her furtive, close-set eyes seeing everything that happened. She sat wrapped in a wool buggy robe, her loose jowls wabbling as she chewed gum. This, and her few snags of yellow teeth and her scraggly hair, gave her a hardcase appearance.

By midnight, the small crowd was noisy and acting giddy. The hall rang with silly laughter. Bottles of white mule were being passed around. I watched this behavior. Uppermost in my mind was what would happen when the folks found out I had gone to a dance of this sort. They would hear about it — Mamie sat six inches taller as she craned her neck, the better to see.

The musicians were so soused they were dancing over the floor while playing their instruments. The fiddle player fell and could not raise to his feet. He sat and sawed the bow back and forth, producing but a raspy squeal. Mamie, Lloyd, and I were the only sober ones in the crowd. The dance ended before daylight because the musicians had passed out and lay on the floor, along with some of the dancers. We left the hall and rode through the storm to the ranch.

The smell of coffee filled the house as we entered. Breakfast was on the table. Mom and Dad looked at us in a way it was hard to understand at first. ''What is this we hear about everyone at the dance bein hog drunk?'' Dad gruffly asked. ''Was you drinkin moonshine?'' he further inquired.

''No! Who said I was?'' I asked.

''Mamie. She called your Ma on the phone before we was up and said it was shameful the way you was carryin' on.''

''There was a lot of people drinkin, I'll admit, but I didn't have one drop, honest I didn't,'' and I turned to Lloyd, saying, ''Did I?''

''No, she didn't, Mr. Aldridge. I don't think you need to worry about her. She's not goin to guzzle a lot of that booze as long as I'm with her, if I can help it,'' he said.

"I'll take your word fer it, young feller; but I'll tell you now, if I ever hear of her takin as much as a drop when she is out with you, I'll take you to task," Dad warned, with emotion in his voice.

"You won't if I can help it," Lloyd promised, and added, "If that old witch, Mamie, would mind her own kids and keep her blabbermouth shut about other girls, things would go a lot smoother around this country."

"That's what I tell Sadie, that she's just a loose-lipped old heifer. To not take too much stock of the gossip she spreads," Dad agreed.

We went to parties and dances all winter after that. Mom still worried over me going with a "moonshiner." Dad upheld me against her protests.

We were feeding the cattle one day, and Dad seemed deep in thought most of the time. "Say, Scrub, is young Kunkler actually makin boose, or is it all hogwash?" he asked.

"Yeah, I guess he is," I said, wondering what would be his reaction.

"Do you reckon you could find out from him how to make the stuff? We could make it in the 'tater house' and no one would be the wiser," he told me.

"I probably could, if I'd ask him," I said. Dad making moonshine — he must be joking.

"I wish you would. All these guys around are makin the stuff and gettin rich on it. That's one of the reasons I ain't let your Mom stop you from goin with him. Anyhow, I don't believe he's a bad sort," he confided.

"I'll say you and me want to get into that business and I'll find out where to sell it, too. Mom will never agree, do you think?" I asked.

"Oh, she may buck like a bay steer — but let her buck, she'll be helpin us if we ever get in the swing runnin it off," he said, with a laugh. "We won't jangle with her; we'll just get makin it, and when she sees the dollars pourin in she'll 'come to her milk' and be willin to help." Going home, we rode several miles without his saying a word. I, understanding his moods, guessed that "moonshinin" was getting a complete airing in his mind.

At last he broke the silence. "Do you think he'll tell you?"

"He may. Anyhow, I'll ask," I answered.

"Are you sure he is actually makin it?" he anxiously inquired.

"Yeah, it's true."

"Where do you reckon he's got his outfit?"

"Well, if you'll keep your mouth shut, I'll tell you somethin." And I waited for his agreement before I said any more. "You remember about a month ago the red sow and her shoats were gone, and you sent me to look fer them? I came home and told you I had found their bed on the canyon rim? Next mornin, I got down there not long after sunup and struck fresh tracks headin into the canyon. I tracked along till I was in the cedar thicket near the big spring and I heard the old sow 'woosh,' and hogs went every way. I heard some feller say, 'Run, you damn fool, run, it's Scott and George!' I looked around, and there by the spring was a lot of fifty-gallon wooden barrels behind a big log in a barrage of brush. By the spring was a still settin on a rocked-up camp stove, and a fire was burnin; but I didn't see a soul. It kinda scared me, so I turned my horse around and got the hell away from there. On top of the hill I remembered seein a coat hangin there on a bush, and it was his coat."

"Zowie!" Dad exclaimed, and struck his saddle horn with his fist. "That's another angle I ain't thought of, is raisin hogs on the mash. We could raise ten times the hogs we do now, and fer practically nothin,'' he said excitedly. ''There's a heap of money to be made if a feller had the savvy to make it. You watch your chance when you see the kid, and find out all about it,'' he added.

On our way to the next dance, I tried to start a conversation about moonshine, but Lloyd eluded every attempt. On our way home, I point-blank asked, ''How do you make moonshine?''

''Why do you ask that?''

''Oh, I was just wonderin. A lot of folks claim you're makin it, and I'm curious how it's done,'' I lied.

''You'll have to ask someone else. I ain't makin it,'' he denied, his voice gruff.

I was dejected and thought of Dad's high hopes in my getting this information. ''Did you find out, Scrub?'' he asked, when Mom wasn't listening.

''No. He says he ain't makin it, and if I want to find out I'll have to ask somebody else. He ain't foolin me, though. That was his coat there on the bush,'' I said.

''He don't trust you, it looks like. That throws a hell of a crimp in my plan. I've a good notion to go down where you seen his outfit and make out I'm huntin hogs and get to talkin to him. Bein's I've caught him in the act, maybe he'll tell and show me how to make it.''

''No! I wouldn't do that — he's buffaloed of you now. Ever since old Mamie told that we were drunk, he's shy of you. Says 'Your old man would like to draw a bead on me.' Can't get him to come in the house no more,'' I said.

''By God, I did notice, the few times he's been here since, he just stayed a few minutes and acted like a wild malamute. If a feller would stomp his foot right quick, he'd jump through a winder,'' Dad said, laughing. ''I don't dislike the boy. Tell him so. I'd like to be friends. I gotta find out some way how to make that stuff. I'm afraid to talk about it to most people around, or everyone will get wise to what I'm fixin to do. Old Mamie would be sayin, 'Old Att's makin moonshine.' I ain't been feelin too good the last couple of years, and I've got to get into somethin easier than cows. Rearin around on a horse and in all kinds of weather is shakin me up awful bad. I was sixty-seven in February, and when a feller gets that old, about all the vinegar is run out of him,'' he said.

Springtime was upon us. The trees sported new leaves. The birds had arrived, and flitted from tree to tree, busy making their nests. Their songs were full of love. Even our old, brown, leghorn rooster, who had been puny all winter, had oiled his feathers and spruced himself. He was quite a feller around the barnyard, as he flirted among the hens and sat on the top rail, crowing like a yearling. The ditches and spring pond was full of frogs. Their croaking echoed about the ranch, both day and night. Wild flowers made the whole outdoors like a fairyland.

When things are thus, with the coming of springtime, most young girls have thoughts of love uppermost in mind. Not so with me. It was merely the right time of year to pick wild flowers, plant garden and crops, mark and brand the calves, cut the pigs, and go coyote-pup hunting. This spring, we had not gone yet.

"Ain't we goin pup huntin, Dad?'' I asked.

"Sure we'll go. I've been feelin kinda not too bush-tailed this spring, but maybe tomorrow we'll strike out,'' he answered with a sigh. But each day was the same, and I began planning to go by myself.

I seen Lloyd downtown, about that time. He surprised me by asking, "Say, do you want to go coyote-pup huntin?''

He must be a mind reader, I thought. "Yeah, been wantin to

go fer a week or more, but Dad's sick and can't go and I've been thinkin I'd go alone,'' I answered.

''I know where there's a hell of a lot of places they sometimes den. You come down right away and we'll go look for them,'' he invited. ''Bring your dogs, cause ours ain't worth a darn lookin fer dens,'' he added.

''I don't know if the folks will let me go or not; but I'll tell you what, if I get a chance, I'll run off. I could tell them I'm goin to do somethin else,'' I told him.

Mom and Dad went on a business trip to Redding a few days after this. While they made plans, I secretly made mine to go coyote-pup hunting. They departed by daylight, and had no more than driven away when I saddled a horse, got the wire hooks and several candles, called the dogs, and was on my way to the Kunkler ranch to go pup hunting.

I realized that going pup hunting with a young man may not be the proper thing for a girl my age to do, but I could not see any harm in it; it would be all right whoever you went with. I was in a reckless state of mind that morning, as I went galloping down the back road, the dogs bounding along in front of my horse. It was good to be alive, I thought.

Lloyd seemed surprised but pleased when I arrived. ''You're surer than hell early. We just finished breakfast. Have you ate yet?'' he asked.

''Sure, hours ago. The folks went to Redding today and ain't gonna be home tonight, and we was up long before the chickens to get them started. Get your horse and we'll get started,'' I urged.

''My horse is runnin down in 'Flat Holler.' We will have to go get her,'' he answered. ''I'll get Prince and we'll drive them in.'' Prince was a stud that belonged to his brother, Cal. We found the horses, some twenty head or more, and when we rode in sight they took off like a herd of antelope.

"How are you gonna catch your horse out of that locoed bunch?" I called, as he took after them.

"Run hell out of them and corral them," he called back.

We chased them in sight of the ranch and they broke across the creek, intending to elude the corral. Lloyd crossed the creek at breakneck speed, the stud jumping logs, chaparral, and boulders. Lloyd was riding bareback, and I had to admire the way he clung to the stud's back. Heading the horses, we ran them into a corral on the flat some distance below the ranch building. After he slammed the gate shut, he tied the stud to a tree.

"You stay here and watch him that he don't break loose, or there will be hell to pay. I've gotta go down here a minute and look at somethin," he said. I nodded agreement.

He went down through the tall grass of a swamp and vanished into overhanging willows. He had been gone but a few minutes when there came a banging sound, as if one board had been dropped on another. The thought sprung to my mind that this was where he was making whiskey. I tied my horse and slipped down through the tall grass and on through the large, overhanging willows. There was no trail, but I had seen where he had gone, and picked my way along. I came to the creek and knew I was going right, because in the damp earth I seen one faint heel print. On around some more willows, I seen him busy stirring his mash. I stepped behind a bush and watched him stir the contents of the ten or more barrels with a long, wooden paddle.

His back towards me, he had no idea I was watching. Cautiously, I made my way toward him. Within a few feet of where he busily worked, I said, "Moonshinin, huh!"

In a flash, he whirled about, his pistol trained at my head. I heard the hammer click back as he turned, and it seemed an eternity that I stared into the barrel of the pistol before he lowered it.

"Don't ever do a thing like that again! You don't know how close I came to pullin the trigger!" he exclaimed. "What in hell you snoopin around here fer, anyway?" he added, in a shaky but vexed voice.

"Oh, figured you was making hooch in here when you left me up yonder," I answered.

"You ain't gonna blab about it, are you?" he asked.

"Heck, no. I knew you was makin it all the time. I was over to the other place on the canyon rim and I knew it was you, cause your coat was hangin there. I heard someone say, 'Run, you damn fool, run. It's Scott and George.' Who said that?" I asked.

"Old Scotty. We was workin together until he started high-jackin me. Scott and George is the revenuers," he explained.

"Now maybe you'll tell me how to make the stuff," I said.

"How come you're so all-fired interested in knowin how it's made? Figurin on runnin it off yourself?" he asked.

"Yeah, that's the idea. Dad and me are goin into hooch and hogs," I blabbed.

"Your old man moonshinin — that's the funniest thing I ever heard! I figured he thought that bootleggin was such a sin that he wouldn't breathe the air where one was," he laughingly said.

"Naw, Mom's the one that thinks that way. Dad's been wantin to get goin on moonshine fer a long time, but ain't found no one he could trust enough to ask how to commence stewin it off," I explained.

"Well, bein's the old man figures that way, I wouldn't mind showin him all I know about it. He'll have to get an outfit — or has he got one?"

"No, he ain't got one. Where can he buy one?" I asked.

"I made this rig here, and it's as good as a boughten one. I know a feller that's gettin scared out, and he's thinkin of sellin

171

his whole shebang. Your dad could buy that, or I'd even make the deal fer him,'' Lloyd offered.

''You buy it and he will pay you fer it, cause we're rarin to get started,'' I said, happy that at last I had got Lloyd's confidence and had set the wheels rolling toward our career as bootleggers.

Down on the lower canyon rim we found two coyote dens, which yielded eleven pups. Our dogs antagonized the old coyotes into fighting and brought them into shooting range, and we killed the two females and one male. It was afternoon before we finished skinning their pelts off.

''There is another place not far from here. What you say we sally over there and look?'' he asked.

''If it don't take too long,'' I agreed.

''Won't take long,'' he answered.

There was no fresh sign at the burrow under an outcropping of rocks there. We hurried on, as it was late afternoon.

''Are you thirsty? If you are, there's a good cold spring yonder in that cave,'' Lloyd said.

''Let's go that way,'' I said.

In seclusion, under the face of a tall cliff, nestled the spring. It was heavily overhung by giant live oak trees. A rocky trail brought us suddenly out to this spot, where the spring bubbled out of the cliff. We stopped, looking at the unexpected activity there.

Two men were busy working. One was squatted, placing small limbs on a fire in a rocked-up campfire. The other was scooping the spring clear of mud with a short-handled shovel. We slowly and quietly backed our horses around to get from their sight. I had seen who they were, in this time. The one at the spring was a neighbor, and the other was Uncle Bill. There was a number of barrels and a shiny copper still. Everyone must be making the stuff, I thought.[13]

"I guess you seen who they was," Lloyd said, after we had ridden away.

"Yeah, I seen, and am I surprised." At the forks of the road, I said, "I'm goin home the back way, so I won't be seen. You take the pelts, and when you cash them in you can give me my share of the bounty."

"How about goin to those other dens?" he asked.

"Well, if you want to come up early in the mornin, we will go over and have a look," I invited.

"That's a date. I'll be there," he said, with enthusiasm.

"See you in the mornin, and come early. It's a long ride over to the sandstone country," was my parting words.

Morning and he arrived early. I was driving the yearling in from the pasture. A steer had his nose white with porcupine quills, and they would have to be pulled. We ran him in the chute and began the tedious operation: first snipping the ends to collapse the quill, then drenching them with vinegar to soften the barbs, which made pulling easier and less painful.

"I'll bet you can't ride one of these yearlins," Lloyd said, as we finished the job of pulling quills.

"I'll bet you I can. I can ride anything that wears hair," I boasted. "You rope one and I'll show you how it's done," I smarty-like said.

"Huh!" he exclaimed. "Get a rope and I'll catch one."

Running to the barn, I got Dad's best lariat, the one he was so particular of how it was handled. Lloyd roped one, a mulie

13. William Lee (Bill) and Att remained particularly close friends throughout life. Bill sometimes stayed at Att's home, and later lived for short periods of time with Anita and Lloyd. Bill died May 12, 1938.

heifer which was bigger and wilder than the others. It took both of us to snub her and get a rope around her middle. I jumped astride, regretting that I had been so brash and "cocksure" that I could ride anything. He loosened the rope from the snub post and the heifer and I flew across the little pasture, going up and down and sideways, her loose hide moving under me.

Before starting the ride, Lloyd had said, with emphasis, "I'll hang onto the rope. When she dumps you, I'll still have hold of her and can take the riggin off without havin to rope her again."

This galled my pride. I'd ride that heifer to a standstill if it broke every bone in my body. Just ahead was a mud-filled depression, and the heifer had her course set towards it. Another jump and she would be in this mire, which would give me opportunity to get better control of my balance. What I did not know was that Lloyd was setting back on the rope. The heifer came to the end of the slack and flipped broadside in the gully. My death-grip tore loose from the rigging, and I sailed across the mudhole, coming to roost on my seat in a clump of bull thistle. There is nothing quite as rough as bull thistle — especially to clamp your backside down on. "You dingbat. What in hell did you do that fer? If I could, I'd kick the pants off'n you!" I added, still smarting from the sting of the thistle barbs.

"Didn't want to see you get muddy," he said meekly, then smiled broadly. "Sorry I stopped her, but the haphazard way you was ridin, I thought you was about to 'fly the coop,' " and he laughed in a way that set my hair bristling.

"Fiddlesticks! I was just getting raired back, startin to ride. The next one you just keep your hands off," I said angrily.

We rode all of the yearlings, forgetting about our plan to go over in the sandstones and hunt coyote dens. "I'd sure like to show you how to ride somethin big," Lloyd said. "I'm use'ta ridin bulls and the likes," he added. I had a mental vision of him on "Bow," our bull, who was in the farther pasture with the milk cows. He had a bad temper and was downright mean when aroused.

"We got a bull you can't ride," I told him. "Come on, we'll go get him over here."

In the chute, Bow bellowed and fought until he broke boards, and I put Dad's lariat around his low-drooped horns and tied it to a post, while Lloyd fitted the riggin about his belly. He dropped astride the bull's back, and I opened the chute door and at the same time slackened the rope from the post. Like a mad devil, the bull left the chute. His rider, with feet thrust forward and body reared back, was riding like a demon.

I had been so fascinated by the performance I had neglected to loosen the end of the lariat from the post. The bull came to the end of the slack in the rope and, with a moan, the big animal flopped to earth and the lariat parted with a snap. Up and going again, Lloyd was astride him once more. The bull, unsuccessful in dumping him, was going wild from the sting of Lloyd's spurs. When Bow gave up and was doing nothing more than galloping along, Lloyd threw one leg over the bull's withers and jumped free of him.

"That's the way to ride them, 'Skeeter Bill,' " he mockingly said. He had given me this nickname. It sounded ridiculous, at first. I gave him the name of "Pocus Pete." We dropped the Bill and Pete, and were known to each other as Poke and Skeeter.

"What time do you reckon it is? We'd better get started if we're goin lookin fer pups," he said.

"Oh, infernal hell, look at the sun. It's almost down!" I exclaimed. "The folks will be home any time, and we've got to get the ropes off the bull and him back in the pasture. The chute's gotta be fixed, and somehow prop that fence straight. The posts are broke off and it's just hangin," I said.

The bull was fighty and mad. He made passes at us and wouldn't enter the chute. One horn was broken loose at the skull; it hung low on his head and was bleeding. We ran the yearlings back into their pasture.

"Now, if we can patch the chute, quick-like, and prop that board fence up straight before they get here, they will never know what's been goin on," I said. "If we could somehow get the ropes off the bull and run him back into the pasture, it wouldn't be likely that Dad would see him until he has stopped bleedin and healed." I could hide the broken rope and it would never be known actually what had happened to it.

Suddenly, I heard the rattle and clang of Old Liz coming at a distance. "Hey, I hear the folks comin!" I exclaimed.

"Holy smokes! I got to get the hell out of here!" Poke said. Running to his horse, he hurdled into the saddle and turned to escape out the south lane.

"Stop! You're gonna help me explain how come things are in such a mess," I called.

"Hell, NO! Your old man's wantin to blow me sky-high the way it is," he answered, and raced out of sight.

I ran up the hill and was nonchalantly standing by the yard gate as Old Liz panted into the barn lot. The folks climbed from the car and beckoned a greeting to me. "Been gettin along all right, Babe?" Mom asked, smiling. Then she seriously eyed me. Until now, I had given no thought to how I looked. I was muddy and dirty and was bleeding from several places on my arms and hands. "Yeah, fine," I cheerfully answered.

Dad was sauntering about the barn lot, his eyes scanning the ground. He was tracking, and learning all that had taken place during his absence. To him, it was like reading the happening as if it was in writing there on the ground. "What was young Kunkler doin here?" he asked, not taking his eyes from the ground.

"Just passing by and stopped a while to talk," I answered.

"He must have been here longer than a while. From the looks of things, I'd say his horse was tied there most all day. Left in a hell of a hurry, looks like," he observed. Then he asked, "What's Bow doin in the clover patch?"

Determined to keep the truth from him if I could, I said, "Well, I'll be darned if I know, Dad. I sure don't savvy," and looked innocent-eyed.

"How in hell did he get there if you don't know? He ain't got wings," he said, taking long strides toward the pasture. He was bound to find out, so I ran to him and explained, "I put him in there, Dad. I didn't want you to know, but Poke bragged that he could ride any bull, no matter how mean he was, so I was tryin to prove he couldn't ride our bull."

"Who in hell's Poke?" Dad asked.

"Lloyd. I call him Poke and he calls me Skeet," I explained.

"Huh!! Why didn't you take the rope off the bull? What's wrong with his head? It's bleedin. You ain't broke his horns, have you?" he asked. "You know I don't want no one ridin the cattle, and especially that bull. You get that contraption off him right now," he said in an angry tone.

"Can't do it, he's madder than the devil. We tried to get him back in the chute, but he's on the fight," I explained.

"Oh, fer Christ sakes. All you gotta do is go in there and drive him in. You just didn't try. You was too busy lollipoppin round with that young feller," he accused.

"No, I was not!" I defended. "I ain't goin in there tonight, I'll wait till morning," I added.

"No, you won't wait. You'll do it now." Dad climbed the fence, saying, "Get in here and head him into the chute when I drive him around."

"Look out!" I warned, as he briskly walked across the pasture. "He's comin your way!"

177

Dad stood his ground, but the bull kept up his charge. With head lowered, he thundered down on Dad. As the bull made his final jump, Dad stepped aside and baisted the brute across the face with his hat. The bull missed his target, but turned, ready for another charge. His broken horn was wobbling around like a big loose banana as he chased Dad, who ran and pounced onto the board fence; amidst the cracking and splintering of wood, Dad fell under three lengths of fence, post and all. I set the dogs on the bull, and they heeled him to the far side of the field.

"What in hell went wrong with this fence!" Dad bellowed, as he dragged himself from under the rubble and looked at the broken-off posts with contempt. "What did you damn kids do? Run the bull into it?"

"No, tied a yearlin to it and he all but took it down."

"Yearlin! What was you doin with a yearlin, ridin it, too?" he yelled. That was a fatal mistake, mentioning a yearling. He was sure to know we had ridden all the cattle. It was almost dark, but his eyes fell upon a piece of his prize lariat lying near the chute.

"What's this?" he said, holding the rope in both hands. "My good 'lass rope, you've broke it all to hell!" he said, as he threw it to the ground. "I'm tellin you right now, if I ever catch that scatterbrained kid around here again, I'll run him to hell," he roared.

"Oh, no, we was just havin fun," I tried to explain.

"Fun! Fun! I don't call this fun," he roared again. "I never did bust you one, Scrub, but I've a damn good notion to, now," he said through clenched teeth, acting as if he intended to strike me.

I ran to do the milking and tend separating the milk before I encountered him again. I passed the back porch with the hog feed, and he seen me and said, "Ain't you fed the hogs yet? It's

178

a hell of a note when you get so busy sparkin you ain't got time to tend the stock.''

''I wasn't sparkin — didn't have time, fer tryin to get the bull fixed up,'' I said.

''You fixed him up all right, breakin his horn like that. You know, I prided the way I put weights on his horns, trainin them to droop just so,'' he said.

Mom and him were waiting at the table when I returned from chores. The atmosphere was strained and chilly as I seated myself. I choked down a bit of food and a glass of milk and retired for the night. I could hear the folks talking as I lay in bed.

''That's what I've been tellin you all along, Att. That boy is no good fer her, she never did crazy things like she does now. You've upheld her moonin around with him and you can't deny it,'' Mom argued.

''Well, maybe I did to a certain extent, Sadie, but I can't see all bad in the boy. He's a hard worker, speaks his mind, and seems honest. That's a heap more than you can say about the ones you would have her go with. Right down in their gizzards they're no good, lázy, and full of loose talk about girls,'' he said.

That's the truth, I thought, as I lay in my darkened room. There was no boy that I knew that I could have more fun with than Poke. Good, clean fun.

Mom said, ''I suppose you're gonna let her keep galavantin around with him like you've been doin, but I'm settin my foot down. Even if you don't think so, there's a lot of nice fellers she could go with. He's wild, and you know the kind of girls he's hung around with.''

''No, I'm puttin a stop to it. It makes me damn mad to come home and they have broke everythin on the ranch,'' Dad said. I lay in my bed, looking out the window at the beauty of the garden in the moonlight, listening to my fate. They could not keep me from seein him. I'd slip out when they did not know it. This would be adventure, and I loved that, I resolved. With this in mind, I fell asleep.

Next morning, they acted as if nothing had happened, outside of Dad's instructions. ''You get out there and take that contraption off the bull. I don't want to hear no excuses. That done, I'll help you set the posts and you can put the fence back up.'' I felt that the gruffness he was displaying was merely an act to prove to Mom he meant to keep his word.

A family meeting was held after that. It began by Mom saying, ''Your Father and I have somethin to tell you, Babe, somethin we want you to listen careful to and mind what we say.'' That was the first time I had heard her refer to Dad as ''your Father,'' and I laughed outright and said, ''Your Father.''

''It's no laughin matter, young lady. What we plan to tell you is ——— '' Mom stiffened, her black eyes smoldering with irritation. ''You tell her, Att, what we have decided,'' she said.

''Well, your Ma has decided, that is, she and I have decided you're to have nothin more to do with young Kunkler. We're just gonna tell him to get, if he shows up around here any more.'' Dad squirmed in his chair and seemed agitated by the words he had just spoken.

Mom's satisfied expression showed her pleasure in what he had said, and waited for him to further tell their decision. Dad went on. ''As a punishment for your behavior yesterday, you can't go to no dances or parties or to town fer three months.''

''Oh, you don't understand, Dad — we ain't 'sparkin,' like you said last night. We like to race our horses and ride cattle. We're just havin fun. He ain't like the other fellers, wantin to make nasty jokes of things. He ain't always wantin to put his hands on me, neither, like the others that Mom thinks is such fine-haired bastards,'' I said, fighting to keep from shouting, I was so angry.

''Maybe you're right, Scrub, but we have agreed on this, so we intend to stick by it. Remember, no dances fer three months,'' he concluded.

If they were to find out I had been coyote-pup hunting with Poke, they would, no doubt, put a ball and chain on me and lock me up for the rest of my life. Shuddering tremors passed through me, thinking of the good chance they had of finding it out, and I quickly banished the thought from mind, as it made me sick with dread.

Three weeks passed and I had gone no place excepting to Hardscrabble and in the mountains, salting the cattle. Mom went after the mail in Old Liz, or sometimes Dad went horse-back after it.

I hadn't heard a word from Poke in this time. To my surprise and somewhat embarrassment, I thought of him almost constantly. Was this love? No, it couldn't be; I was only missing the good times we had when together. His devil-may-care personality acted as a drug to me. I felt free and alive, and in an entirely new world, it seemed, when with him.

I was beginning to believe, from his actions, that Dad was relenting about the corrective measures they had piled upon me. Then, one day after he had returned from town, I overheard him talking to Mom, and I was sure of it. ''I saw the kid downtown,'' he began.

''What kid?'' Mom snapped.

''Poke, the Kunkler boy. You know, Sadie, I think you have that boy pegged wrong. He was friendly as a hound pup and asked about Scrub. Wanted to know if she'd been sick, said she hadn't been around.''

''Did you tell him what you thought about his comin up here when we was gone, breakin everythin to pieces?'' Mom urgently asked.

''Well, no, I hated to mention it. When I get to thinkin back, I've done about the same durn things myself in my younger days, and I ain't much on givin someone hell fer the same tricks I've been guilty of.''

There was silence for a few seconds, and then Mom came back: ''Ridin the stock and breakin the fences and rope ain't so bad. I wouldn't have said a word if it would have been one of the nicer boys in the country, but I don't hold with her goin with that moonshiner.''

''You keep harpin about his moonshinin, Sadie, but do you know that I've been figurin serious on goin into that business myself. I got Scrub to find out from him about how to make it and he consented to show me how it's done. He told her he would even buy me an outfit that's for sale. There's a heap of money to be made in that stuff. Besides that, we could raise a lot more hogs on the mash than we do now, and all fer nothin. That's shot to hell now, with us takin the stand we did with her. It knocks the props out of all my plans,'' he complained.

''You ain't about to lower yourself doin that. The first thing that would happen to you is you'd get caught and took to jail; then everybody would be sayin 'Old Att's a jailbird.' How would you like that? I seen Mamie in town the other day, and she told me Lloyd is intendin to go back to Oregon and work in the woods right away. She says she heard he's quit makin the stuff. He's scared out since the revenuers caught that layout over in the flat woods,'' she prattled. ''If he leaves, I'd be willin fer her to go places again,'' Mom told him.

"You and Mamie's stories she peddles make me have a pain where I sit. You know good and well all this supposed inside dope she tells you is all phony, that she gets it from talkin to a Ouija board. I don't think he's leavin very soon. He's haulin posts now, or is today. Him and Cal are fencin a quarter section of land," Dad informed her.

"Posts!!" I wildly thought. The Kunklers had a bunch of posts they had split out not too far from our ranch.

Next morning, I started for Hardscrabble to regulate the irrigation water. The posts were but a short distance out of my way, so I nonchalantly rode along the little-used road, pretending I was just accidentally going that way. Poke was busy loading posts when I came into sight. When he seen me, he came a few steps to meet me.

"Hello, Honeychild. I was just thinkin about you. How have you been? I was afraid your folks had locked you up. I ain't seen you since I was up there that day, and I was afraid to go see," he confessed.

"Honeychild," he had called me, and I felt my face go crimson to my hair roots. "I've been pretty good, only I can't go nowhere anymore. Can't see you or go to no dances fer three months. I can't even go to town," I explained. For the first time, I felt sorry for myself.

"Well, hell, I seen your old man in town yesterday and he seemed more than friendly. Who's doin this to you, your Mom?" Poke asked.

"More or less. She's after your scalp," I laughed.

"Get down and take a shot with my new pistol," he invited. "I just got it yesterday and it's a pip," he proudly said.

"It is a beauty. That's the kind I'm gonna get some of these days. This would kill a bear, you hit him right," I appraised.

"I bet you can't hit that white spot on the oak yonder," he bantered.

"Think I can't?" And I raised the gun to fire, but quickly lowered it, letting the hammer back in place. "Can't shoot it here — it's no more than a mile straight through to the ranch, and the folks would hear it and guess I'm up to somethin again. Gotta be careful or I'll never get out of the dungeon," I said seriously.

"Oh, hell," he said, seating himself on the pile of posts, and I sat beside him, admiring the pistol and practicing aiming it.

"If the folks will allow it, I'm gonna get one like this right away. I'd rather have one of these than anythin I know of," I confided.

"You seem to let your folks govern every move you make. You'd be buyin it with your own money. Say, talkin about money, I've got some money of yours. I cashed in the bounty on the coyotes," he said. He gave me thirty-five dollars. "I've been keepin it in my pocket, thinkin I'd see you in town," he said.

"You don't think your folks will tell my folks that we went coyote-pup huntin, do you? If they do, I'm as good as a dead pigeon," I said anxiously.

"You never can tell," he answered.

We sat in silence for some time, me sighting the pistol and him deeply engrossed in carving an arrow out of a piece of cedar bark. "Say, how would you like to get married?" Poke asked, not looking up from the carving.

"I don't know. It's accordin to who I was marryin," I said, blushing.

"Well, I've been thinkin, why don't we run off and get married?" he asked again, not looking up from the carving.

"Where would we run off to?" I asked.

"Anywhere. I'm goin back to Oregon as soon as Cal and I get a fence made. You might as well go with me," he said, handing me the finished arrow point.

"The folks would have a S-Q-U-E-A-L-I-N worm. I ain't eighteen yet. But I'll go as soon as I am," I answered.

"Yeah, but that's over a year yet, ain't it?" he asked.

We spent several hours planning to get married when I was of age. "A feller is suppose to give a girl he's engaged to a ring, ain't he?" Poke asked.

"Yeah, I think they most always do, but I couldn't wear a ring if we are gonna keep our runnin off a secret," I reasoned.

"Which would you rather have, a ring or that pistol?" he asked.

"Oh, the pistol," I quickly answered.

"That's what I thought. I believe you're the worst tomboy of a girl I ever saw. That's what I like about you," he added. His eyes fondly caressed me as he said this, and very sweet and gently he kissed me for the first time.

As foolish as it seems, I had an inspiration to run through the woods, jumping about like a kangaroo, I was so happy. This must be love. I had never felt this way before. I fought this crazy impulse and tried to act as normal as possible, while he buckled the pistol belt about my waist.

"Just the fit, Skeeter," he said, stepping back to admire me as if I was a model in a fashion show. I had the feeling that I was the only girl with the distinction of wearing her engagement ring about her waist, but it was as binding as if it was a ring of solid gold, studded with diamonds of fabulous value.

Again he kissed me, as he helped me mount my horse. "Bye, Honeybunch. I'll be out at the forks of the road tomorrow evenin at sundown. If you want to see me, be there," he said.

"Be there come hell or high water," I promised.

15

MY CRUMPLED WORLD

I CAME IN WITH a few head of beef steers which I found back in Choke Cherry Canyon and Snow Shoe Flat. Tied out front by the gate was Poke's bay, and standing by the water trough was Dad and Cal, looking at the steers as I drove them by.

"Where did you find them?" Dad asked.

"Choke Cherry and Snow Shoe," I told him.

"Any more up there?" he asked.

"Just cows and calves and yearlins," I answered.

"I wish you would have brought all of them in. Cal's got a buyer fer all of his cattle and ours, too, if we wanta sell them. I think, with me all bunged up till I can't get out and ride, the sensible thing is get shed of the whole herd. How long do you reckon it would take you to gather everythin?" he asked.

"They're scattered far and wide. Maybe two weeks," I guessed.

"I know it's a big territory and is a hell of a job by yourself. There's not a soul I know of I could hire to help you," Dad lamented.

"I'll tell you what I'll do, Att," Cal offered. "I've sent for Lloyd to come home from Oregon and help me, and we'll come up and gather your cattle as soon as we get ours in." Dad showed pleasure and appreciation at Cal's offer, and said he would be glad to pay for the job. This was a surprising turn of events, and I tried to conceal my feeling of excitement.

Fire and brimstone showed in Mom's eyes at Poke coming to the ranch to help round up our cattle. She sat idly holding the sock she had been mending and began slowly rocking, setting stiff as a chipmunk in her chair. I could read her thoughts and could tell she intended pouncing onto both Dad and I when she got us alone. The encounter was not nearly as rough as I had supposed it would be, because Dad stopped her griping before she started.

"Now, Sadie," he said, "I can see you've got your hackles up and rearin to give me hell over acceptin Cal's offer, but I think it's damn neighborly of him to offer to help us. I don't want to hear one thing you got to say about it," he concluded, with a look in his eyes that he meant every word spoken. Mom's expression was filled with a desire for vengeance, and she muttered something in an undertone, the last of which I heard: "Hang up your hides."

When Poke and Cal came to start our roundup, I was aflutter with excitement. The first time we were by ourselves Poke kissed me, and I was sure he loved me as much as I loved him.

"You ain't forgot about us runnin off, have you?" he asked.

"Heck no, that's all I could think about while you've been gone," I confessed.

"You know," he said, "I don't understand why your Mother dislikes me so, but I'm gonna start playin up to the old gal and see if I have better luck with her."

For more than a week, I and Poke and Cal searched the hills for cattle, some days riding as far as fifty miles. During this time, Poke made himself the "golden haired" boy with Mom. He helped her wash dishes of evenings while I would be down milking the cows. Mornings, he was up grinding the coffee and slicing ham and stoking the range with wood. Mom was being won over, I could tell. She smiled to herself and at him as she seen him do these tasks in such a workmanlike manner. When she spoke to him now, she did not address him with "Hey you," or speak of him as "that kid," or "what's his name." He was "Poke" to her, now.

The evening of the last day of riding, when the cattle was all accounted for and corraled, Mom had a special supper prepared for us to celebrate a task well done.

Returning to the house after doing chores, I seen Mom, Dad, and Cal setting on the front porch in the easy chairs, chatting. Poke was replenishing glasses they each held, from a pitcher. "Must be havin pink lemonade," I thought. Entering the house from the back way, I found Poke was back in the kitchen, busy refilling the pitcher.

"What are you makin?" I asked.

"Shhh — I've got your Mom drinkin hooch," he said, with a grin.

"Does she know what she's drinkin?" I asked.

"Yes, but she don't know how much," he said, as he poured a generous amount of moonshine into cherry juice and added sugar and the juice of a lemon.

"Where did the stuff come from?" I asked, indicating the jug of liquor.

"Some of my brew. It's good stuff, more than a hundred proof. Cal and your Dad and I have been havin a snort out of it once in a while. I think maybe your Dad dips a little when I ain't around, from the account that's left," Poke said, holding the jug up to scrutinize its contents.

"Want some?" he asked.

189

"Just juice," I answered.

"Gotta go fill their glasses again," he said, and carried the pitcher to the porch. I followed with a glass of cherry juice.

"Bottoms up," Poke said cheerfully. They all drank the little remaining in their glasses, and were ready for another round.

Mom's eyes were a bit glassy, and there was a distinct white ring around her mouth, and her upper lip seemed too long. "Sure's good drink," she said, as Poke filled her large glass to the brim.

"Down the hatch," Dad exclaimed. His eyes sparkled and his voice was a bit loud. He and Mom were talking at once and nothing they said made much sense.

"Here, have another drink," Poke said, after Mom's glass was empty.

"No, I don't think I'd better, Poke."

"Oh, come on, it will put hair on your chest. It won't do you any harm," he coaxed.

"I know when I've got enough," she answered, as she arose on legs a little unsteady and went indoors humming "Tipperary." I followed to see what she planned to do. She got in bed and was gazing wide-eyed at the ceiling.

"Honey, I'm full as a goose," she said, not shifting her stare from the ceiling, and hiccoughed quietly.

"Good night, Mom," I said, and closed the door.

Next day, the cattle buyer arrived and had a cowboy with him that I soon learned to avoid. He was a brash individual with a vulgar mind, and I had the feeling he was a gink kind of a fellow.

With these men's arrival, I was brought to face the fact that selling the cattle was taking from me all the enjoyment I had known through the past years. Until now, I had not known I liked them with all my heart and soul. As unworldly as I was, my heart told me I could never regain the wonderful fun I had enjoyed caring for these animals, regardless of where I should go, or if I lived to be a hundred years old. A part of my soul moved away as the long line of cattle crowded through the lane and set their course north over Tamarack Mountain. Dad would not let me go, on account of the buyer's cowboy.

I sat on the uppermost limb of the old oak on the knoll and watched through tear-dimmed eyes, glad that I was saying farewell from my familiar perch, glad there was no one around to question why the tears. Not that I was ashamed of crying, but it seemed more befitting I should grieve here alone in the one spot I could call my heaven.

I had barely recovered from giving the cattle up when another grief-striking blow came. The folks sold Hardscrabble.[14]

It was bought merely for the hay and pasture it afforded. If it could have passed into the possession of someone who would make their home there, they too would have learned to love it as I, and perhaps add to its magnitude.

Poke went back to his job in Oregon after the cattle had been delivered at Fall River. I was lonely without him around to take me places. Now that the cattle were gone, except for twenty or so cows, there was little to do. I did help with the sheep, driving them to winter range that fall.

Poke came home just before Christmas. He had bought another car just before coming home. I was so enthused, I thought it rode like a feather and purred like a kitten. Really, it rode like a bucking bronco and sounded like a thrashing machine as it went bouncing over the road.

Christmas, as usual, was celebrated with a "blow out" at

14. Hardscrabble was sold to Att's brother, Jefferson Davis Aldridge.

Whitmore, and all the hill people were there.

Most every day I rode to town for the mail. Poke would meet me there and we would ride home together. We target practiced with our pistols and ran horse races and, once in a while, talked of getting married the coming fall, at which time I would be eighteen.

16

LAST HUNT

NE MORNING, about the last day of January, Fritz Lukenbacker called on the telephone, saying that a panther had killed a newborn calf in his barnyard the night before. Would we bring our dogs and trail him down?

Dad had been moping since the cattle and Hardscrabble had been sold. Gone was the spark and determination he had always displayed. Only a few minutes before Fritz's call, he had said to Mom and I, "Guess I'm about ready fer the boneyard. I feel tolerable well some days, but I peter out easy. Just don't amount to nothin no more." He sighed at his situation.

Mom had answered the phone when it rang. "That's too bad, Fritz, but Att's in no shape to go trackin a lion over the hills. He just ain't well enough," she said.

Dad's eyes glowed eagerly, he stood up, saying, "The hell I ain't! Tell him Scrub and I will be there in an hour." He squared his shoulders and marched into the bedroom, coming out with his pistol strapped on and his rifle in his hand. "You get our raincoats, Sadie." To me he said, "Get our horses saddled and be ready to go."

193

Between two and three inches of snow blanketed the ground, and it was sure to be much deeper at Fritz's place, as it was some higher elevation there. Mounted, we called the dogs and discovered that only one was home; so we took out with one dog "Tip," a small but good hunter. He was a fox terrier and bull, mixed.

"That damn 'Zar' — he would be gone sparkin," Dad complained. Putting Tip behind my saddle, we rode along. It was necessary to save the little dog's strength if we were to tree that cat with this one dog. We took the panther's trail where he had gone over the fence when leaving the barn lot. We followed his tracks, which took us across the five forks of Dickenson Creek above Lonca Meadows. He hadn't stopped but once; that was to roll in the snow. On the north rim of Bear Creek, we at last jumped him. He had bedded in some big rocks which overhung each other, producing a dry place out of the snow. Tip winded him and Dad told him to go, and the chase began.

The ridge from which the cat was jumped continued on into a low saddle; then up into some broken, benchy country, heavy-timbered in places with thickets of small fir and pine; then, on to more big rocks and big timber.

Tip began barking "treed" back in a cove, and we hurried the horses up the steep mountain to get where he was. Long before we came in sight of this place, we heard the dog begin yipping and running in pursuit again, and we knew the cat had jumped. Back on a bench, we heard Tip begin barking "treed" again, and spurred ahead, confident we would get there in time to shoot the cat. It was no use; the same thing happened. Tip was unable to keep the wise old monarch treed.

"That damn Zar. If he was here, they'd keep that bastard up a tree. It's just like him to run off when we need him," Dad said.

On and on we went, the cat treeing and jumping, until we

were into the headwaters of both Bear Creek and Camp Creek. Again, we were in bench slide country. Tip was almost exhausted when Dad called him back, and he lay in the snow, panting. Despite the coldness and the feather-like dry snow that was drifting down, the horses were white with lather. A few minutes rest, and Tip wanted to go again. After a time, we could hear him barking "treed."

"The only way we're goin to get that smart old cougar is outsmart him. I'll circle around and get where I can watch that bare ridge yonder, and get a bullet into him. After I've had time to get set, you go on up and jump him, and I'm likely to get some shots. If you get in range with your pistol, shoot the daylights out of him," Dad said, as we parted.

I waited, then rode cautiously up the hillside. The horse's footsteps muffled in the snow, I was in closer range than we had gotten before. There, about a hundred yards above me, I seen the big cat, skillfully hanging on the side of a sugar pine tree. He was around thirty feet above the ground, intently looking down at the dog. Keeping my eyes upon him, I continued up the hill. If I did not attract his attention until I was closer, I might at least cripple him with a shot from my pistol.

Just then, my horse found it necessary to blow his nose and let out a blast that resounded. In a split second, the panther hurled himself, a yellow streak, toward the ground. I fired one shot as he flitted down, and again as he leaped into the brush nearby.

Near the tree I found a tuft of fur, and across the hill I came upon three drops of blood in the snow. I had only grazed him, but felt proud that I had done that, he was such a fast target. It had been like shooting at a streak of lightning. The excitement set my nerves jumping, bringing on a sudden attack of "panther fever." I might ride him down, so I spurred off on his trail.

Then I seen Dad, silhouetted against the cloudy, grey horizon on top of the ridge. A sharp report from his rifle, and he went racing along the hilltop like a madman, riding to gain a spot where he could see the cat again. Yesterday, I would have wagered he would never ride like that again. His horse was running as if its life depended upon it, and Dad was spurring for more speed.

After the shot, the cat circled below me, keeping to the brush thicket. In there, I found I could make more headway on foot, so I left my horse and hurried along, thinking of getting another shot. A while of this, and I discovered the big cat was playing hide and seek with me. He was traveling in a circle, following precisely the same trail every turn. Instead of being in front of me, he was behind, but keeping well covered.

Dad called, and I found him back where I had left my horse. "We ain't gonna get him this way. Tip has 'flew the coop,' " he said, indicating the little dog, who was laying on his belly, panting as if he would never get his breath. Water was streaming from his eyes. He was exhausted. "I'll tell you what I think we orter do," Dad thoughtfully said.

"What's that, let him go to the devil and go home?" I asked.

"Christ, no! We'll get that cat if it takes a week. I ain't never let one get away from me before, and I ain't fixin to do it now. This is no time to give up the ghost and pull in your horns. You go home and get Zar, and go by Ben's and get that yeller dog of his, and get back here," he said.

"I can't be back much before dark. We're to hell and gone over here, you know."

"I know, but you fan that nag right along and ride another horse back. That way you should be back some before dark and we'll tree him quick. That's all it will take, is enough dogs. Get goin," he urged. "Maybe you better bring my toothache medicine — my tooth is jumpin to beat hell. I'll get his trail straightened out while you're gone and find out where he's figurin to go. I'll be waitin fer you someplace. You'll see my tracks,'' he added.

I spilled off the mountain, across all the canyons and ridges that lay between me and home like the devil was hot on my trail. I found that Zar had not returned home from his courting trip.

Packing a few sandwiches and a few oats in a sack, I saddled Steamboat and hurried up to Ben's to get his dog. When he called, his dog ''Catch-em'' did not come. Ben found that he had crawled to the lowest place under the house and refused to come out, due to the fact that Ben had, that day, given him a bath in sheep-dip, for fleas.

To return with no dogs was unthinkable, but it was the only thing to do. Arriving in the locality of where I had left Dad, it was a short hour before dark. I rode to a spot where I was sure he could hear me, if he was still on the Bear and Camp Creek side of the mountain. I expanded my voice as loudly as possible and gave out with several shouts of ''Yeah-hoo,'' but got no answer. I guessed he had crossed the ridge and was now someplace high up in Snow Creek Canyon.

Cutting across country, not bothering to try and follow his trail, I reached the top of the canyon wall, where I could see into the deep, wild canyon of Snow Creek. Each tree stood like a snow-capped sentinel. There I found his trail, where his horse had plowed through the deepened snow. Again, I loudly called, but got no answer — just the echo and reecho of my voice as it bounced from canyon rim to canyon rim.

Following his tracks down the canyon wall, I found that he had crossed Snow Creek and up the other wall. The cat's tracks were visible even in the semidarkness. Topping that rim, the country leveled out into flat, level expanses, which were timbered with giant pine trees with but little underbrush. Not too far, I seen the glow of Dad's fire. There, in a place ideally designed by nature, I found him. He was back under the protection of some overhanging rocks, and had started burning a dead tree which grew within feet of the shelter. The flames licked high on the big tree as I rode up out of the darkness.

"Where is the dogs? Didn't you get them?" he asked.

"No. Zar ain't home yet, and Ben sheep-dipped his dog and he'd gone under the house and refused to come out."

"Well, fritters, I thought fer sure you'd at least fetch one back with you," he said, and set thoughtfully thinking. I gave the horses the oats and Dad and I nibbled on the sandwiches, sharing with the little dog.

"Tooth achin bad?" I asked, noticing he was keeping his mouth closed exceptionally tight and running his fingers through his hair as if in pain.

"A little," he muttered, and applied more medicine from the vial I had brought.

We slouched down against the rocks to await the coming of tomorrow, enjoying the warmth of the fire and listening to the conversational crackle of the fire. An occasional star glittered in the heavens, but without doubt the storm was far from settled.

I drifted to sleep, and was awakened by Dad's saying, "Scrub, are you awake?"

"Yeah," I answered. "What do you want?"

"My tooth's getting worse. Do you reckon you could take my pliers and yank the damn thing out?"

"Oh no! I can't do that," I said, a shuddering tremor passing through me. I was startled at his asking such an unthought-of thing.

"Infernal Hell, kid, there ain't nothin to it. I can stand having it yanked a lot better than this pain I got now. Here, yank her out," he said, offering me the pliers. "It's this bastard, here," he said.

"Too dark, I can't see which one," I answered.

"You don't have to see. I'll get the pliers fastened on and you pull," he said, agony in his voice.

I took hold of the handles and he muttered, "Now, just sashay it back and forth hard to loosen it up, then pull fer all that's in you. But don't get haphazard and break the others out," he instructed.

It was an upper front tooth, and by the feeble light from the fire, I could see that it was bleeding. He had been trying to pull it while I had been asleep. I suddenly grew faint, my knees buckling from thinking of this thing he expected me to do.

"I can't do it, Dad. Let us start home, where you will be dry and warm," I said.

"Hell, no!" he said, taking the pliers off the tooth. "A feller expects you to have a little savvy and guts, but I ask you to do one thing that's a little out of ordinary and your tail flies up and you say, 'I can't.' What kind of a kid are you?" he asked, anger in his voice. "A tooth ain't any more than a doo-dad stuck in your jawbone. It will come right out if you surge on it quick and hard."

I felt sick and did not answer.

"I'll do it myself," he said, and in the darkness I could not see what he was doing. A snapping sound and a slight moan. "The damn thing was clinched," he mumbled.

"Get it?" I asked.

"You're damn right," he answered.

The grayness of a new day appeared soon after this. Snow began falling, and the quietness of the snow-laden trees was broken by a vicious wind coming from the north.

"We'd better get home, hadn't we?" I urged. "Your face is swelled bad," I said.

"Well," he hesitated, "I reckon so, but I think we'll take a little circle around first and see if that damn cat stopped anywhere close and hung out fer the night. I was right on him last night when I stopped,'' he said.

We tracked on, and the tracks were rapidly being filled with snow. Several miles, and the cat was still traveling, had neither stopped nor slackened his pace. Our horses were chest-deep in snow, and it was pounding down until you couldn't see but a short distance.

''It ain't no use, Scrub, that guy is headed fer Battle Creek as sure as you're born and he ain't stoppin until he gets into that canyon of iron. We'll turn back now,'' he regretfully said. He was saddened at his failure. ''I'll tell you, if I was ten years younger and Old Shep or some of the other dogs I've had was alive, I'd get him yet.'' Old Shep had been dead several years.

We arrived back at the ranch in the afternoon, the snow storm still raging. Mom did not scold, as she would have done back in the years before. She saw that we had not gotten the panther. Her actions expressed her feelings of sadness that Dad had, at last, failed on a hunting trip. Her thoughts were only sorrow for him in his old age.

Without a word, after coffee and a little food, he went to bed, sick from a body overcome by age, and sick with defeat — a thing new to him in his many years of life.

17

IT COST BUT FIFTY CENTS

YOU'RE WANTED on the telephone," Mom called to me.

"I'll be there," I said, thinking it was Poke calling.

"Hello there." I said.

"Hello. This is Mabel. I'm calling to invite you to a sewing party and chit-chat we girls are having tomorrow at my house. I thought you might like to come." This was startling, to be asked to join this group of girls. They had held these get-togethers for years, and had not invited me before now.

"Well, I ain't got nothin else to do, so I'll be there," I accepted.

"Bring whatever you happen to be working on at the present time," she said, meaning fancy work. I worried, wondering what I might do to cover up my ignorance about sewing. At last, I decided on taking a tatting shuttle and "outshining" the whole bunch. I could make a straight, single edging that looked good to me.

Among the other girls, I felt out of place. I had come horseback and wore my Levis, while the others had either come in buggies or by car, and were dressed in crisply starched and beautifully ironed dresses. My hands were dirty, but I hesitated to ask where to wash them. It won't matter much, I thought, as I took out my shuttle and pink and white variegated thread, and began tatting.

The conversation, at first, concerned the fancy work each was doing. It drifted into small talk about their boy friends.

"My Joe, he brings me the most exquisite gifts," Susanne said. "Last week he surprised me with the darlingest watch. See," she said, displaying a small wrist watch. "Last evening he came with a beautiful, big box of candy. The price tag he had forgotten to remove. It cost five dollars," she boasted.

"That's not big, at all," spoke up Isabelle. "Henry did the same thing, and it was marked twelve dollars."

Candy. Poke had never bought me candy. I was beginning to think he was as tight as Dad about spending money. I'd tell him about the boxes of candy the other fellers bought their girls.

Toward evening, I had about a foot of tatting done and, with shame, I noticed how uneven, scraggly, and dirty it was. Hastily, I rolled it around the shuttle. I put it in my pocket so the others could not see it.

The young ladies began showing their achievements of the day. Undoubtedly, they were geniuses, despite my opinion of them, with their scatterbrain talk and make-believe ways.

Hells bells, I thought, I'll bet there ain't a one of the bunch that would know what to do fer a horse with bots, a bloated cow, or a hog with kidney worms. If you did not know how to cope with commonplace things like that, you were not very smart, to my way of measuring. "I believe I'll be startin home," I nonchalantly stated.

"Oh, must you go so soon? Do come again," Mabel said, in her small, sedate voice, but not meaning a word she had spoken.

"If I find time, I'll be back; but you see, I'm awful busy with my knittin at home," I answered, meaning it as a joke.

"I'd love to see it sometime," she came back, and I wondered if she sincerely thought I sat in the house and did stitchwork. However, that was my last attendance at their sewing parties.

In a joking way, I told Poke about the sewing party and what a "dingbat" I'd been for going and revealing how I had been trying to outdo the other girls in fancy work.

"You know, I think they was tellin untruths about their boy friends. They say that their fellers bring them big boxes of candy every week and that they cost from five to twelve dollars. I just don't believe what they said. The first place, they couldn't hold that much candy every week," I added, hoping he would maybe take a hint and buy a box for me.

"I was thinkin just the other day I should get you some candy, but darned if I can remember to buy it," he matter-of-fact said, and the issue was closed.

The next Saturday, we were passing through town and he stopped the car, saying, "I've got to run in here a minute," and went into the store. In seconds, he was back. With a beaming grin he handed me a green- and red-striped paper sack, a small one. "All for you, Sweetpea," he said, with a smile. Inside was a handful of old-fashioned peppermint candy. "Next time, I'll maybe get a whole box," he said, as we drove on.

Next time, true to his word, he brought me a whole box. I set it aside, after admiring the lavender box and the bow on its top. But as soon as he had gone home, I ran to look at the box to see if it had cost five or twelve dollars.

Marked boldly on the bottom was "fifty cents."

I didn't mind too much that it had cost so little, but kept the thought running through my mind that in a short while I'd be married to this geniune, dyed-in-the-wool "Squire Skimp" — and what then?

203

18

GLAMOUR ON THE HOOF

EBRUARY AND LAMBING time came, and I went down to the sheep camp to help Al and Ivy. The lambing range took in most of the territory between Anderson and Cottonwood. Headquarters was on the Aloha Ranch, near the Sacramento River. Al and Ivy lived in a shack that provided but few comforts in life. A herder's life is a very severe one, I found, even on the valley range.

Lambing lasted about one month, and in this time none of us got the proper amount of sleep. At lambing's conclusion, Mom came after me, and I was thankful that I wouldn't be needed with the sheep until the drive to mountain range began.

On our way home, I seen a car coming to meet us and recognized it as Poke's car. "Stop! There's Poke!" I exclaimed.

Mom pretended she did not hear, she was so preoccupied with guiding Liz over the road. We were traveling at a ridiculous speed, and there was only time to wave and call "hello." We flitted around a bend and were out of sight.

"Why didn't you stop?" I asked.

"Didn't hear you in time. Anyhow, I wanta get home. Ain't got time to doddle around," she muttered.

"Is there gonna be a dance tonight?" I inquired.

"Don't know," she mumbled again.

"Don't suppose Poke will be back in time to take me if there is," I lamented, half to myself.

We had just driven into the yard when Poke drove in beside us. "Say, do you want to go to a rodeo?" he asked, by way of greeting.

"Sure, when is it?" I asked.

"Tomorrow. I was on my way to the sheep camp to ask you when I met you on the road. Why didn't you stop?" he asked.

"Well, you know Mom. When she's under the wheel, there's nothin that stops her, outside of a blowed tire or out of gas," I laughingly answered, glancing at Mom to see if what I'd said seemed funny to her.

She had not heard; she had the hood up and was busy with a wrench, removing the magneto post.

"Need help?" Poke asked, as he sidled over to view what she was doing.

She held the magneto post up for inspection before she answered. "Nope."

"Broke?" Poke asked.

"Nope," she came back.

"Dirty?" he inquired.

"Naw," she mumbled, as she tightened it into place, slammed the hood down, and hurriedly walked up the path.

Poke looked puzzled and asked, "What was she doin that fer?"

"Nosin, waitin to hear what we might say," I answered.

Morning and he came early, but I was ready and waiting when

he rounded the turn, the motor roaring, the muffler wide open, announcing his arrival with the nerve-wracking toot of his exhaust horn. ''Why does that boy have to be so rowdy?'' Mom asked, with a scowl.

''That ain't so, he ain't rowdy,'' I defended.

''Plurt! Plurt!'' again came the rattle-scream of the horn. I ran out to the car and, in a cloud of dust, we went racing down the lane on our way to the rodeo. This was the experience of my life, as I had never attended a rodeo. The affair was being held at Bella Vista, a small village northeast of Redding.

People were arriving at the grounds by droves when we got there. The atmosphere was tense with the excitement of the day. Horse-buckers hurried about the grounds, dressed in their flashiest riding costumes. A band was playing loudly.

Angora chaps were in fad. The long, curly, mohair was dyed colors varying from black to orange to brown, or left its natural color of silver-white. Here, a man wore a pair colored a shocking, bright pink. To further enhance his glamour, he wore a purple shirt, green sleeve-holders and scarf, a black ten-gallon hat, and black britches; also, a wide, back-supporting leather belt, studded with silver conchos. Matching this, he had leather cuffs, which fit from elbow to wrist. His horse was black, and to further enhance its appearance, its bridle was decorated with green ribbon and conchos to match the color of his green saddle-blanket and scarf. To me, this entire thing was ''glamour on the hoof.'' He rode by and I stared, hardly believing what I saw.

Poke nudged me. ''Your mouth's open,'' he said, which brought me back to reality.

The show had not started, as yet. People thronged about the pink lemonade stand, which was near the barbecue pit. Bottles containing a drink more refreshing than lemonade conspicuously showed in the back pockets of two-thirds of the men there. In the shade of the oak trees these merrymakers sat on the grass, shooting dice, boxing hats, and Indian wrestling.

Before the rodeo got underway, there were several fist fights. One man was so badly cut with a broken bottle, he was taken to a doctor. The law, if it was there, did not present itself.

The opening of the rodeo came. The man with pink chaps galloped his horse to the center of the arena and fired six shots from his six-shooter. His horse kneeled and the man bowed to the crowd, then rode helter-skelter back to the corrals. The first saddle bronc came bucking from where he had been saddled, the cowboy on him spurring high on the bronc's neck and shoulders. He whooped like a locoed Indian and fanned the horse with his hat. The rider was Bob Stuadnick, better known as "Bronco Bob."

During the day's performance, we saw Tye Stokes, "Montana Red," Jessie Stall, Patty Ryne, Hugh Strickland, "Soda Water Bill," "Bronco Bob's" wife, Ann, and many others. Ann made a ride, I believe, equal to any of the men's. She was colorful in a leather riding skirt, offset by the glamourous trappings worn by celebrated women rodeo performers of that era.

Besides riding broncs and bulls and roping, "Montana Red" did a spectacular act — trick riding on a bareback horse. I was deeply impressed with this, and determined to try doing the things he did when I got home.

No seats were provided for the spectators. People watched the show from any vantage point they found. We, among others, sat on the top rail of the arena fence.

Toward the end of the show, I had to go. Supposing there was no privy, I entered a pasture which looked as if it held places of privacy. I found a spot which seemed to afford the shelter I desired, but to my dismay, at almost the fatal moment, I heard a giggle and a laugh and discovered, in the brush nearby, a courting and drinking party was going on. Shocked over what I had seen, I hurried further into the bushes. Returning to the rodeo grounds, I noticed women walking to and from a frame structure covered with burlap. Tacked to its door was a shingle sign which read, ''Ladies.'' A woman emerged as I passed and I heard her say to another about to enter, ''It's out of catalogs in there, not even a cob.''

''I've seen such,'' said the other, waving a newspaper.

Back on the fence with Poke, he bluntly asked, ''Where have you been?''

''Walkin,'' I answered.

''It was a hell of a time fer you to go walkin. You've missed the best part of the show. There was a dinger of a fight a minute ago. One feller gouged the other's eye practically out,'' he said, still excited by what he had seen.

For some days after the rodeo, I practiced trick riding in the fashion I had seen ''Montana Red'' do at the show. The seemingly reckless way he had gone about it looked easy, or so I thought at seeing it. I would learn to be a trick rider if it killed me. I took spills that shook my bones, and I had black and blue spots as big as a bucket on my body. I was gimpy in one leg and I was sure several ribs were cracked. Through this pain I suffered in silence, because I was learning to become a trick rider on the sly from Mom and Dad. They must never find out unless I could perfect the stunt.

19

WICKED BARBS OF LIFE

DAD SPENT MOST of the time now laying on the cot or seated in his comfort chair on the front porch. The aches and pains of old age dulled the sparkle of his once clear, sharp eyes. But this had not stopped him thinking. He fretted that money was not coming in like it had before we sold the cattle.

"You know, Scrub, we've got to start doin somethin to get money comin in again. Ain't even a cream check comin anymore. I believe you'd better get all the cows in and start milkin and sellin cream. Get all the cream out of them you can wihout stintin the calves. I ain't plannin on takin money out of the savins, cause it will go hellbent if I do," he said, with a troubled look. Listening to him, you would have gotten the idea he was ready for the poor house.

"Don't you intend for us to start makin booze?" I asked.

"Hell yes, I'm rearin to get into anythin that makes money."

"Poke has brought in a lot more barrels and made himself a big concern. He says if you want his old rig you can have it. Says he will move it in and show us how to run off the first batch, if you say so."

211

"You just bet I'll say so. He's a good kid fer takin us into his confidence and offerin such a thing. Your Mom keeps sayin it's wrong doins, that I'll make the hoose-gow; but I'm willin to run the risk," he said with a laugh, and spat far into the yard, hitting a stone dead center.

"Do you know Uncle Bill's been shinin fer a year or more?" I asked.

"No. Hell, no. How do you know?" he asked in disbelief.

I could not disclose the fact I had seen him, so I said, "I've heard tell it's so."

"That old scalawag. Why ain't he told me? I wondered where he got money to buy a horse and saddle, and that silk, flowered vest, and that hell of a big new watch chain. I never knowed it was in the old son of a gun," Dad said, acting as if he was proud of his brother. "Where is he doin all this?" he asked.

"I hear it's down in that broken country, where Mill Creek forks with South Cow Creek. There's a spring there where they hang out called Shot Gun Springs," I answered.

"Do you know where it is?" he asked.

"No. Gee, no. I ain't got no idea," I stuttered, fearing somehow he had heard about Poke's and my coyote hunting trip.

"I'd like to go down and find that place, ride right in on Bill and watch his eyes bulge," he laughed.

"I'd be afraid to do that, cause him and Sim Sontag are in cahoots. If that guy seen someone snoopin around, he ain't to be fooled with and might blow a hole in you as big as your fist," I cautioned.

"Yeah, you're right. A feller had better be lookin a little bit out where that guy is concerned, and play close to his belly. I'd better forget it and stay up here on my own dung hill," he decided. "I've been setting here, thinkin: when we get that still, we'll put it in the tater house like we planned. You can make the stuff while I stay here on the porch and watch for suspicious-lookin characters. We'll fix a wire runnin out there and tie a cow bell on it, so if someone shows up, I can give it a jingle and you'll know somethin's up and lay low. No one would ever suspect you of moonshinin,'' he added thoughtfully. The wildness and unlawfulness of this adventure was to my liking. I could hardly wait to get into action.

"You had better get out there and dung the place out, and we'll run water in from spring ditch and get our warnin signal fixed and be ready to move the barrels and the contraption in,'' he planned.

Two days later, the tater house was spick and span, and the warning signal, bell and all, was ready for use.

Mom was helping me put the pipeline in for water. She was athrob with anguish and misgivings over this new and lawless thing we were planning to launch into.

"I can't see what your Dad's thinkin about, gettin mixed up in such a shameful business. He's a darn muttonhead where money is concerned. This thing of you makin that stuff cause you won't be suspected is what gets my goat,'' she stormed. "I've been in a jangle with him ever since I heard about it, but it's like pourin water on a duck's back. All I can get out of him is, 'she wants to do it, and you just wait and see the pile of money we'll make.' Him and you are just bullheaded Aldridges, is all I can say. What runs me about bugs is, what is people like Mamie gonna say when you two get pinched?'' she faunched.

"Oh, to hell with Mamie! She's nothin but chaff, just dirty chaff. Her morals ain't too pure if you could see her in the right light, Mom,'' I broke in. "You know, it's said that she was once caught red-handed stealin a bunch of horses,'' I reminded.

"Oh, flitter-flatter, that's just loose talk of your Dad's,'' she defended.

"It ain't only him that says it, and I think it's so,'' I argued.

213

"You believe it if you like, but what I'm against is you two gettin yourselves drug off to jail and fer somethin where there's just a piddlin amount of money to be made and runnin such a big risk," she said, her words coming out like a torrent.

"Piddlin amount!" I ejaculated. "Poke's makin eight hundred dollars every four days. He's set up with an outfit that comes and gets all he can run off, and he's fixed it so they will come here, too," I explained.

"That much!" she exclaimed. "At that rate, we'd be coinin the dough. I could buy a new car and a lot of stuff I've been cravin to have. I want one of those new-fandangled kind of cars. One with a shiftin rod and a self-starter and battery in it," she planned, with a look of pure fanaticism in her black eyes. "When we get started good and I get the hang of the thing, I'm fer gettin one a lot bigger than the one we're gettin," she excitedly said, referring to the still. Glancing about the tater house, she said, "What else could I do to have the place more ready when we start?"

"Well, it's a must to have a big paddle, like fer a boat. You stir mash with that," I explained.

"I'll get right at it and hack one out and smoothed down," she said, her voice pleasant.

Before we got started in this money-making business, Dad took seriously ill and was confined to bed. Agnes came and persuaded him to go home with her and see a doctor. She lived in Dunsmuir at that time. Mom went with them to nurse Dad. I was almost eighteen years old, so they said I was "big enough" to stay at the ranch and care for things.

As they were almost ready to depart, Dad spoke to me confidentially: "Now, while I'm gone, you ask around and find out if anybody's got a bunch of 'piggie' brood sows fer sale. If you

214

find some, tell them to hold on about sellin, that I'll be home in a few days and want to go into hogs in a big way. Don't get anythin moved in before I get back. I've got to be here fer your lookout man.''

They had been gone a few days when the truth dawned upon me that I was undoubtedly the world's worst cook. Mom had left food cooked, and when this was gone I was compelled to cook or go hungry. It was startling how little I knew. To fry eggs taxed my culinary knowledge to its utmost. This was a frightful awakening. I was to be married in a short while, and knew hardly enough to boil water. How a woman kept from killing herself cooking was a mystery to me. After cooking not more than four snacks for myself, I had numerous cuts and burns on my hands. It appeared as if I might have been stirring in the fire with my hands, and maybe got mixed up in a sausage grinder.

I went on long horseback rides every day, and done the chores about the ranch. Poke and I had gone to several dances, and to the circus in Redding.

Two weeks passed and no word had come from the folks. By this time the kitchen, in fact the entire house, was a disheveled mess. Mom was going to have a squealing worm if she come home and seen how I had burned things in her pots and pans. The dishes were not washed, nor had a floor been swept since she had gone.

Sunday, Poke invited me to his house for dinner. Gladly I accepted, although my intentions had been to clean and wash everything in the house that day. ''I can do that tomorrow,'' I decided. Poke's Mother was a good cook. This was the first time since Mom had gone I had actually had anything fit to eat.

In the afternoon, everybody was going swimming. ''I can't swim. I'll watch,'' I said.

215

"Heck no, I'll teach you!" Poke remonstrated. "Get this bathin suit on, everyone is ready to go," he said.

Bathing suit! I had not had one on in my life, had seen but a few. The folks had swum in old overalls. I was hurried into the guest bedroom to change into the suit and was shocked by my reflection in the mirror. This was indecent. I could not face all those people with this scant thing on.

"Hurry, Skeeter," someone called.

Something must be done. Bringing my stocking tops up to meet the legs of the swimming suit, I pinned them there, slipped a long-tailed, slipover sweater on, and was ready to go. They eyed my silly get-up when I emerged from the room.

A lady in the group said, as we were walking to the pool, "What have you got that sweater on for in this warm weather?"

"You should see me in this suit. I'm practically naked," I half-whispered.

"That's all right, everyone has on a swim suit like that, and no one notices how bare the other is. Take that sweater off, you're dripping with sweat. Take the stockings off, too," she commanded.

Despite what I thought was better judgment, off they came. Above all in my mind was Dad's disapproval if he could see me.

After the swim, I found it hard to leave the party and go home to do the chores. A freezer of ice cream had been made and everyone was enjoying this, when the phone rang, and Poke's Mother answered. Suddenly I was all attention when I heard her say, "Yes, she's here. Skeet, your Mother's on the phone and wants to talk to you."

Oh, those dirty dishes — why hadn't I stayed home and washed them? She seemed vexed, as I thought she would be.

"Yes, I'll be right home," I promised. "How is Dad?"

"Not too good. He didn't come home. The doctor wants to examine him further," she said.

It was nearing dark when I got home, although I jogged my horse right along all the way. Mom was seated in her rocker on the porch and I knew I was in for a lecture.

"Hello, Mom," I began.

"Hello," she answered, but said nothing more.

"Been home long?" I asked, striving to ease the tension.

"Quite a spell," she answered through stiff lips, and went on rocking. "Long enough to see that you ain't washed a dish, swept, or done nothin while I was gone," she added, as she rocked. "When you get your chores done, you march into that kitchen and wash every blasted thing you've dirtied. A little soap, water, and elbow grease won't do the entire house any harm," she said, her black eyes snapping in anger.

"Yes, Mom," I agreed. Although it would take me most of the night to clean everything, the penalty could have been worse.

The day before she was to leave and go back to Agnes' house to see Dad and perhaps bring him home, Al came by the ranch to pick up supplies for the sheep camp. I was not home the time he spent there. When I returned, he and Mom had turned every horse on the ranch out on the open range.

"What did you do with the horses?" I asked Mom.

"Albert and I turned them outside. We've gotta save the feed for the sheep when he brings them here this fall. We couldn't see no sense in havin them here, because we don't use them since the cattle are gone."

"Don't use them! I ride every single day, and you both know it!" I exploded. "You two think you're big shots since Dad's up there. You just wait till he gets home, he'll show you which side of your cake's dough," I said, my voice choked with emotion, my eyes full of tears. "He's the only one that keeps things runnin right around here," I added.

"Watch your tongue, young lady," she said.

"It's true!" I exclaimed. "You just wait, he'll stop all this little 'behind the back' stuff that's been goin on since he's been sick. I'm goin tomorrow and find my horse and bring him back," I told her.

"No you ain't. You leave that horse where he is," she answered. She spoke with more determination than I had ever known her to. With Dad gone, it left me with a feeling of defeat.

"You and Al just done this little underhanded stunt so as to stop me ridin," I accused.

"Well," was all she said.

I would be stuck here on the ranch with no transportation for a long time, as she would not be back until the doctor said Dad was well.

Next morning, she planned to go back to Dunsmuir. Before leaving, she lectured me on how she expected me to behave.

"You go see the neighbors around as often as you like, but don't go runnin all over the country," she said pointedly. What she was meaning was not to go down to Poke's ranch again. A plan was already forming in my mind, and as soon as the dust settled from her leaving, I planned to carry it out.

No sooner than she had gone, I went down the valley to a neighbor's and asked them if they would let me borrow one of their saddle horses, and they agreed. I had no misgivings of this thing I was doing. This wasn't getting my horse back, and she had said nothing about borrowing one. Having this horse was just a temporary thing. Dad would make quick work of this selfish idea of turning my horse out when he got home.

Time went by, and letters and phone calls from Mom informed me that Dad was no better. One day, she came home unexpectedly and broke the news to me that they had decided to sell the stock we had left and move to where Dad's doctor was.[15]

One by one, the animals were sold. We packed the things she thought we would need to start housekeeping in the new place.

---

15. Att sold his lease on the Schearer farm to one of Lloyd Kunkler's brothers.

20

GONE ARE THE DAYS

WITHOUT TELLING MOM where I was going, I saddled the borrowed mare and rode to Hardscrabble. For what reason, I did not know. Slowly, I rode past the cow barn above the ranch, on across the ford where Dad had so nearly drowned. It brought back vivid thoughts of that memorable day. Although the creek, at this time of year, was a pleasant, placid brook, I only saw it as it was that day — a rushing, death-dealing devil, its milky-white water entangled with drifting logs and vines.

The house sat lonely, bleak, and gray, its curtainless windows gaping like unseeing eyes. I went onto the front porch to set a while, to be near all this that held such sweet memories of my childhood. The old cot still occupied a spot on the porch. It had been my favorite place to sit, in the past.

The perfume from the cabbage and moss roses, mingled with the sweetness of the honeysuckle vine climbing around the porch edge, came to me as I watched a hummingbird pierce its bill into each little wax-like, white flower of the vine.

I arose and found that the door was unlocked and went inside

221

the house to bid each room farewell. I could almost feel the cozy warmth of winter as I went into the big, square living room. Music from the old organ seemed to fill the room, and I could hear voices singing as it played.

In the kitchen, I half expected to smell fresh bread baking and the smell of preserves simmering on the old range. But there was only the smell of mice, and no preserves on the old stove. Its top was rusty and dirty. The oven door was broken and hung at an angle.

Peeking into the bedroom which Agnes and I had shared, I found that the roof had sprung a leak and water had stained and loosened the rose-patterned wallpaper. A window pane was broken, so a long cane from the climbing rose outside extended into the room.

Back in the living room, I could not hear the music and singing in my imagination now, and saw only the rusty old heater stove, and the chips and shavings littering the floor which Mom had scrubbed and kept so spic and span.

With sickness in my heart, I went into Mom's and Dad's bedroom. Only the smell of mice confronted me here. There was not even one trace of the perfume of Mom's sachet, or Dad's chewing tobacco. It was in this room that Estella, the sister I had never known, had passed away.

Al's room was littered with grain sacks and junk.

The wagon shed held no wagons, and the shake pile was there no more. The grain house was empty. Even the old muskets which had belonged to Granddad Aldridge were gone. The stable was a foot deep with manure, and the pegs where harnesses hung was still there, but bare of anything.

Back by the smokehouse, I seen that the currant patch was dead from lack of irrigation, and the majestic old apple trees had been brutally browsed by cattle. The smell of smoke still lingered in the smokehouse. The rafters were blackened by the smoke where the folks had cured the bacon and hams of years, and the big salt box remained in one corner.

A rattlesnake buzzed his warning from under the sill as I was leaving. Not bothering to look for him and take his life, I left, saying, "She's all yours, now," not bothering to think whether I said this to the snake or to myself.

The spring down near the corral was as cold as ever, and the moss around it as green and soft as before. Hippity, the pet frog, did not plop into the water as I stooped to drink. He was the guy which had run Mom "about bugs" because he sat on the lid of her butter crock and plunged into the spring when she came near.

I mounted, and rode through the ford at the lower end of the swimming hole and on through and past the flat where our bull, Pitt, and the Spanish bull had had their fight. Skirting around the hillside, I didn't stop to look down on the ranch until I was at Lick Flat. From here, you commanded a view of the entire place and its background. High Rock Springs Mountain stood boldly in the southern background, and far under it, not far from the house, stood the sandstone cliffs over which I had slid and played every day when I was little. With a catch in my throat, a sob in my voice, I looked for what I thought was perhaps the last time at this place, where as a child I had known all the peace, warmth, love, and happiness that had been bestowed upon me.

"Good-by home, good-by Hardscrabble. May you forever keep your magnitude and charm. I shall always love you, wherever my steps may lead me," I sadly said.

I was not ashamed of the tears that fell, or the heartbreaking sobs which came, as I turned the horse and slowly rode over the ridge past Alamine Peak, leaving a part of my soul behind. Mind in a turmoil, I began passing familiar landmarks. Yonder was the wild hog bed where, in the past, wild hogs bedded. There, not far to the right, was where Old Red, one of the milk cows, had died giving birth to a calf.

I passed the tree by the trail where I, for the first time, seen a lynx cat treed. It seemed I could still hear the bawl of the hounds as they circled about, and the report of Dad's rifle, and could still see the big, tawny cat as he fell to earth, and hear Dad say, "Get back, Jack!"

I came to the road on the north side of Alder Springs Grade, and was soon rounding Jackknife turn, which was a hazard to travelers in anything larger than a buggy or spring wagon. But Dad had made it without one "bobble" on our move from Hardscrabble.

Here, at Garden Gulch, had come the first catastrophe — when the chain broke, letting the buggy lurch ahead into the wagon and break Mom's fancy dishes and the ducks' necks. The log where Mom had sat, pouting, still lay by the roadside.

The flat woods was an exalting place of beauty at any time. The ground was covered with devil's carpet, which was, at this time of year, full of rust-colored seed pods. Now was no comparison to its fairy-like beauty the first time I'd beheld it, with its endless expanse of lavender flowers, the very air felled with their perfume. It was here that deer kept to their traditional trail when moving to and from their summer and winter ranges. The ground, for a belt several hundred yards wide, was cut deep from the millions of hooves of generations passing this way.

I could see the time Dad and I were riding by this place in a cold fall rain, and he had sat his horse and fired six shots at deer that were passing and killed six bucks — enough meat, when jerked, to fill three flour sacks. Seemed I could still smell the acid smell of gunsmoke in the damp air of that day.

Why was I remembering and seeming to see all the happenings of years gone by as I idled along? The past few days I'd had a foreboding, for the first time, that Dad would never return home, in spite of his past laughing remarks that he was as immortal as these hills. I'd passed this way thousands of times since these happenings, but had never visualized them or let them linger in my mind as they did this day.

On into "No Name Gulch." Memories of the time a coyote had jumped forth in front of me and I and Old Shep had tried to run him down as he raced through the flat woods, hellbent.

There, by the trickle of water of the gulch, Dad and I had come upon a king snake who seemed demented. He came at our horse's feet, striking and restriking as he followed us across the water. As we watched his peculiar actions, Dad said, "Get off and kill that dingbat. Anything as nuts as that ain't got no use livin." After he was dead, we saw a rattler not more than twenty feet away that the king had, no doubt, killed. Dad had said, "that orta teach a feller to never get his hind sights first and do something he will be sorry fer later."

At Cow Creek Canyon's rim, I again seen the three laden wagons on the day of the move, and there was Dad, his foot pushing hard on the brake lever, holding the many lines as if he was truly a skinner, and Mom setting sideways on the high seat beside him, pulling with all her might and main on the brake-rope on the wagon following. I could hear the squall of the brakes and smell the brimstone smoke as the wagon tires dragged over the rocks. I could see the runaway's fire-colored body flash as he reared and bolted when the doe went bouncing across the road with Old Shep hot on her heels; Mom's look of helplessness, as she pulled on the rope; and Dad, in desperation, guiding the team to keep the wagons on the narrow roadway.

I could feel the stifling smother of the feathers as they billowed out in my face, the clatter of hooves upon the bridge, the crash and upset of the wagons, and the startled faces of Mom and Dad as they got down from their seat. "Dilly-dally," Mom's voice rang in my ears. No, that was not here; she had said that before we got here.

I could see the broken-legged runaway hobbling across the bridge and around the turn, and hear the report of the rifle.

On across the bridge, I seen the rat-chewed and bleached-white thigh bone of the fire-colored sorrel, and felt deep remorse as once more he was a colt and I a lonely little girl. I seen him galloping through the meadow, his four white feet flashing in the sunlight, his mane and tail a fiery plume. In a small child's voice, I'd say to Dad, "He's mine."

As I drew near home again, and reached the gate to enter the south lane, I seen Mom standing on the front porch with our old telescope to her eyes, looking down the valley; and I knew, without doubt, she was looking to see if I was at either of the neighbor's. How am I going to explain this day to her? I wondered wearily. She would not understand how I felt. If she had seen me crying over past memories, she would have said, "Fiddlesticks, Babe, what are you bawlin about? Your mouth is square as a box."

"Where have you been?" she asked, with accusation in her voice, as I came up on the porch. Seating myself in Dad's rocker, I said nothing, and gazed at the fields, so bare-looking without the animals there now. "I know where you have been. You've been galavantin around with that bootleggin kid again," she accused. "I've been slavin all day, gettin last-minute things picked up while you fly the coop and go helter-skelter like you're wild. I'm glad we're leavin this dump and gettin you out of the country he's in," she said.

Fighting to retain my composure and say nothing, I arose and

226

carried a box of packed things outside to the car.

"Now tomorrow it's gonna be different. You're gonna stay home and you're gonna help me if I hafta break your neck gettin you to do it," she informed me.

"I'll be here," I answered soberly.

"Your job will be to get all the farm tools into the shed and lock them up. Get the water regulated to keep the grass growin fer the sheep. Another thing I want done fer sure is you take that horse back to the neighbors, cause you ain't gonna go ridin off no more," she added.

I had not seen or heard from Poke for near two weeks. Cal, his brother, had been killed in an accident, and of course Poke must be grief-stricken. Somehow, I felt that our romance had withered on the vine. Despite this feeling, I must see him and tell him how I felt about this abrupt change. Perhaps he would say something that would take some of the sting out of my being torn away so abruptly from all I held dear.

Mom had held a firm rein on my coming and going since the day I'd stolen away and gone to Hardscrabble. She kept me on the jump with all our preparations of moving. The evening before we were to leave, I returned the borrowed horse to her owner. I let her pick her way slowly along, as this might be my last horseback ride, I tearfully thought. I was like a comdemned-to-die person, as they look for the last time at the sunfilled world.

That evening, I called the switchboard and asked the lady to call Kunkler's. I'll only tell him I'm leaving, I thought. But the wild beating of my heart told me this call meant a good deal.

He was surprised that I was leaving and explained that circumstances since Cal's death had kept him from coming to see me. "I'll be up to see you as soon as I can get there," he promised. When he came, he finished carrrying the heavy boxes to the car for us. Mom was all smiles with him, making me feel she, at last, had buried the hatchet and was seeing him as he really was. We gave him Tip, our one dog we had left. With Mom always present, we did not talk in private. When he left to go home, he merely said, "Bye, Skeet, I'll be seein you."

"Good-by," I answered, my heart feeling like a piece of lead. "I'll be up there," I added, in a stupid manner, pointing northward with my thumb. What I was meaning was, I would be up at Agnes', at Dunsmuir, and please, oh please, come see me.

Without further ado, he drove away. As Mom and I walked up the path to the house, my eyes smarted from unshed tears. I was filled with apprehension concerning our romance. All I had to show for all our plans of "runnin off" was the pistol.

"You know, I like that darn kid, when he's around. But I've heard such stories about his wildness, I've a feelin he's no good for you," she added. Dear old Mom. If she but knew how tame and gentle he actually was, she would love him as I did.

Next morning at sunrise, we were ready to go. I sat beside her in Old Liz, with an empty feeling in my innards. Tabb, our old lady cat, was setting near the stable door, as we were making ready to go. I seen a look of question and accusation in her big yellow eyes, which seemed to say, "Abandonin me, huh? Who is gonna be around to pet old Tabb and see that she gets the proper amount of milk each day?" Without doubt, she knew we were leaving for all time.

Tears poured down my face like a flood as Mom drove away. She boldly looked at me and said, in aggravation, "What are you bawlin about, Babe? Your mouth's as square as a box." Sobbing, unable to control myself, I hid my face in shame, as Dad had taught me from a small child that tears were a sign of weakness.

228

''Are you bawlin because you ain't gonna see the kid again?'' she asked.

''No!'' I exclaimed in disbelief. ''I'm gonna go on seein him forever, Mom. You nor no one else can stop me!''

21

A VOW THAT FOREVER SOUNDS

GNES' HOME was on the ground floor in an apartment house. Dad seemed listless, and kept to an easy chair most of the days. He seemed in a worse condition than when he had left the ranch.

Life here was more confusing to me than I'd thought possible. The first Sunday, I was hustled into my best clothes and told I was attending church. "Church," I exclaimed, "I ain't goin to church! Never was in one but once, and that's when a preacher came and preached at the church near the cemetery. I couldn't understand a blessed thing he said. One of the kids at school said that there was a lot of preachers that talked like that so people couldn't comprehend what they were talkin about. He claimed it was pig Latin, so I ain't goin," I told Agnes.

"Why, Babe, why are you such a dummy?" she asked. "I don't believe what you are telling me, but anyway things are different here, honey. We have ministers of high intellect. That 'pig Latin' you talked about was Latin," she explained.

"It wasn't any such thing," Mom broke in. "He was a German preacher and was talkin German."

"All the young people your age that amount to a hill of beans attend church regular," Agnes explained.

She drove me to the very steps of the church of her choice. "I believe we may be a little early, as the congregation is not going in. I'll stay here until they begin arriving," she said.

"If goin to church is so all fired good, why don't you go in?" I asked.

"Oh, I have. I go quite often. I'm older, and my character is not being formed, like yours. Your soul and outlook on life is badly in need of correction. You just go inside and quietly set down and listen to the good man's sermon. If anyone should talk to you, be polite — don't get off a lot of that lingo talk of yours. Whatever you do, don't swear. I'll be waiting for you when church is over, and drive you home," she promised, and drove away, leaving me standing on the church steps. Throngs of people were going in by this time, their faces solemn. I thought someone near and dear to them had passed away.

Dread of going inside came over me until I stood trembling. The church bell began slowly tolling, and I stood moon-eyed. I could see the high hills which closed in around town and wished with all my heart I was on top of the loftiest and fartherest one away. I was reminded of the majestic mountains at Hardscrabble I was so familiar with. I was tempted to walk to the outskirts of town and explore the woods nearby, but I would not know when church was over so I could be there when Agnes came to pick me up. A multitude of excuses flew to mind that I might tell her if I didn't go to church and wasn't back when she arrived; but they were all a bit far-fetched. I had a mental vision of what she would do and say to such behavior.

With throat dry as dust, I ascended the steps and slipped inside. For this once, I'd see for myself what the good church would do for me.

Having never read the Bible, the preacher's sermonizing about things taken from the Holy Book held little meaning to me. But the choir inspired me with their singing. With their voices, if they would swing out on songs with pep, they would be a knock-out. The ideal song in my mind was, "Show Me The Way To Go Home."

My thoughts were interrupted by the minister saying, "We shall all pray." He and the congregation began praying aloud, while I sat fidgety, not knowing what to do. I was as different and apart from these people as a bluejay is from a flock of doves.

Praying aloud was a foreign thing to me. Dad had always said that talking to your grub and begging to some supposed-to-be Supreme Being that you'd never seen was a bunch of "hog wash," to his way of thinking. His belief, in his words, was: "A feller don't have to go to church and beller and faunch in public to be the right kind of person. That only goes to show what a hypocrite a person really is. If you wanta worship something, you'd better make it the sun, moon, rain, and wind. These things are the substantial things that keeps this world goin round. These things are real; you can see and feel them all, and you are the reaper of their harvest. You don't have to make a big horseplay about the thing. Just keep it in mind, Scrub. Always keep in thought and action to do unto others as you would like to be done unto. Don't go about makin a lot of false promises and waggin your tongue concernin a bunch of false junk. You can't go wrong doin and actin like that," he would say.

I thought of his words as I sat listening to the people so earnestly praying aloud. Honestly, I weighed the two courses of belief, and my conclusion was that Dad's way was the most likely to be right. When church was over, I couldn't see that I felt any different than before — maybe just a little more confused.

Within a week, Agnes had me joined up with a Young People's Club. She also introduced me to a score or more of the nicer boys about town. My social outlook was very limited. I came to the conclusion there must be something drastically wrong in my way of behaving and thinking. What seemed to thrill and completely captivate the girls of my age I came in contact with at the club and church did not interest me one bit.

Agnes was forelady at the town's laundry. One morning, shortly after she had gone to work, she suddenly returned to the apartment. ''Get a better dress on, Babe, I need you over at the laundry. One of my girls, the little sap, run off last night and got married. Hurry up!'' she snapped.

''What will I be doin?'' I asked.

''There's plenty to do in a laundry,'' she answered.

''Yeah, but I ain't goin over there and iron clothes,'' I remonstrated.

''You'll be on the flat work. I'll show you how. Hurry, I need you now,'' she said.

She put me to work shaking sheets on the poling crew. My working partner was a large pleasant-faced colored lady. I was a bit awed by this for a time, but soon learned that she was the most tolerant person in the crew concerning my lack of know-how. The two things that made life bearable, as I slaved through the long days, was that quitting time was bound to come, and that I received a check every Saturday for the fabulous sum of sixteen dollars. After a few weeks at this job, I began to wonder if I could find another. Something outdoors was to my liking.

I noticed an ad in the local paper for a milker in a big dairy. The ad did not state whether they wanted a man or woman, but it did say the pay was one hundred and twenty-five dollars a month; also that you had to be an experienced milker, and sober. I pretty well filled these requirements, and was anxious to get

234

this job. That evening, I made the excuse that I was going for a walk. I hurried to the dairy, which was at the edge of town. The cows were in their stalls and being milked when I arrived.

"What can I do for you?" a bold-eyed man asked as I entered the barn.

"I've come fer the job you have advertised in the paper," I matter-of-fact said.

"For yourself?" he asked.

Embarrassed by his searching eyes, I giggled and said, "Yeah, I've been milkin cows since I've been knee-high to a grasshopper, and I figure I can milk better and faster than most people. Where is a bucket, and a cow to be milked? I'll show you I'm just not 'flitter-flatterin' you, Mister," I told him.

"No, I couldn't hire you. I have men to do the milking. It's no job for a girl," he said, finishing all the hopes I had for this job.

I went home, sick with disappointment. People are plain stupid around here. "No job for a girl," he had said. I could "rear back" and take it easy part of the time and yet beat that feller I'd seen milking. This was my first lesson that a girl is destined to live within the bounds of her supposed abilities.

My eighteenth birthday came. In honor of the occasion, Mom baked a birthday cake and cooked a special dinner. In the evening we were in the act of setting down to the feast, when a rapid knock came upon the door.

"I'll get it," Agnes said, going to see who might be calling. "How do you do?" I heard her say.

"Is Skeet home?" a man's voice asked.

"Who?" she asked.

"Yeah, I'm here, come in," I called, going to the door. "Agnes, this is Poke. I don't believe you two have met," I chattered excitedly.

"No, I don't believe we have," she said.

"Come on in," again I invited. "We are havin my birthday dinner, and you are just in time to help celebrate my independence from my elders." I added.

"Hello, kid!" Dad exclaimed. "Come shove your feet under the table. Scrub is eighteen today, and that's all I've been hangin on fer."

"You're lookin pretty well to be figurin on shovin off very soon," Poke said in encouragement. "How have you been, Mrs. Aldridge?" he politely inquired.

"I'm fair, since I've got away from the endless work at the ranch. Havin to chug over those rough roads is the thing that kept me bushed. We lived so fer back, a person had to drive hell fer leather to get there and back. I'm just sick of such a place," she complained.

The dinner over, Poke asked me, "Would you like to go to the show?"

"You bet," I answered, "but we will have to hurry, it begins in a few minutes."

Uptown, we decided the picture being shown was not to our liking, and drove north along the highway. It's amazing, when you're in the company of someone you love, how different and beautiful everything becomes. This is how it was with me, as we drove along.

"I brought you somethin I believe you will like," Poke said.

"Oh, yeah? What is it, another pistol?"

"No," he laughed. "Did you want another pistol?" He was still laughing, and a look of admiration was in his eyes. "Would you wanta see what it is?" He stopped by the side of the highway. "Shut your eyes, and no peepin," he said.

"I won't peek," I promised, as I sat, my eyes closed, my heart beating like a horse with a bad case of thumps. Upon the ring finger of my left hand he placed a ring. "See," he said.

"Oh, it's beautiful!" I exclaimed. It was a dainty little ring set with diamonds and ruby stones. "I'll give you a kiss for that," I said softly, leaning toward him to kiss him on the cheek. But he spoiled my aim by hugging me tightly to him. We kissed like the two lovesick kids we were.

"Why don't we run off tonight and get married?" he asked.

"No, I can't. Dad's bad sick, and if I don't go home, it would make him sicker," I objected.

"But you said you'd go with me as soon as you was eighteen," he reminded.

"I know, but he will have to be told when we go that I ain't comin back, so he won't worry," I explained.

"Then the whole damn tribe will pounce on you and keep you from goin," he said, his voice deep with disappointment.

"I won't tell anyone but him. He's no blabbermouth."

We planned about our future until it was far past time to go to the late movie in Weed, which was where we were going after leaving Dunsmuir.

Poke got a job near town. Weekends and evenings we went to places of entertainment of interest to us, returning sometimes rather late in the evening. A "watchful eye" is a mild description of the vigil that was kept upon my comings and goings by Mom and Agnes.

Our good times ceased shortly, when Poke received a letter from home asking if he would return and help "log off" a certain forty-acre strip before winter storms came. Again, we parted without naming any certain day we would be married.

To date, I had not told Dad anything concerning our plans. I'd simply promised Poke I'd be ready to go when he came after me, if he would let me know in advance, so I could tell Dad.

Mom suspiciously eyed my ring. "What is that, an engagement ring?"

"He gave it to me on my birthday." I eluded.

"If it's not an engagement ring, why do you wear it on your left hand?" Agnes joined in.

"One hand's same as the other," I muttered.

"Oh, honey, you are such a dummy!" she exclaimed.

"I'm tickled he had to go home and get away from you," Mom triumphed.

"You're so right. He is a bad influence on her, and she's too blind to see it," Agnes said, then added, "I can't imagine what you see in him you think is so fine."

"I love him, damn it!" I exclaimed. This sent both the dear souls into the kitchen, clucking like two setting hens. Dad sat in his chair, and from outward appearances he was dozing; but as they rushed from the room, he opened his eyes, grinned in satisfaction, and said, "That's the shot that buckled them up, Scrub;" then closed his eyes.

Poke had said when he left that he would not write me unless it was important. A week before Christmas, and quite by accident, I went after the mail after work. To my amazement, there was a letter for me from him. "Important" flew to my mind as I ripped the envelope open and began reading.

Dear Little Sweetpea:

As usual, I'm in a hell of a hurry, but I've found time to scribble off a few lines.

I'll be through with fallin timber in about three or four days, if I work hard. Anyhow, I'll be after you the morning of the twenty-fourth.

You get your Dad primed to the idea of your leavin by that time.

If you kinda figure on dressin up special fer the occasion, you had better have your clothes ready.

I guess you aint changed your mind about things.

238

Anyhow, I'll be there after you when I say, and if
you still wanta marry me, be ready.

I've missed you since I've been back from there,
and was glad to get your letter.

See you when I said.

With all my love and a big kiss or two,

Your prospective husband

Poke

My heart leaped in excitement, and I rushed to the dry goods
store and bought a lace dress, stockings, and very exquisite
undergarments and high-heeled shoes. I marched home with
them and placed the large box containing my finery on the shelf
atop my closet, arranging a blanket over the top of the unopened
box.

I still had not found courage to tell Dad of my leaving. One
evening, a day or so later, when everybody was gone but he and
I, I decided to show him my wedding clothes and thus break the
news to him. Removing the box from its hiding place, I discovered it had been opened and gone through.

When I showed Dad my dress and told him our plans, he
matter-of-fact said, ''Yes, I've seen it before and I think it very
pretty, Scrub. Your Ma and Sister have been throwin cat fits
about it. They know damn well what it's fer. I'm surprised they
ain't jumped you about it,'' he said, smiling. ''Me and them, we
had quite a tussle about you and the kid gettin married. I told
them they ain't got no say in the matter. I told them he might be a
little uncurried and hot tempered, but that time will mellow that.
They think cause he don't slam on fancy clothes several times a
day that he's shiftless. I tells them that bein slicked up all the
time don't make a man. When did you say you figures on gettin
married?'' he asked.

"He's comin the mornin of the twenty-fourth, and we'll go to Redding and get married," I confided. "It's kinda funny — you was the only one I planned tellin about this. We thought it would be fun to run off, but with you feelin a little 'on the hog,' I didn't think it right to go and not tell you and cause you worry. Now they all know it, and it's gonna kinda spoil the fun."

"We don't have to tell them," he said.

"But they know," I answered.

"They don't know when," he laughed; then added, "We'll just keep them in the dark about the date, and they will be like a feller before a firin squad — they'll know it's comin but from what gun they can't tell."

The morning of the twenty-fourth came, and I had accidentally told Mom that Poke was arriving, and she had guessed the rest and told Sister. Agnes and I went to the laundry to receive Christmas presents. Our employer was giving a turkey to each employee. We were returning with the birds when she remarked, "I'll bet you five dollars to one your feller don't show up today."

"Get your money where your mouth is," I said, and stopped to clinch the bet, but it was too late. At that moment, Poke came driving across the bridge, "plurting" his horn so loudly it rent the cold, still air. "Remember your bet, I'll collect it," I called, as I ran to the car and jumped in beside Poke and gave him a kiss.

I had previously packed my belongings, and had only a few last things to do before leaving. Hand-in-hand, we went storming into the house, talking and laughing like two magpies.

"Hello," Mom said, looking up from the newspaper. The pages gradually slipped to the floor and she sat with immobile face, as if, body and soul, she had been locked in a tomb. I felt deeply sorry for the agony I was causing her; she was my darling Mother.

Dad came in from out back and greeted Poke with genuine gladness.

"I was afeared you wouldn't show up and we'd have to put up with Scrub fer years," he said with a grin.

My things were stowed in the car, and we were ready to go. Leaving, I kissed Mom and Dad goodbye. Tears found their way down my cheeks; Mom's eyes were swimming in tears and she had a catch in her voice.

Dad smiled and said, "Anytime you kids want to come home, the latch string is out fer you. Now, get goin."[16]

We drove to Redding, and in a jewelry store we bought a ring, priced fifteen dollars and fifty cents.

"Are you young people getting married soon?" the jewelry clerk inquired.

"Yeah, just as soon as we go to the court house and get a license," Poke answered.

"You will have to go quickly, as they close in just four minutes," the man said, glancing at the ponderous clock on the wall.

"It does? Come on!" Poke exclaimed, grabbing my arm and half dragging me through the store door.

We hadn't time to go seven blocks up Market Street to get the car. We went running towards the court house, which stood back on a hill about six blocks away. High heels were never made to race in, but the necessity of reaching the court house within four minutes, or not get married that evening, prompted me to put on a burst of speed that would have shamed a track champion. I was at Poke's side as we went flying up the court

16. Att died at Dunsmuir on August 1, 1926, only a few months after Anita's marriage. Sadie became a maid in a hotel in Dunsmuir. Later, she lived and worked in Chico, and eventually died at the home of Agnes on May 25, 1949.

house steps and into the records office. "We've made it," I rejoiced to myself.

A man was placing books on a shelf. "Could I do something for you?" he asked.

"Yes. We wanta get a marriage license," Poke panted out.

"I was just closing," the man stated, looking at us as we gasped for breath from the six-block spring. "You youngsters must have come from far and fast," he said, with a smile.

"We did. The feller down at the jewelry store, when we was buyin a ring, told us we only had four minutes to get here, so we came hell-a-hoppin," Poke answered. "Where can we find a justice of the peace?" he asked.

"Judge Albert Ross lives but a short way from here. Would you like for me to call him and have him come here? He could perform the ceremony right in my office."

"That would be fine," we agreed. Getting married was developing into more of an ordeal than I had thought. I was trembling — and why, I did not know.

The judge agreed to be right over.

"Now, we will get the license," the clerk said. He began asking questions and filling in the blank spaces on a legal-looking paper.

"Your age, Miss Aldridge?"

"Eighteen," I choked out.

"White?" he asked, glancing at me.

"Mostly," I half-whispered. "Mom's got some Indian blood in her, but I guess that wouldn't count against me sayin I'm white."

"A little redskin blood don't make any difference in us California people," he smiled, and said, "I suspect that most of us, if we would admit it, have some. I'll put 'white,' " and he wrote out the word in the place provided for it.

Poke seemed composed as he was asked questions concerning himself.

The judge arrived, and the clerk introduced us. "Judge Ross, this is the young folks I called you about. Miss Aldridge, Judge Ross; and Mr. Kunkler, Judge Ross."

"I am pleased to make your acquaintance," came the pleasant voice of the man. "Your names seem familiar. Could it be that you are related to the Aldridges and Kunklers at Whitmore?"

"Yes, that's where we are from," Poke said.

"Well, by George, I'm acquainted with your people. I went hunting with Cal Kunkler at this mountain cattle camp about six years ago."

"Cal was my brother. Did you hear about him bein killed this last summer?" Poke asked. "A high-tension wire from the power line fell across the phone line. He tried to call on the phone and was electrocuted," Poke said sadly.

"I deeply regret hearing that. Cal was a good man," the judge said. "I must know your parents. Which of the Aldridges is your family?"

"Dad's name is Att," I said.

"Sure, I know him. A real old-timer," he answered, taking papers from his briefcase. "Now, I believe we are ready to begin the ceremony."

When I had bought my wedding dress, I had a vision of myself being married looking like the pictures of brides in magazines and the newspapers. But the weather was cold and stormy, and I had a long coat on, and it buttoned to the throat, which completely hid my beautiful dress. Just as the judge began our wedding vows, I said, "Wait a minute," and ran across the room. Taking off the coat, I hung it upon a tree hatrack.

"Oops," I exclaimed, as the rack crashed to the floor, scattering hats all about. Red-faced, I picked the hats up and set them back in place. With my coat folded across my arm, I walked back to Poke's side. Everybody, including Poke, laughed; but I seen nothing funny about my ignorant blunder.

"Ready now?" Judge Ross asked good-naturedly.

"Ready," Poke said, squeezing my hand in encouragement.

It came time to put the ring on my finger, and Poke could not find it. He earnestly searched his pockets with a blank expression on his face. "Did I give it to you?" he asked.

"I don't think so, but I'll look." I searched my coat pockets. My handkerchief, with my ten dollars tied up in it, I found in one pocket. From the other, I produced the white satin box of the ring. "Here it is!" I exclaimed.

"It ain't in here, it's just the empty box!" Poke ejaculated. "I still think you've got it," he said in an accusing tone. "I've got so damn many things in my pocket, there could be a bull elephant in there and I wouldn't know it." He began dumping the contents of his pockets on the counter: car keys, a small screwdriver, a handful of silver money, four rusty bolts, two lock washers, four bolt nuts, three sticks of gum, a pocket comb, and a bottle of Carter's Liver Pills, which he placed on the top of the pile. Oh yes — the ring was there, snugly fit around one of the rusty little bolts.

The judge looked at the assortment on the counter and, picking up the liver pills, he laughingly said, "Son, I believe you are going into this thing better equipped than anyone I have seen. You are prepared for about anything."

With the ring on my finger, the judge uttered the fatal words. "I now pronounce you man and wife."

"I reckon this is all there is to it," Poke said.

"Yes, my boy, you now belong to each other," the judge commented, and slapped a friendly hand upon Poke's shoulder. "I wish you all the happiness in the world."

"What do I owe you?" Poke asked.

"Whatever you think is right," he answered; then added, "How much do you think she is worth?"

Poke gave him a twenty, saying, "This is the smallest I have."

Judge Ross accepted the bill and painstakingly put it in his billfold, while Poke stood by with an expectant air about him. I guessed he expected the judge to give him no less than nineteen dollars and fifty cents in change.

Outside, it was dark and storming. Hand-in-hand, we hurriedly went down the hill to the main part of town.

"What are your teeth chatterin fer?" Poke asked.

"I'm gettin scareder every minute," I confessed. "This gettin married is sure nerve-wrackin. If I'd known it would be such a 'whoop-up time,' I'd never had the guts to try it," I further confessed.

"It's all over, Honeybunch. We'll go have supper, our weddin supper," he consoled me, as we dashed through the storm. My heart sang a brand new song as he looked at me in a loving way, as if he had just married the Queen of all Queens — which was far wrong when considering me as a cook and housekeeper. I could sit tall and straight in a saddle, but was just a puny shadow in front of a cook stove. He had not captured the queen of all girls; a poor bargain he had got, who did all sorts of dumb things, and one who could not even sew a button on his shirt.

The wind was bitter cold as it rollicked through the streets and howled around street corners. Snow had taken over the rain. Speeding clouds rolled overhead. The lights of the town reflected upon the clouds and the driving snow. This made the entire storm seem no higher than the building tops.

If I had not been overwrought with excitement, I would have revelled in the beauty of the storm enveloping the town, which was so brightly and beautifully lighted with Christmas lights of many hues. I felt like it was not I who hurried along at her husband's side, in this gaily lighted, storm-drenched place. I can remember but a few things that was said and happened from the time we left the court house until we gave our orders at the restaurant. The fury of the storm and the beauty of the town all but missed my notice, when compared to how I would have seen it under calmer circumstances.

"Run, Sweetpea, you're gittin your tail feathers wet," Poke said, his grip firm upon my arm as we went racing around a street corner, my spike heels slipping and sliding in the slush snow.

There, not more than two feet before us, came a lady. There was a shuddering crash, and she went sprawling to the sidewalk and rolled into the curb's gutter. She was an unbelievably fat squaw. Her cape coat was swept away by the mad wind. "Uhh," she grunted, as we collided.

I stood dumbfounded, too startled to say or do anything. Poke gently helped her to her feet, saying, "We are sure sorry, lady, we didn't see you! We didn't mean to hurt you."

He retrieved her cape and placed it about her shoulders. She hugged it tightly about her and, without a trace of emotion in her moon-shaped face, muttered, "Ugg, white girl in heap big hurry." Without further ado, she went walking down the street.

We walked up the street in silence, until Poke looked at me with a grin and remarked, "You damn near killed your blood sister." Then, "Here's the place I figured we'd eat. It looks a little highfalutin fer stump-jumpers like us, but maybe we can get out of the place without showin our ignorance too much," he said, as he opened the door and ushered me inside.

We seated ourselves at a table by the front window. After our orders had been given, Poke repeatedly glanced toward the window and door.

"What are you tryin to see?" I asked.

"Injuns. That squaw you run into didn't act too happy about you knockin her in the gutter. I figure she's gone to round up her kinfolks and the whole tribe will come lookin fer you and get on the warpath. If they see you settin here, they will pounce on you like a chicken hen on a June bug. They'll take your scalp the first thing; and if I was in your boots I'd keep my eyes peeled, or the first thing you'll know, that gal will be leavin here with your scalp danglin from her belt," he said, in seemingly deep concern.

"You're a bag of wind," I accused. "You've forgot that me and her are blood sisters, and she don't want my scalp. They only take scalps of the palefaces, my dear," I said, laughing.

"Oh? That's where you're far wrong. Ain't no squaw goin to get my hair," he said, quickly brushing his hair with his hand.

"Huh. I already got it, so to speak. I have it danglin from my belt right this minute," I nonchalantly said.

When our supper was served, it tasted better and different than any food I'd ever had before.

"Good grub," Poke appraised.

"Ugg! You tastum good, long time you no get food like this. Me can't boilum water," I soberly said.

He chuckled at my little joke, and a million devils danced in his dark eyes. Then, with a somber expression on his face, he said, "You heap strong squaw. You fetchum game, me cookum."

No words can express how wonderful I thought he was, or how right it was for us to be pledged to each other by the recent words spoken by the judge: "To have and to hold, until death do you part." We were content to wander down life's crooked road, hand-in-hand, until thus parted.

AFTERWORD

ONCE DISLODGED from their beloved hill country and with no further Western frontier left to explore, Anita and Lloyd became part of the great mobile society which has characterized the Pacific Coast. Lloyd had driven to Portland, Oregon, many times as a rumrunner for an illicit whiskey distributor in Sacramento, and before the couple were married in Redding on December 24, 1925, they had agreed to live in Portland, where Lloyd would train as an electric welder and Anita would study comptometer operation. But after settling in Oregon, the young couple soon changed their minds about welding and business machines, and both decided to attend barber college; they envisaged a life of travel throughout the world while they earned a pleasant living from this exciting trade.

After graduation from barber school, both were employed for about three years in Portland's unionized shops. Anita became particularly expert in the use of the razor. They soon tired of barbering, however, and Lloyd started working for the forest service while Anita enrolled in a detective school. She became interested in psychology and the reading of the human mind; but within a few months they moved to Medford and earned a living by plucking and dressing chickens and selling them door-to-door throughout the community. From Medford, the Kunklers drifted back to Dunsmuir. Anita cooked for the Southern Pacific Railroad, worked in a laundry, and finally became a telephone operator. By the late twenties, they were working in their hometown of Whitmore, where Lloyd helped at a sawmill and Anita milked cows on a ranch. A year later they were in Red Bluff, working in construction and for a concrete contractor. In 1930, they purchased a ten-acre farm near Anderson; but the next year they moved again — this time to a forty-acre ranch nine miles from Junction City in Trinity County.

Over the following decade-and-a-half, Anita and Lloyd worked at a score of jobs in as many different locations; but they tended to view Junction City and the ranch with its placer mine as home. They moved from Redding and the Shasta Dam site to Klamath Falls, to Crater Lake, back to Redding, to the Pitt River mining country, to Richmond, to Eureka, and to other camps and towns. Anita worked at a dozen laundries, at Montgomery Ward's, J. C. Penney's and various construction sites, and was a welder in shipyards, a farmer, and a miner. At the end of World War II, the Kunklers moved back to the Junction City ranch and engaged in placer mining. In addition, they grew and canned fruits and vegetables and exhibited produce, meats, and canned items at Hayfork, Anderson, McArthur, and other local fairs.

The placer mine produced a small quantity of gold which was sold to Portuguese and Greek agents in San Francisco for about eighty dollars per ounce (almost three times the twenty-eight dollars per ounce allowed for such impure gold by American officials). Money was made in additional ways: Christmas trees were cut for San Francisco truckers; herbs were gathered and sold; rocks, onyx, and Indian arrowheads were traded; and coyotes were trapped for the bounty. In the early fifties, the Kunklers sold their holdings in Trinity County and bought twenty-three acres at Paynes Creek in Tehama County. The move was occasioned by a stroke which left Anita partially paralyzed; but she quickly recovered, and they operated a combination bar, gasoline station, restaurant, and grocery store at Paynes Creek. They sold the businesses in 1964, but retained most of the property.

Throughout the fifties and early sixties, Anita and Lloyd searched the hills of Northern California looking for Indian artifacts. For a time in 1953 she lived at Weitchpec and worked with the Hoopa Valley Indians. She collected implements, studied the methods of Indian doctors, and kept a diary in which old legends and stories were recounted (unfortunately, this material has been lost). On the eastern side of the state, she roamed over the mountains from Truckee to Alturas searching for arrowheads, axes, and other remains of Indian life. Anita died suddenly at their Paynes Creek home on December 11, 1967, and is buried near the graves of her father and grandfather in the Ogburn-Inwood Cemetery near Shingletown, California.

Anita was always active, inquisitive, and versatile. United States Senator Clair Engle awarded her a prize for winning a Northern California crosscut sawing contest; and at the same time, she was writing an article on flying saucers. She was the mother of three sons. Sometimes she was seriously ill, but she continued to train dogs, trap, and hunt; and she rode horseback with the reckless abandon of youth. Anita maintained the self-reliance, ingenuity, and endurance of her ancestors, and she would neither accept nor tolerate intrusions into her life by relatives, the community, or public officials. And, most fortunately for her readers, she was able to create a historical and literary entity from the conflicts, the deprivations, and the pleasures of childhood. The environmental integrity, the vivid lifestyles, and the humanizing experiences reflected in *Hardscrabble* give it an arcadian, an artistic, and a very personal flavor.

W.S.S.